Refiguring
ENGLISH
STUDIES

Refiguring English Studies provides a forum for scholarship on English studies as a discipline, a profession, and a vocation. To that end, the series publishes historical work that considers the ways in which English studies has constructed itself and its objects of study; investigations of the relationships among its constituent parts as conceived in both disciplinary and institutional terms; and examinations of the role the discipline has played or should play in the larger society and public policy. In addition, the series seeks to feature studies that, by their form or focus, challenge our notions about how the written "work" of English can or should be done and to feature writings that represent the professional lives of the discipline's members in both traditional and nontraditional settings. The series also includes scholarship that considers the discipline's possible futures or that draws upon work in other disciplines to shed light on developments in English studies.

Volumes in the Series

David B. Downing, editor, *Changing Classroom Practices: Resources for Literary and Cultural Studies* (1994)

Jed Rasula, *The American Poetry Wax Museum: Reality Effects, 1940–1990* (1995)

James A. Berlin, *Rhetorics, Poetics, and Cultures: Refiguring College English Studies* (1996)

Robin Varnum, *Fencing with Words: A History of Writing Instruction at Amherst College during the Era of Theodore Baird, 1938–1966* (1996)

Jane Maher, *Mina P. Shaughnessy: Her Life and Work* (1997)

Michael Blitz and C. Mark Hurlbert, *Letters for the Living: Teaching Writing in a Violent Age* (1998)

Bruce Horner and Min-Zhan Lu, *Representing the "Other": Basic Writers and the Teaching of Basic Writing* (1999)

Stephen M. North, with Barbara A. Chepaitis, David Coogan, Lâle Davidson, Ron MacLean, Cindy L. Parrish, Jonathan Post, and Beth Weatherby, *Refiguring the Ph.D. in English Studies: Writing, Doctoral Education, and the Fusion-Based Curriculum* (2000)

Stephen Parks, *Class Politics: The Movement for the Students' Right to Their Own Language* (2000)

Charles M. Anderson and Marian M. MacCurdy, editors, *Writing and Healing: Toward an Informed Practice* (2000)

Anne J. Herrington and Marcia Curtis, *Persons in Process: Four Stories of Writing and Personal Development in College* (2000)

Amy Lee, *Composing Critical Pedagogies: Teaching Writing as Revision* (2000)

Derek Owens, *Composition and Sustainability: Teaching for a Threatened Generation* (2001)

Chris W. Gallagher, *Radical Departures: Composition and Progressive Pedagogy* (2002)

Robert P. Yagelski and Scott A. Leonard, editors, *The Relevance of English* (2002)

Shari J. Stenberg, *Professing and Pedagogy: Learning the Teaching of English* (2005)

Linda S. Bergmann and Edith M. Baker, editors, *Composition and/or Literature: The End(s) of Education* (2006)

Critical Literacy and the Aesthetic

Transforming the English Classroom

RAY MISSON

University of Melbourne

WENDY MORGAN

Queensland University of Technology

National Council of Teachers of English
1111 W. Kenyon Road, Urbana, Illinois 61801–1096

Cover photography: © Karen DeWig

Staff Editor: Bonny Graham
Manuscript Editor: Jane M. Curran
Interior Design: Jenny Jensen Greenleaf
Cover Design: Evelyn C. Shapiro

NCTE Stock Number: 49510

© 2006 by the National Council of Teachers of English.

Library of Congress Cataloging-in-Publication Data

Misson, Ray, 1945-
  Critical literacy and the aesthetic : transforming the English classroom / Ray Misson, Wendy Morgan.
      p. cm. -- (Refiguring English studies)
  Includes bibliographical references and index.
  ISBN 0-8141-4951-0 ((pbk))
  1. Language arts (Secondary) --Social aspects--Great Britain.   2. Critical pedagogy--Great Britain.   3. Aesthetics, Modern.   I. Morgan, Wendy. II. Title.   III. Series.
  LB1631.M48 2006
  428.0071'273
                                                                    2006001310

CONTENTS

Acknowledgments

We would like to thank the Australian Association for the Teaching of English and its constituent associations for the opportunities they have given us at various times to try out some of the ideas in this book in keynote addresses. We have been encouraged by the positive response and hope that this book fulfils the expectations of those who encouraged us in the project.

Wendy would like to thank the School of Cultural and Language Studies in Education, Queensland University of Technology, for some release from teaching in the final stages of writing the manuscript.

We would particularly like to thank Kurt Austin of the National Council of Teachers of English for his continuing enthusiasm for the book, and for the courteous and professional help he has provided. Jane Curran and Bonny Graham have provided careful, sympathetic, and altogether exemplary editorial work on the book, and we are grateful to them both.

We thank Faber and Faber Ltd in London, and Farrar, Strauss and Giroux in New York for permission to reproduce the Robert Lowell poem "Women, Children, Babies, Cows, Cats," in Chapter 2, and to Les Murray, c/o Margaret Connolly and Associates, for permission to reproduce the quotations from his poem "The Quality of Sprawl" in Chapter 8.

INTRODUCTION

This book sets out to investigate a very simple problem. Both of the authors are known in their home country, Australia, as proponents of *critical literacy*. The range of what might be meant by this term is looked at in the first chapter. Suffice to say for the moment that the salient feature of critical literacy as far as we are concerned is that it conceives literacy education as ultimately concerned with giving students an understanding of textuality (i.e., of the way texts work). In particular, it is based on a poststructuralist understanding that all language is socially contextualised, and so texts are inherently ideological, and that texts are fundamental to the construction of our identity.

We have both been active in promoting the critical literacy agenda through publications, plenary addresses, professional development workshops, policy work with government curriculum bodies, and in our teaching of student teachers in teacher education programs. And yet both of us, perhaps in differing ways and to differing extents, had concerns that there were major areas of the English curriculum that critical literacy, as currently constituted, was not able to deal with adequately. By 1997, Ray was confessing in print that he was uneasy about some aspects of critical literacy, particularly that its theoretical framework had "the effect of making the whole concept of personal difference suspect, pretty much unavailable for serious consideration" (Misson, 1997, p. 18).[1] Wendy's concern was focussed starkly when a well-known critical literacy guru said to her that he could not see any place for poetry in the critical literacy curriculum. Understandably, this gave Wendy, a committed, published poet, considerable food for thought. When she discussed her reaction with Ray, it coalesced with his concerns, and this book is the (rather delayed) result. It is an attempt to answer the question of why critical literacy feels uncomfortable with aesthetic texts like poetry, and whether it needs to be. This is used as leverage onto questions of what are the limitations of critical literacy in terms of its conceptualisation of significant matters such as individual identity, human emotion, and creativity, and whether it can be reconfigured to answer those concerns while retaining its acknowledged and vital strengths.

There are two major strategies employed in this project. The first is to try to understand the aesthetic in the poststructuralist terms that are current in critical literacy (*discourse, genre, subject position, resistant reading*) or that might be compatible with its poststructuralist framework (*desire, performativity*) in order to investigate the value it has, and ultimately to make a case not only that it is far too important to be neglected, but that it can be reconciled with the critical literacy agenda. The second is to consider how a poststructuralist understanding of the aesthetic might be worked with in a critical literacy classroom. These strategies are often employed simultaneously, but implicitly. In fact, there are many implicit assumptions and decisions on which this book is built, so it is worth making some of them explicit here at the beginning.

Assumptions

Poststructuralism

It will be noted that the poststructuralist framework is never questioned, or even explicitly argued for, but implicitly the whole book is making the case that poststructuralism provides the best framework we have for understanding texts and their relationship to human society and identity. If the discussion of textuality and individual texts in poststructuralist terms does not demonstrate satisfactorily how poststructuralism can be illuminating and how it can be the basis of an engaging and significant English curriculum, then the argument is lost.

One of the problems we have confronted with this, as with many other matters, is what kind of knowledge we can assume in our readers. Should we assume that our readers are familiar with the fundamental concepts of poststructuralism (even if they do not necessarily subscribe to them), or should we back up and explain what we are talking about? On the whole we have taken a conservative line on this, going back to first base on many of the concepts. This is not because we think that they will be unfamiliar to our readership (although the strategy allows that this might be the case), but because most of the concepts with which we are dealing are broad, multiply defined, and often contested, so it is useful for us to indicate where we stand on them by giving an introductory explanation, however brief. It also, of course, allows us to define the concepts strategically for the purposes of our argument.

Incidentally, we have used the term *poststructuralism*, although what is understood by this term in the United Kingdom and Australia is more often subsumed under *postmodernism* in North America. Apart from wanting to follow what is our familiar domestic usage, the reason for doing this is that it does enable at times a distinction between the formation of theoretical understandings that is known (to us) as *poststructuralism* and a thesis about our inhabiting a particular historical period, the features of which are gathered under the term *postmodernism*.

Critical Literacy

Just as we have not argued for a poststructuralist framework, we also have not explicitly argued for the importance of English/literacy teaching adopting a critical literacy framework. We have assumed that if the poststructuralist understandings of textuality are valuable, then critical literacy as an attempt to base English teaching on those understandings must be worthwhile, whatever its limitations might be.

The standard procedures of the critical literacy classroom are, on the whole, also assumed, although we have been careful to give enough detail to ensure that those who are unfamiliar with the pedagogical model will understand what is going on. We are very aware that critical literacy is more current and institutionalised in Australia than it is in either North America or the United Kingdom, and we are also aware that readers will be interested in the pedagogical practicalities. However, it needs to be asserted upfront that this is *not* a general critical literacy handbook, however practical its implications might be (see below).

Literature Teaching

Similarly, we have assumed that a critical literacy model is *not* the current norm in literature teaching, but that literature teaching generally proceeds on a more conventional model of narrative, thematic, stylistic, or issues-based analysis, alongside a regime of tasks that may ask for creative responses but in the end values most the analytical essay or the book report.

We have assumed that the explosion of "theory" that happened in the 1980s and 1990s has had some effect on literature classrooms, so that, for example, a feminist or postcolonialist reading would not be found extraordinary, but that, on the whole, most literature classrooms are operating on broadly liberal humanist principles, aiming at a general, "non-tendentious" reading of the text.

Decisions

As well as working on particular assumptions, inevitably there were a host of other decisions made on how to develop our argument and where to place our emphasis. Some of the major ones that have been particularly significant in shaping the book and that it might be useful to make explicit to our readers are discussed below.

The Aesthetic versus Literature

It may well be asked why we have framed the book as an investigation into the aesthetic and critical literacy, rather than simply talking about literature. There are two reasons: the first is because we felt it important to achieve the level of generality given by taking the argument back to the aesthetic. This is not a book about literature teaching, but about the importance of acknowledging in the English classroom the range of aesthetic experiences that texts give, whether such experiences occur in literary texts or elsewhere. Indeed, it is a small but important part of our argument that critical literacy cannot achieve its aims without acknowledging the aesthetic element in the nonliterary texts that it is ostensibly comfortable dealing with.

The second reason for focussing on the aesthetic and critical literacy has to do with the eternal problem of defining *literature*. Again the practice in the various English-speaking countries seems to be rather different, but certainly the tendency worldwide at the postsecondary level and increasingly in secondary schools is to conceptualise English in terms of cultural studies and so expand what is meant by literature to include movies, TV programs, hypertexts, popular publishing (comics, magazines, newspapers)—indeed any kind of text that is read for leisure purposes. We would support this explosion of the category, but rather than become embroiled in the often pointless discussions of what might or might not be considered literature, it seemed best to go back to the underlying notion of the aesthetic, especially since we did want to argue that the aesthetic was potentially an element that needed to be acknowledged in all texts. It will be noted, however, that our definition of literature is the broad one, and when we use the term we intend it to cover movies, TV shows, comics, and all those other kinds of leisure texts.

This also means that we have a broad view of reading and writing. When we use the word *reading,* we intend it to cover viewing, game-playing, or any other kind of decoding and responding that relates to making sense of or taking pleasure in the range of texts that we are covering by the term *literature.* Our use of the term *writing* can be taken to cover the production of all such texts and so could include such things as creating a hypertext, performing an improvisation, or producing a video.

Choice of Texts to Discuss

Anyone writing on teaching texts knows the problem of choosing which texts to use as examples and how much reader knowledge of them to assume. Our solution has been pragmatic. We have largely talked about classic texts, poems that can be quoted in full, or, in a couple of cases, popular texts that most people are likely to know. This has meant that the range of texts discussed might seem very limited and conservative and not particularly appropriate across the levels of education. In any country there are texts that are particularly favoured for work in the class-room, texts that speak particularly to that country's concerns. Teachers and curriculum bodies in each country will be concerned to ensure that the texts chosen acknowledge appropriately the presence and importance of indigenous people and groups from other than mainstream cultures. There will be a concern to acknowledge the special value of contemporary literature written specifically for young people in that country. We would certainly hope that most teachers would go well beyond the range of texts that we have covered in making choices for their classrooms. However, in writing for an international audience, one cannot easily discuss the favoured local texts without providing a great deal of background, and so we made the decision to work with texts that are likely to be familiar to most English teachers in English-speaking countries. Even so, we have tried to give enough context for any quotation that a reader who did not know the text would still be able to get a sense of what was going on and have some chance of confirming whether or not the point being made was valid.

Some chapters have been built around a broad range of examples drawn from various genres, media, and countries (e.g., Chapters 4 and 9), whereas others have deliberately been limited to a few texts (e.g., Chapter 3, which is built around a novel, a poem, and an episode of a TV sitcom) or even just one (Chapter 6, which uses only *Huckleberry Finn*). It is perhaps worth saying that while we were concerned to vary the strategy in the various chapters, the decision to work on a large range or just a limited number was almost arbitrary: the decision could have gone any way. It is not that it is easier to talk about the way texts put us into subject positions on a range of texts (Chapter 4) and the value of the aesthetic on just one (Chapter 6): it was almost a test of what we were saying to see if it could work either generally or particularly in any case.

Textual Interpretations

It is one of the basic tenets of poststructuralist thinking about literature, as it was of reader-response theories, that there is no absolute single "true" meaning of a text. Any reading is the result of complex negotiations between a reader and the text, as we will see in Chapter 5, and not only will different readers make quite different sense of a text, but one's own reading is inevitably shifting, tentative, and subject to change over time as well as from moment to moment. However, as Stanley Fish has pointed out, while we may be aware that our current reading of any text is provisional, at any moment we are of necessity actually inhabiting a reading (or a reading is inhabiting us), and that reading is what we believe about the text at that particular point (1980, pp. 364–365). Our sense of the "obvious" (at that moment) meaning of the text playing against our knowledge of its provisionality provides a dilemma for anyone writing a book such as this. Does one make constant acknowledgment that other readings of the text are possible, and humbly and persistently insist at every point that the reading and judgment one is proposing are just one's own and that no claim is being made for absolute authority, or does one simply talk about the text from the position one is currently inhabiting and make the points about it that one currently believes to be "true"? We have decided on the whole, to take the latter path, and so we would hope the reader will keep in mind that when a statement is made about the meaning or value of a text, it is surrounded by the unspoken acknowledgment that the reading or judgment is provisional and only one of the nearly infinite number possible, but that, on the other hand, it is how the text is being experienced at the time. In fact, one of the things that we hope this book achieves is reassuring people that there need be no sense of an embarrassing failure in poststructuralist purity when they make statements about a text's meaning and its value. Texts matter to us because they mean things and we like them. Such statements are a basic element of our interactions around texts in everyday life, when we see a movie or read a novel, and they are part of classroom activity around texts, always with the proviso that it is the teacher's job to keep the possibilities of meaning and judgment open and not impose her or his meaning or evaluation on the class.

Pedagogical Implications

As noted above, it is a major strategy of this book to look at the implications that a consideration of the aesthetic might have for classroom practice. One of the most difficult decisions was how explicit to make this. In the end, we have developed only one chapter (admittedly by far the longest) that is specifically examining what a pedagogy embracing the critical and the aesthetic might look like (Chapter 9). However, we would claim that the whole book is, in the end, implicitly geared to what might go on in the classroom. There are many incidental comments about classroom practice, but more importantly, much of the book is committed to articulating the kind of understandings that we think could be valuably developed in the classroom, albeit not always in explicitly theoretical terms. The strategies by which this might be done are not made explicit, but we assume that the readers of this book will be good, innovative teachers (or prospective teachers) who will know how to go about implementing lessons that draw on what is given here. If a teacher finds interesting the analysis of the discourses in *To Kill a Mockingbird* in Chapter 3, then she or he will know how best to set up their students to investigate that aspect of the novel. If someone else finds interesting the discussion of the physical importance of rhythm in Chapter 7, they will know the strategies by which to develop these understandings in their students on the texts that they have assigned in their classrooms (or had wished upon them).

We do acknowledge readily that teachers are not free agents. They work within particular curriculum and assessment regimes that strongly influence (if not determine) what they are able to implement in their teaching. We hope, however, that all teachers will find in this book ways of thinking about aesthetic texts that open up possibilities for their practice, whatever the adaptations that might be necessary to fit in with the institutional constraints under which they are working.

Reading versus Writing

One of the things that we have been very aware of is that this is largely a book about reading, and we do not say a great deal about writing. We do talk about it here and there, but rather in an apologetic, supplementary fashion, guiltily conscious that we are not giving it more time. The reason for the comparative neglect of writing is simple: critical literacy is preeminently a pedagogy of reading, and since critical literacy was our starting point, reading is what we have tended to concentrate on. Critical literacy is not alone in tending to divorce the writing curriculum from the reading curriculum: classical literature teaching has not generally been intimately meshed with creative writing, perhaps because it was felt that students could not possibly compete with the greats. Creative writing has generally been seen as a sideshow, irrelevant to the development of the kind of understandings that the literature classroom taught. If we had wanted to develop a proper account of creative writing within the critical literacy context, it would have almost doubled the size of the book, and the editors were rightly anxious about the size already. We acknowledge that the hints here about the creative writing curriculum are inadequate, but we hope that they will at least be a beginning to set readers thinking.

The Book's Structure

Although the various chapters can, of course, be read separately, and we hope that they can stand interestingly on their own, this is a book with a very strong overall argument mirrored in its structural development.

Chapter 1 gives a historical survey, locating the development of socially critical versions of literacy in relation to English and literary studies, thus establishing why we think it important to consider the place of aesthetic texts within critical literacy.

Chapters 2 to 5 as a group develop a view of the aesthetic and the reading of aesthetic texts within the kind of poststructuralist framework that is underpinning critical literacy. Chapter 2 establishes the basic view of the aesthetic on which the book is built. Chapter 3, largely through a discussion of the concepts of discourse and genre, examines the ways in which the aesthetic is inevitably implicated in particular social contexts and values. Chapter 4 turns to the individual and looks at how individual subjectivity is socially constructed through texts, and at the ways in which aesthetic texts engage readers through playing on their desires, thus bringing them into particular subject positions. However, we are not simply subject to texts, reading them as they demand to be read—there are complex negotiations that go on as we accept, reject, or qualify what the text is saying. Such negotiations are investigated in Chapter 5.

Chapter 6 picks up the suggestions implicit so far in the book on what might be the value of the aesthetic and makes a case for its significance by reconsidering in poststructuralist terms some of the answers traditionally given. This leads on in Chapters 7 and 8 to a consideration of two aspects of the aesthetic that would seem to be beyond the realm of critical literacy as currently constituted. Chapter 7 looks at recent theoretical work on the body and argues for the importance of acknowledging the embodied aspects of the aesthetic. Chapter 8 considers the aesthetic as a productive phenomenon, generative of different kinds of pleasure.

In Chapter 9, the pedagogical implications of the book's arguments are considered in terms of what might practically be done in the classroom, while Chapter 10 rounds off the argument by articulating how critical literacy might be transformed by taking account of the aesthetic.

Our Positioning

We speak a great deal about positioning in this book. It is a good indication of how the positions any of us takes become thoroughly naturalised that in some ways only in retrospect has it become clear how we have positioned ourselves and what possible positions our readers might take.

Those readers coming from a traditional literature teaching background who pick up this book to see what critical literacy has to say to literature teaching will find a quick introduction to a certain amount of basic theory that they may well find very useful in reconceptualizing and extending what they are doing in their classrooms. If they have previously looked into critical literacy and rejected it because it seemed to miss so much when it came to literature, we hope that they will find the version of critical literacy presented here much more interesting, persuasive, useful, and even liberating.

Those readers coming from a critical literacy background are, in fact, as likely to be as challenged by the book as are the traditional literature teachers, although they will understand much more readily the discourse we are using and the position we are coming from. For these readers, the challenge will be to remain open-minded as we argue about the limitations of their current position and about what critical literacy is not doing well, and as they come to terms with thinking about literature as a highly significant area of textuality worth their very serious attention. We hope these readers too will find the version of critical literacy presented here interesting, persuasive, useful, and even liberating.

Of course, these are the two extreme positions: most of our readers will come somewhere along the continuum ranging between them, pragmatically using in their teaching whatever seems to work best. It is our hope that these readers will find it helpful that we are trying to accommodate a breadth of literacy practice here in a properly theorised way, and that they too will find the model convincing.

In some ways, we could have simply written a book for literature teachers, arguing that critical literacy had something to offer them, but, of course, that would not have been responding to the major impetus behind the book, which is to reconfigure critical literacy so that it can cope with the aesthetic and all the attendant aspects of human experience. Such an alternative book would have left critical literacy practice unquestioned and unchanged. Our positioning is in some ways a little odd: we spend a great deal of time showing up what is wrong with critical literacy and criticising its practices, whereas we are ultimately aiming to promote its interests. There are, no doubt, those who

will read the book as being against critical literacy and will perhaps see us as recanting our earlier commitments. We think this
would be totally mistaken. We are both still thoroughly committed to the critical literacy agenda. If we criticise it, we do so as
insiders, concerned to ensure that its understandings are seen as
basic to the whole English/literacy curriculum. We have found
that bringing the aesthetic into its realm and conceptualising
what this might mean for critical literacy practice in general is a
significant thing to do. We can only hope that all our readers,
whatever their initial positioning, do so too.

The Cultural and the Critical, the Aesthetic and the Political

The words *valuing* and *evaluating* share a common root. We value what we prefer, and we discriminate between this (which we like) and that (which we like less). And—whether it's a pair of shoes, or the current blockbuster, or the latest prize-winning volume of poems—we try to enlist others to share our taste. But across the years, in secondary and postsecondary English classrooms, the activities of praising and appraising texts have been carried out in very different ways, on different objects, and with different ends in view. These differences of valuation have been the cause of a major quarrel in English studies over much of the last century. And although the terms may have differed somewhat during that time, and different parties have gained the upper hand in particular times and places, the fallout from this quarrel has not yet subsided.

In 2004, for instance, the metropolitan daily newspaper of Australia's third largest city, Brisbane, featured an article whose subhead asked, "Could Bart Simpson do as much to help students attain a good English education as reading the classics?" The opponents in this debate were a local media studies lecturer and the national education minister. The former first argued that television programs should be at the heart of English education: "Teaching that Shakespeare is good while reality television is bad imposes on school students the values of one culture rather than embracing the diversity of different cultures." By contrast, the federal minister for education, Dr. Brendan Nelson, asserted that traditional philosophy, literature, and poetry, "from Socrates to the more modern works of Jane Austen and Thomas Hardy to the poetry of Wilfred Owen and the war poets," should be fundamental to secondary schooling. Without such a curriculum "students' lives will not be enriched as they could be," since the classics help students to "find their soul and give them the courage to do what is right" (Livingstone, 2004).

In the United States, the chair of the National Endowment for the Arts, Dana Gioia, has recently made a similar case for the reading of literature. The Endowment's 2004 research report, *Reading at Risk: A Survey of Literary Reading in America,* makes a clear distinction between the "active, engaged" reading of literary texts and the "passive participation" in electronically mediated texts with their "accelerated gratification" (National Endowment for the Arts, 2004). And a causal link is drawn between such literary reading and not only the health of individuals ("focused attention and contemplation that make complex communications and insights possible," p. vii) but also the well-being of the nation ("As more Americans lose this capability, our nation becomes less informed, active, and independent-minded. These are not qualities that a free, innovative, or productive society can afford to lose," p. vii).

These views are consistent with a conservative line about the value of literature that dates right back to the work of F. R. Leavis some seventy-odd years earlier and beyond to the nineteenth-century views of Matthew Arnold. In this book we do not concern ourselves primarily with the debate over Great Books versus popular texts, but with more fundamental issues underlying it. These involve questions about the aesthetics, ethics, and politics of the texts of both high and popular culture, about the capacities that are to be developed in student readers and writers, and indeed about the ultimate aims and benefits of a literary education.

By these early years of the twenty-first century a shift *has* occurred in many high school and college English classrooms. This can be focused around the terms *cultural* and *critical*. For most teachers it is no longer possible to say the words *culture* and *cultural* unproblematically and take them to refer to the products and activities of "high" culture—of cultivated people who are the arbiters of taste in the fine arts. These days the terms *culture* and *cultural* have a sociological flavour: they are taken to mean any of the practices of everyday life by which members of a group make a shared meaning, whether text-messaging, shopping in a mall, surfing the waves or the Net, going to a barbeque or a bar mitzvah, watching the football finals in the pub, or wearing a particular brand of designer jeans.

A similar shift has occurred in many English teachers' use of the terms *critical* and *criticism*. Before about the 1970s, and in some more conservative classrooms still today, you could use the word *critical* comfortably, secure in knowing that your hearers would understand that you were referring to the work that literary critics do and that students were to emulate. This work entailed explicating the literary text under consideration: interpreting it, explaining what it "really" meant deep down (the meaning that an expert reader like the critic could extricate), and evaluating the worth of the text based on the way its literary features enhanced or made that meaning. These days, in a number of classrooms, the term *critical* is no longer mostly joined to *literary*, in *literary criticism*, but has migrated to join up with *literacy*, in *critical literacy*. Criticism, or critique, now entails a quite different activity, based on understanding that texts are deeply implicated in the cultural contexts in which they are produced and read. It means identifying the ideology inscribed in any text, determining who benefits from the very partial representation of the world offered in that text, resisting any invitations to comply with worldviews that are socially unjust, and taking verbal or other action to redress such injustices.

These shifts broadly encapsulate two different views of the purpose of English teaching, which the Kingman Report of 1988 in the United Kingdom identified by the terms *cultural heritage* and *cultural analysis* (Cox, 1991). The first model assumes that the responsibility of an English curriculum is to bring students to an appreciation of the finest works of literature; the second, that students need to be brought to a critical understanding of the culture within which texts, and they, are produced. One model encourages readers to yield to all that valued texts offer: insights into human nature, guidance in making ethical discriminations about characters' interactions, and aesthetic satisfactions. There is a payoff for readers who give themselves attentively, submissively, to such aesthetically charged works: they become discriminating, subtle readers with a mature moral awareness. By contrast, the other model, cultural analysis, encourages readers to resist the seductions of texts that offer various kinds of gratification, including aesthetic, but that slip noxious, ideologically suspect drugs into that pleasing cocktail. The benefits of such disengagement for readers lie in their ability to see through the text's blandishments: they too become discriminating readers, but in a very different way from those who value high over popular cultural texts and give themselves to such texts.

These simplified versions could be accused of caricature, but they are ones that each side has conjured up about the other, while denying that their own position is so simplistic. We will scrutinise their arguments at various points in the book, in particular, the position each takes regarding the aesthetic and the critical. Cultural heritage teachers see a cultural analysis curriculum as clearly inadequate because it does not, cannot even, satisfactorily deal with the aesthetic dimension of texts or comprehend the worth of the pleasures they bring. Cultural analysis teachers meanwhile accuse their conservative colleagues of promoting a naïve reading of texts in failing to engage with the fundamentally political agenda of texts and the ways in which readers are positioned to accede to the ideologies they offer.

This book attempts to bring together the aesthetic and the sociocultural model of English in a synthesis that is not eclectic but theoretically coherent. It tries to show how an awareness and valuing of the aesthetic can, indeed must, be incorporated into a critical sociocultural model of English pedagogy. The aesthetic and the socially critical are not opposed to one another but, rather, are necessary, complementary components of a rich literacy practice, one that can lay claim legitimately to benefitting both individual readers and writers and the society to which they graduate from English classrooms. To provide a context for the book's arguments, this chapter traces the main theories about culture and critique, the aesthetic and the political, and sketches how they have been taken up in various educational settings.

New Lamps for Old

Since about the 1970s, university departments of English, human-
ities, and social sciences have been engaged with a consortium of
theories, enthusiastically embracing them in some instances,
locked in bitter conflict in others. These include Marxist, feminist, postcolonial, poststructuralist, and semiotic theories and
their "post" derivatives.

There are a number of reasons, historical and theoretical,
for the challenges that were mounted against the study of classic literature. The great Christian narrative that elevated
"Man" and offered him his soul's salvation through religion or
its later substitute, literature, was in some quarters looking very
tattered after the Second World War. As higher education
expanded from the 1960s, it could no longer remain an exclusive club of the elite. The student masses included more women,
members of the lower classes, and ethnic minorities, whose
access to higher education often coincided with an increased
political awareness. These new groups had little reason, perhaps, to genuflect before the altar of high culture.

This less deferential generation found new energy to assert
the worth of their culture counter to that of their elders and
"betters." And for their instruction and delight in their everyday lives they carried with them the songs and stories and con-
sumables of a proliferating popular culture. They and some of
their teachers began to ask questions of the literary criticism
they encountered: Whose culture? Whose texts? Which kind of
reader is assumed here? Who speaks for and about me? What
pleasure and profit, for individuals or society, are to be gained
from reading, according to what values? And what is the nature
of the society in which such texts are produced and consumed?

Two broad confluent streams carried answers to these questions. The first had to do with textuality and textual politics;
the second with identity politics.

According to developments in semiotic theory (Barthes,
1968), everything in the world could be said to signify—could
be read as a text. Moreover, according to this theory, and to
poststructuralist theories that drew on it, what any text signified

was not inherent in it, but was constructed within a society. Meanings could therefore change in different times and places, as the text was read by readers in different circumstances. And insofar as those meanings were produced within a society, they inevitably shared the assumptions and values—the ideologies— of that society. Now—so the theories went—since all societies are inequitable, the texts sanctioned by the groups that have political power and social influence will present a version of the world that works to legitimise their position, culture, and taste.

This was heady stuff for many students and their teachers. The world of texts was no longer an exclusive preserve patrolled by a hieratic caste of guardians of Literature. It was instead a world in which everything was a form of language, was mediated by language, and was to be read by a myriad of readers generating a plurality of readings. And one could do important political work by uncovering in even the most formerly sacred texts the ideologies by which an inequitable order was shored up.

The second stream was a turbulent current of those claiming their place in the sun: women, people of colour, the working class. Marxists had long championed the cause of those who had only their labour to offer to society. (We see more of their views later, when we come to the work of cultural studies critics.) And Marxist literary critics set out to trace in texts the ideologies that shored up an economically unjust order. Their tactics were taken up by feminists who wanted to redress the patriarchal order that offered them a place as "the second sex." They also critiqued their invisibility in classic Marxism, which saw only class divisions. Gender was put back firmly on the agenda, including of the committees that set the texts for study in English courses. Women writers were brought into the light from the shadowy silence in which they had languished, and a place was claimed for them alongside the Great Male Authors, whose tenure on the canonical lists looked increasingly less natural or proper and more the result of unjustifiable privilege. And the kinds of texts previously scorned as women's (romances, soap operas, and the like) were offered for re-evaluation. In both ways, the canon was split open.

Feminism was one species of identity politics. Increasingly, politically active people aligned themselves with the cause of their particular social group—whether gays or lesbians, blacks, diasporic nations, or a range of Others on the margins, who now demanded that their differences be respected, not subordinated to the one standard of judgment and discrimination handed out from the Centre by those with power and privilege. "Culture" could no longer be represented as singular, in any society. People from a plurality of cultures each proclaimed that their ways were authentic, valid, and valuable. In increasingly multicultural, democratic societies, no less could be expected. (More recently it has been recognised that these identity groups were always fractured: there are differences within, not just between, groups—and even within individuals too: our identities are much more volatile than identity politics could admit.) Advocates of these various groups demanded that their voices be heard alongside or even instead of "His Master's Voice" in the canon of works set for study. They insisted on their right to "appreciate" texts that validated their experiences and culture.

A parallel charge against the canon and the educational practices that supported it was first levelled by Raymond Williams in 1973 (1980), then taken up and developed by Terry Eagleton (1983). They argued that the criteria by which texts were admitted to the category of "good" literature could no longer rest on claims about the author's "genius" or the work's "high moral seriousness" (terms of praise typical of Leavis and his followers). Rather oddly, they noted, these criteria had picked out only those (white, mostly male, bourgeois) authors who were members of the same class to which the arbiters of taste belonged. Instead, said these critics, the category of "literature" and the stamp of literary value given to such works were not intrinsic but derived from the institutions that had created the category. "Literature" was a creation of history, not of absolute standards of taste, and the aesthetic was a product of the ideology of a hegemonic group.

Indeed, it could be said that "literature" is dependent on literary criticism, which has created it, rather than criticism being the servant of the literary texts. That is, we learn to read books, and we have been taught how to read certain books in certain ways, as literature. This learning occurs within institutions such as schools and colleges and is supported by lecturers' explications of texts and by books of critical commentary, examinations, and the like. The long-honoured practice of "close reading" or "practical criticism" (Brooks, 1949; Ransom, 1941; Richards, 1929), for instance, is a set of techniques for producing particular kinds of reading and valuing certain kinds of meaning. Such techniques also thereby form certain kinds of readers who can perform this reading and evoke in themselves the specific desires, pleasures, and satisfactions such close reading offers. These practices produce versions of the texts under discussion that lend themselves to this treatment: they draw attention to particular features, value some, and neglect or denigrate others.

Are we readers merely deceived when we believe we have had an aesthetic experience and have acquired a taste for particular pleasures in our reading? Must the aesthetic experience be no more than an ideologically driven effect? Can an aesthetic experience be bad for one's moral health? Eagleton for one seems to think so, when he talks of literature as a "moral technology" (1985/86), a specific set of techniques and practices for shaping readers' beliefs, values, and attitudes, and argues that "the task of the moral technology of Literature is to produce an historically peculiar form of human subject who is sensitive, receptive, imaginative, and so on . . . *about nothing in particular*." So too in his *Literary Theory* (Eagleton, 1983), he accuses I. A. Richards's practical criticism in the United Kingdom and New Critical reading practices in the United States of being a "recipe for political inertia," because they encouraged the illusion that all a reader needed to do was focus on the words on the page rather than on the contexts that produced and surrounded them.

These are serious charges. They can be summed up as follows:

◆ Literature is a hitherto exclusive, politically motivated category, which has shored up the idea of one exalted culture.

◆ There are instead many cultures, each legitimate, which each produce a range of texts worthy of study.

◆ Indeed, all the practices of a culture can be seen as signifying.

- There is no innocent aesthetic experience of a text: readers, like texts, are shaped by their ideological assumptions and agendas.

- Hence there are many possible, competing, readings of any text.

- Texts, and readings, do political work, in promoting or discouraging social justice.

This manifesto offers a radically different sense of culture and criticism from that offered by conservatives like Leavis or his latter-day disciples quoted at the beginning of this chapter. In this new order the old (great) texts are differently evaluated, and sometimes devalued; other texts are revalued in this cultural stock market. This new order did not go unchallenged. Here, for instance, is Bloom, in a classic statement of nostalgia for a time of grace now almost departed:

> Men may live more truly and fully in reading Plato and Shakespeare than at any other time, because then they are participating in essential being and are forgetting their accidental lives. The fact that this kind of humanity exists or existed, and that we can somehow still touch it with the tips of our outstretched fingers, makes our imperfect humanity, which we can no longer bear, tolerable. The books in their objective beauty are still there, and we must help protect and cultivate the delicate tendrils reaching out toward them through the unfriendly soil of students' souls. Human nature, it seems, remains the same in our very altered circumstances because we still face the same problems, if in different guises, and have the distinctively human need to solve them, even though our awareness and forces have become enfeebled. (A. Bloom, 1987, p. 380)

But it is simply not possible, after the theories and politics we have been tracing, to return to this prelapsarian state. A question remains to be asked, however: if all aesthetic responses to texts are produced within particular practices, and if those responses are thereby entangled with the ideological, is the only possible answer to substitute a politically motivated critique for that old-style self-satisfied aesthetic that promotes inaction? Or can the aesthetic be (re)conceptualised in sociocultural terms? These are questions to which we will return in later chapters.

Meanwhile, we need to trace the uptake of those theories in various secondary and postsecondary educational institutions. In particular, given the demise of an unquestioned elitism of texts and taste, we will need to see how educators have dealt with the popular culture of their students, whether it is to be deplored, or accepted, even celebrated, and how they engage with literary texts.

Instituting Cultural Studies

The critiques of traditional literary culture we have been exploring were given an institutional home in cultural studies. This interdisciplinary discipline claimed a university place in Britain from the 1970s in the Birmingham Centre for Contemporary Cultural Studies and in Open University courses, though it had been founded as a form of study previously in the writings of people such as Raymond Williams (1958), Richard Hoggart (1957), and E. P. Thompson (1968). It was soon exported to the United States and given prominence in postgraduate courses by the likes of Lawrence Grossberg. It also found a hospitable home in Australia. Again, there is no need here for even a short history of cultural studies (Easthope, 1991; Grossberg, 1997; Hartley, 2003; Morris, 1997). Amongst the various forms of investigation that cultural studies inaugurated, concerning how people lead their lives, what we do need to examine are two very different views of culture, especially in its popular manifestations: the critical; and the appreciative, even celebratory.

The first view, the critical view, followed from the left, even Marxist, leanings of a number of influential early cultural studies practitioners, such as Williams (1958, 1980), Hoggart (1957), Thompson (1964), and Hall and Whannel (1964). These made sustained critical inquiries into the operations of power and the control of opinion by those who held sway in society. They traced the workings of ideology in culture, including the making of "common sense," and the shaping of people subject to these ideologies. They asked that now classic question of Raymond Williams regarding various cultural institutions and practices:

"Who benefits?" In many ways, they were aligned with the Frankfurt School of Marxist theorists, including Theodor Adorno, Max Horkheimer, and others. These critics tended to denigrate the masses as duped or doped by the culture industries whose mindless entertainments manipulated them with propaganda and encouraged them to consent to their economic and cultural impoverishment. This critical view could encourage strange bedfellows. As Hartley notes (2003), "It didn't matter whether the critics were on the political Right (Leavis, T. S. Eliot, Wyndham Lewis) or on the Left (Hall, Hoggart); mass culture was a common enemy." This attitude underpinned the educational agenda of the critical wing of cultural studies teachers: to enlighten students by revealing the ideologies in popular texts that hold them in thrall and so laying bare the falsity of the common sense offered in those texts. Frank Lentricchia (1983) encapsulates this view, arguing that "the point [of literary criticism] is not only to interpret texts, but in so interpreting them, change our society," and that this will be accomplished if teachers can through their work produce a "culturally suspicious, trouble-making readership" (p. 11).

This is very different from the more open agenda set by Grossberg (1993); he takes the popular to be "a field of questions" that demands that we examine how power works where people live their lives. Power may indeed not be simply imposed on the people through the texts with which they engage but may rather be exercised by them. Which brings us to the second cultural studies view of the popular. This has to do with what Hartley (2003) calls a founding principle of cultural studies, its "philosophy of plenty," as opposed to the restrictive practices of an exclusive high culture that was "designed to preserve scarcity and therefore value (price) in a market not only of works like paintings, but also of repute, symbolic power and representativeness (cultural capital)" (p. 4). A more inclusive cultural studies practice is broadly accepting and appreciative of a range of cultural forms and practices. (Recall the media studies lecturer quoted at the beginning of the chapter.) It looks at how people engage with popular entertainments, how they construct their leisure activities, and how they manage their everyday domestic lives. In such matters people are seen as agents, actively investing in and shaping their environments, culture, and selves, and negotiating their responses to the texts they choose. Hartley (2003) characterises this strand of cultural studies as "more preoccupied with meanings (story, song, spectacle, speech) than with power, more optimistic in mood, more inclined to take ordinariness as an end of democratisation, not as a means to power" (p. 33).

Since cultural studies proponents had from the outset established an educational agenda (Grossberg, 1997), it is not surprising that both of these attitudes towards the culture and lived experience of people who are not members of the elite were taken up by secondary and postsecondary teachers.

After Cultural Studies: Radical Pedagogy, Critical Literacy, Media Studies, and Multiliteracies

Certain aspects of cultural studies have been especially attractive to some teachers of English and media studies: an extension of the range of texts legitimate for study, an awareness of the social grounding of those texts, and a concern for the ideologies implicit in them. It is a legacy that has been unevenly taken up in high school and college classrooms in the United Kingdom, the United States, Australia, and elsewhere. The account that follows will not attempt a full history, only follow some of the major strands.

Critical Pedagogy

The critical strand of cultural studies could be plaited quite neatly into that movement of the 1980s and 1990s called radical or critical pedagogy. Like cultural studies, this movement for radical educational reform inherited much from neo-Marxism, feminism, and other forms of identity politics. And postsecondary educators such as Henry Giroux (1983), Peter McLaren (1989), Ira Shor (1980), and others also saw themselves as following in the footsteps of the Brazilian literacy educator Paulo Freire

(1970, 1985; Freire & Macedo, 1987), who aimed to help his peasant students understand the world in the word—that is, the politics of their labour and poverty in even the most neutral seeming names for things in their daily lives.

Radical pedagogues have adopted this process of "conscientization" or politicising of consciousness, for their first-world classrooms. They advocate opposition to the inequitable status quo. Their stance is activist, even revolutionary, if not armed: the "transformative intellectual" will help inaugurate a new, more democratic order within and beyond the school walls through ideology critique. Struggles in the community and the classroom become the sites for learning not only literacy skills but also political awareness and counter-hegemonic strategy. Students are taught how to critique the very bases of knowledge offered to them in the "commonsense" texts of their culture and schools. And the "voices" of marginalised minorities are to be heeded and validated.

In their writing they do not discuss specific literary texts and only occasionally discuss those of popular culture (e.g. Giroux, 1992b, on the film *Dirty Dancing*). McLaren, however, offers a lengthy polemic about popular culture, in his *Critical Pedagogy and Predatory Culture* (1995). His voice at times becomes almost hysterical as he condemns "the myth-machine, television," and other popular media:

> The pulsating beams from the T.V. screen become the shifting and perilous ground on which we form our judgements and decisions which forge our communal vision; a ground in which desire is infantilised, kept separate from meaning, and maintained in a state of narcissistic equilibrium. (p. 60)

By contrast, Giroux (1992b) recognises that teachers need to engage with the pleasure students take in the popular texts of their culture, although he still defines such engagement as a "struggle." It is the same ambivalence of his attitude towards popular culture and mass media texts that we find in much cultural studies writing.

In general, the radical pedagogy movement seeks to cure students of their investment in popular texts through arming them against the false values these convey. This has been critiqued by Buckingham as "fantasies of 'empowerment' and 'liberation'" (1998).[1] Against such oversimple theorising Buckingham sets the realities of classroom practice, the complexities of young people's engagements with media texts, and the limits of a rationalistic analysis to change students' consciousness.

In discussing public schooling, the critical pedagogues offer the same cultural critiques of the canon we have traced earlier in this chapter (e.g., Giroux, 1992a). They call the teaching of traditional "cultural literacy" the practice of "pedagogy as domestication" (Lankshear & McLaren, 1993). They tend to agree with McLaren (1995), following Eagleton, that literature, as a moral technology, "serves to create a bourgeois body/subject which values subjectivity in itself" (p. 72). And Giroux (1992a), is similarly dismissive of the practice of textual interpretation: "How we read or define a 'canonical' work may not be as important as challenging the overall function and social uses the notion of the canon has served" (p. 96).

This book argues that such reading *is* important and is not to be so quickly dismissed. Not all aesthetic responses to texts are hopelessly compromised by the reading practices traditionally associated with canonical texts. If those who advocate politically based critique fail to engage with the multifarious aesthetic aspects of both literary and popular texts, they cannot give an adequate account of the workings of such texts in the lives of readers.

Critical Literacy

An affiliate of radical pedagogy goes by the name of critical literacy. This movement has also inherited some characteristics from a critical cultural and media studies. All of these draw on similar strategies of ideology critique based on a social justice agenda; however, critical literacy concentrates on texts (both literary and popular) and language use rather than addressing the broader schooling-reform agendas of critical pedagogy.

> Critical literacy teaching begins by problematising the cultures and knowledges of the text—putting them up for grabs, for critical debate, for weighing, judging, critiquing. Learning the linguistic structure of texts can be a crucial part of this process. But a social analysis of texts also requires classroom frames for talking about how and in whose interests social institutions and texts can refract and bend social and natural reality, manipulate and position readers and writers. Such analysis can also provide the groundwork for "changing the subject" of texts, and for strategically intervening in social contexts. (Luke, O'Brien, & Comber, 1994, p. 141)

The critical literacy movement recognises that texts are made and read in particular cultural, historical, and political contexts that condition what meanings can be made. It scrutinises the selective representation of people, places, and events and examines the partiality of those textual constructs—their tendency to foreground or privilege some matters and marginalise or occlude others. It is interested in what is not said—in the politically charged silences in texts. It identifies the position readers are offered, in order to make sense of the text; and it encourages readers to take up a resistant reading position—to be suspicious of the ways texts may serve the interests of some groups to the disadvantage of others. (See also Knoblauch & Brannon, 1993.)

Such critical literacy is akin to the "radical" version of English characterised by Ball, Kenny, and Gardiner (1990) as

> class-conscious and political in content. . . . The stance is oppositional, collective aspirations and criticisms become a basis for action. Campaigns and struggles in the community become vehicles for learning social and literacy skills. Children are taught how to "read the world", to question the grounds and origins of knowledge. . . . Attempt is made to confirm the voices of the oppressed: anti-sexism and anti-racism become a crucial part of this. And the emphasis is upon shared experience and collective struggle: the state is challenged. (p. 80)

Critical literacy as theory and practice is also generally aligned with the more specifically linguistic concerns of critical linguistics (Fowler, 1986; Kress & Hodge, 1979), critical discourse analysis

(Fairclough, 1989, 1992a), critical language awareness (Fairclough, 1992b), and critical applied linguistics (Pennycook, 2001) in the United Kingdom and elsewhere. These are part of a larger movement to reintroduce an explicit and socially critical focus on language in classrooms. Although significant critical language work has been done by some committed teachers, in general this movement has not had much impact on curriculum in mainstream classrooms. A significant exception is the uptake of Fairclough's critical language awareness in the curriculum work of Hilary Janks in South Africa (1993a, 1993b). These linguistically focused movements have not, however, taken high or popular cultural texts as their central concern or dealt at all with the aesthetic.

A species of critical literacy has developed within accommodating niches in parts of Australia (and in New Zealand). In Australia through the 1980s and mid-1990s more left-wing Labour governments were in power at state and national levels, and they still predominate in the states (which have direct responsibility for educational curricula). Given their broad general alignment with social justice agendas, these governments allowed a version of critical literacy to take hold in policy, in educational theory and rhetoric, and (unevenly) in a number of classrooms (A. Luke, 2000; Morgan, 1997). This version is less overtly politically oppositional and radically activist than critical pedagogy. (Whether this has facilitated the uptake of critical literacy in curricula or followed from it is unclear—it is probably a bit of both.) In the analysis of texts that goes on in critical literacy classrooms, a social justice agenda, and sometimes a left-leaning politics, is for the most part covertly assumed rather than openly debated. Analysis is often thought to be the sufficient endpoint of critical literacy and its justification; political activism is considered beyond the scope of English teachers.

By contrast, in American high schools there seems little evidence of a widespread uptake of radical pedagogy or critical literacy, at least in mainstream English classrooms, though aspects of it may appear in critical media literacy courses. Certainly such radical movements are institutionally less endorsed in the United States than (say) in Australia, whatever individual teachers are able to do in their classrooms. It can be hard to identify general trends at the grassroots level across rather fragmented and localised school district norms. (But see O'Malley, Rosen, & Vogt, 1990.) Critical literacy is, however, on the radar screen of some teachers' organisations. For example, the International Reading Association in the United States has established a page on its Web site devoted to a "Focus on Critical Literacy." In some cases, however, such critical literacy is more narrowly equated with critical reading skills—that is, with more traditional analytical work on the substance and form of texts.

In the United Kingdom, for historical reasons having to do with the imposition of a conservative National Curriculum, critical literacy has similarly made few if any inroads into more traditional literary study. Chris Searle (1998), however, provides a salient if almost solitary instance of radical English or critical literacy at the secondary school level. His teaching of ethnically diverse working-class pupils in northern England involved them directly in political community action. The title of his book, *None but Our Words,* sums up his emphasis on pupils' giving voice to their own cultural concerns and their solidarity with those who are oppressed locally or globally. Thus his pupils' poems are quoted extensively in the book. Searle's emphasis on speech and writing reveals his allegiance to "voice" in radical pedagogy—but also with the progressive tradition of English teaching, which valued students' experiences and local knowledges and encouraged students' self-expression. Searle writes of a tradition of poetry very different from the "great" tradition of the official curriculum—one allied to the lives and movement of working-class people that "gave the heartbeat of the struggling communities" (p. 6). He finds his role as an English teacher in

> a whole new literacy, a new curriculum of poetry and life embracing each other for the betterment of those whom it served, and I was determined to make this noble and purposeful use of language and the imagination the centre of an 'English' teaching in my classroom. (p. 6)

Like Holbrook too, Searle finds in the mass popular culture to which his pupils are subject "the opposite of life, generosity, empathy and people's solidarity. It subsumes the truly human and projects a new barbarism which threatens to smother social life and the very bonds that keep us capable of being one human race" (p. 9). As we have seen, this case against popular culture is a very familiar theme amongst critical pedagogy and cultural studies theorists.

Media Studies

In various places an attenuated version of media studies appears under the umbrella of English, but it is also a secondary and postsecondary subject in its own right. (For an itemising of the differences between media studies and English, see Buckingham and Sefton-Green [1994, pp. 132–35].) Some aspects of a critical cultural studies had a marked influence on its development, not least in the United Kingdom, though they have been taken up selectively and are now undergoing change. In this older strand of media studies in schools the study of texts has been emphasised, rather than everyday practices, the influence of English teachers being apparent here. This study has characteristically taken the form of putting on trial "deceitful" media texts (Mellor & Patterson, 1994), which stood accused of bias, distortions of reality, manipulation of audiences, and the like. The prosecution was led by the teacher, with the students enrolled as junior counsel. That is, the media have been seen as channels for society's dominant ideology, and the young have been regarded as particularly vulnerable to their influence. The point of this kind of media studies has been to "interrupt students' unreflective acceptance of [TV] text" (C. Luke, 1997), since students have characteristically been seen as the passive dupes of the media.

Such critical analysis, modelled by the teacher, has been considered the most effective form of "inoculation" against the insidious diseases communicated by this means, or as "demystification"—of bringing into the light of critical reason truths that usually lie hidden under the bright, alluring qualities of media texts. (For a critique of this approach, see Buckingham, 1998.) In this form of media studies the field of study may be broader than in English, but the evaluations have been based on similar assumptions about value and culture offered by Marxist or even Leavisite critics. So too the pedagogy has been similar, with the teacher as the bearer of the light of pure, critical reason, bringing students out of their darkness.

More recently, many British, Canadian, and Australian media studies theorists and practitioners have begun to move beyond this view of media as purveyors of "false consciousness" and consumers as dupes. They recognise that students are expert and discriminating users of media and that knowledge and power are less securely and exclusively held by the teacher. Buckingham and Sefton-Green (1994), for instance, critique that older, critical form of media studies because "it neglects the pleasurable or emotional dimensions of that relationship [of young people with popular culture]: pleasure, it would appear, is highly dangerous, and can only be dispelled by a good dose of objective, rational analysis" (p. 130; see also Bazalgette & Buckingham, 1995). Turnbull (1993) also examines the "largely overlooked" aesthetic dimension of media texts in schools. We explore these matters of aesthetic pleasure in later chapters.

In the United States, by contrast, that older critical approach to the media appears still to persist in critical media literacy policies and practices. (For the history of media literacy education in the United States see Tyner, 1998.) By comparison with Britain, Canada, and Australia, for example, American media education is marked by "top-down, protectionist rhetoric" (Tyner, 1998). And media literacy educators still generally aspire to "inoculate" students against the dangers of media texts.

Multiliteracies

This account of the legacy of critical cultural and language studies would be incomplete without brief mention of an allied theory and practice. A group of influential scholars drawn from the United States, England, and Australia (often called the New London Group after the place of their first meeting, New London, New Hampshire) set out a coherent theory of language practice as multiliteracies (New London Group, 2000). This stemmed from and attempted to develop critical literacy in two main ways: by giving full recognition to the multimodal nature of literacies in a technologically and visually saturated world of texts; and by working with the understanding that all literacy practices are situated within particular cultural and social contexts. Among other things, their manifesto attempted to develop a comprehensive social view of what subject English, or literacy education, should be. In particular, Gunther Kress's (2000) notion of a design element as central to English could provide support for the significance of the aesthetic understood in social terms. However, *design* as it has been conceived focuses rather on the processes of production of language, text, and teaching. The multiliteracies program has been taken up in the rhetoric of policy and curricular documents in some places, particularly Australia, and has informed some teaching practice within existing areas of literacy and English education.

A number of species of critical literacy have been described here—critical media studies, critical pedagogy, critical linguistics—as well as the largely Australian curricular movement within the subject of English that goes by the name of critical literacy. At the heart of them all are two connected ideas: of language as socially situated and produced, hence as inherently ideological, and of our subjectivities as socially and ideologically constituted through language. This is the sense in which the term *critical literacy* is used in this book.

A Dilemma for English

In various parts of the English-speaking world, a division often persists in secondary English education between more traditional interpretative study of literary texts (even if the list of texts now includes those from minority cultures) and a more critically suspicious analysis of media texts. Indeed, when they take up literary texts, many teachers still practise what Jane Tompkins (1985) called a "modernist reading" derived from practical and "new" criticism. Here the literary text is treated as a self-sufficient object, an end in itself. All elements of the text are taken to be significant and to contribute to the overarching, unifying theme of the work. Meanings are therefore valid if they can be shown to contribute to the work's thematic unity. And readers are invited to respond to such works by entering into their richly realised imagined world and to learn with or from the characters' experiences (Belsey, 1982). The same consideration is not, of course, extended to films, television dramas, or narrative computer games.

There is often a lag, or even an unbridgeable gap, between the theory and analysis of literary and other texts practised in universities, and what goes on in school classrooms. Whatever encounters preservice teachers have with current literary and cultural theories, when they move into schools they find a particular, and sometimes peculiar, set of institutionalised practices of teaching texts. Syllabuses and curricula, resources (books, worksheets, textbooks, and the like), and assessment regimes encourage or require teachers to conform to the norms of their school and their profession. Busy teachers are not expected to read, reflect, theorise, and "translate" those theories into classroom activities. By such means, teachers learn how to teach in ways that do not promote questioning of the assumptions on which their practice rests.

The United Kingdom offers a salient instance of the persistence, or reimposition, of a certain form of literary study in secondary English. With the development of a National Curriculum and a testing regime in the 1990s, English was reframed in accordance with that older, humanistic view of the value of literature study. As the Cox Report stated, such study is to help students to

> 'grow' through literature—both emotionally and aesthetically, both morally and socially. . . . An active involvement with literature enables pupils to share the experience of others. They will encounter and come to understand a wide range of feelings and relationships by entering vicariously the worlds of others, and in consequence are likely to understand more of themselves. (Cox, 1991, p. 76)

That view is still apparent in the current UK National Curriculum for English (DfES, 2004). Pupils at Key Stage 3 (12–14 years) are, in "Reading for Meaning," to "identify the perspectives offered on individuals, community and society," but not, apparently, to critique these. They are to focus on "understanding the author's craft," in which "language is used in imaginative, original and diverse ways." And—most revealing to an outsider—under the heading "English literary heritage," pupils are to be "taught . . . the characteristics of texts that are considered to be of high quality." The qualifier "considered" does little perhaps to dint the solidity of that category, since pupils are also to be taught "the appeal and importance of these texts over time." The notion of the universality of great texts remains virtually unchallenged.

High quality and importance over time are not, however, characteristics that are extended to "texts from different cultures and traditions." Under this heading pupils are merely taught "the distinctive qualities of literature from different traditions." And when it comes to media and moving-image texts, pupils are taught the semiotics of the formal characteristics of such texts and engage with questions of audience (both typical of media studies approaches). They do not apparently need to consider aesthetic quality, except insofar as "form, layout and presentation contribute to effect" and how "readers choose and respond to media." The advice given in the document concerning the range of texts to be studied makes a clear distinction between literature and nonfiction and nonliterary texts. Under literature the traditional categories are observed (drama, fiction, poetry, with Shakespeare in a category all his own), and a division exists between texts written before and after 1914 from which teachers are to select. Very few instances of genuinely popular texts are available for study.

Teachers who work within these directives may over time come to take their categories, emphases, and valuations for granted. Or they may accede to the status quo as inevitable. In either case this, like any curriculum framework, governs their work, not least since they are accountable for their pupils' achievements.

If we look at an instance of an Australian state-based curriculum document, we can see how radically different "English" as critical literacy is from that which prevails in England and

Wales. In Western Australia the *English Learning Area Statement* (1998) identifies two forms of literacy that students need: a functional literacy and a critical literacy. Although functional literacy includes "the conventions associated with literary texts" (p. 83), critical literacy entails "appreciation of and sensitivity to sociocultural diversity." Those terms typical of a more conservative version of English, *appreciation* and *sensitivity,* have undergone a remarkable displacement: they now grace the work of critical literacy, which is defined very much in the terms spelled out earlier in the chapter. When students come to discuss a poem, for instance, they will "analyse the construction of gender" in it (p. 87). And while they may read "for enjoyment" (this is mentioned only once), it is evidently much more important that they should respond critically: "they identify values and assumptions within a text and the ways in which a text may seek to elicit particular responses from readers" (p. 91).

The National Curriculum and the *English Learning Area Statement* take seemingly irreconcilable stances towards aesthetic appreciation or political critique of literature and popular texts. Each version of English concentrates on a different range of texts, attends to different aspects of them, aims to develop in students different capacities for reading, seeks to generate and regulate certain desires and satisfactions, and has in view a different society for which students are being prepared and to which they will contribute.

Teachers who work within that older paradigm, whether in the United Kingdom or elsewhere, tend to resist the introduction of popular texts, from advertisements to sitcoms, on equal terms with literary texts, arguing that this breadth takes attention away from more "worthwhile" works. Very often, it appears, they simply do not know how to teach them productively. It does not seem to such teachers that they can or should credit the texts of popular culture with such artful design or aesthetic satisfactions as literary texts offer (Abbs, 1989). Indeed, they have learned from the legacy of Leavis to deplore such texts and to train their students to resist their blandishments. In such cases, two types of critical work are practised on two types of text. Texts of the first category are to be highly valued for aesthetic qualities that are taken to be intrinsic, and the work of literary criticism performed on them. Texts of the second are to be evaluated critically in a manner that more closely resembles critical literacy. It is a divisive practice.

By contrast, as we have seen, some teachers who locate themselves within a sociocritical paradigm embrace the use of popular texts, although, as we have seen, they are often united with their more conservative colleagues in their scorn of the deadening effect of such texts. They often seem less comfortable working with those traditional literary texts, unless they know how to bring to bear a political criticism and trace the workings of the text's informing ideologies, or unless the texts are to be exempted from such political critique, since they give "voice" to interests previously silenced by the literary establishment, such as Indigenous rights. Except where curricula and booklists direct them, such teachers would often prefer to engage their students with causes and texts that seem to matter more urgently, and on which they can bring to bear the full weight of their politically grounded critique. This too is a divisive practice.

This book takes the position that no text is the ultimate source of its own meaning or value. Any text is a site on which various meanings are generated, all of which need to be enjoyed, argued over, and critiqued. So too our acts of valuing and preferring need to be evaluated, and on grounds that need to be made explicit. Meaning and value, pleasure and engagement, are produced within practices of reading, of teaching, and of learning. We therefore need a theory and practice of reading and teaching that work with these assumptions and allow for the generation and evaluation of meaning and pleasure.

The aesthetically appreciative and the politically critical can be reconciled, in approaches to English. The rest of this book considers how an awareness and a valuing of the aesthetic can be incorporated into sociocultural and political models of literacy. Indeed, it argues that any model of literacy that does not encompass both an aesthetic and a sociocultural awareness is flawed. The two are not in opposition but are necessary and complementary components of a rich practice of English education. In order to launch this argument, we must first consider what is meant by the aesthetic. This is the work of the next chapter.

Defining the Aesthetic

The first step in our investigation of how the aesthetic can be accommodated within socially critical versions of literacy must be to examine the aesthetic itself and establish some common understanding of what might be meant by the term, what are some of the major features by which we recognize its presence, and what are some of its most common ways of working.

Aesthetics as a philosophical discourse has a long and distinguished history, which in itself suggests the difficulty of coming to terms with what exactly the aesthetic is. *The aesthetic* is a slippery and protean concept, and much of the philosophical writing is, in fact, geared to trying to pin it down, define the essential elements, and generally make it manageable.[1] Since there is not time to engage in this philosophical venture here (nor much likelihood of success), it seems advisable to make a virtue of necessity: rather than attempt a tight and comprehensive definition, we will take advantage of the indeterminacy and work with a flexible understanding of the concept, especially since our attention is on its relevance to education, and education is likely to call on pragmatic everyday understandings of the term rather than those found in refined philosophical discourse. For our purposes, it is more likely to be productive in the end to acknowledge the complex and shifting nature of the aesthetic and the variable ways in which it can be seen than to limit the argument artificially by defining some of the common understandings out of consideration because they are philosophically impure.

The term *aesthetic* is used in many different ways. Much of the writing on it is abstract and concerned with mapping out its defining qualities, and we too will start with looking at it as a concept. However, there is also frequently a concern in the literature with the aesthetic in experiential terms—that is, what is happening when one is involved with the aesthetic, how the aesthetic text is produced, and how it is recognized and understood—so we will then go on to examine the aesthetic as a process.

The Concept of the Aesthetic

It is perhaps most profitable to consider the aesthetic not as a particular range of content and interests but as a way of knowing. We have many ways of knowing (ways, indeed, in which "knowing" means many different things). There are the basic means of knowing through sensory input, and there are the simple categorisations of the sensory material into useful organising concepts—food, day, weapon, shelter. Then there are the more abstract ways of knowing, where the categorisation moves into theorisations, where basic principles are intellectually abstracted from phenomena—philosophy, theology, science. The aesthetic is another of these more sophisticated ways of knowing, but as opposed to the "philosophical/scientific" ways, there are two major differences with the aesthetic:

◆ The intellectual is not (necessarily) privileged over the emotional/sensory/affective; and

◆ The movement is not to abstraction, but to particularisation, knowledge coming from a more intense focus on the particular rather than by abstracting from particulars to general rules.

This is not to say that the intellectual is excluded, nor that the general is not aimed at. Indeed, it is one of the constant claims of the aesthetic that it is its capacity to encompass the intellectual and the affective, the particular and the general, that makes it so powerful. Equally, however, such claims indicate that there are major tensions within the concept. In fact, one cannot go very far in reading on the aesthetic without becoming aware that the claims for its essential character are rife with oppositions and contradictions. Rather than this being the grounds for despairing of ever reaching a definition, it in fact points to the essential feature of the aesthetic as a way of knowing. The argument here is that the power of the aesthetic is grounded in these tensions that have the potential to be seen as binary oppositions but that do not become contradictory in the aesthetic. Rather they are genuinely held in balance.

We next examine some of these tensions.

Universal/Particular

Leaving aside purely formal abstract works, characteristically with the aesthetic we are presented with a representation of some particular experience. We are involved in the particularity but at the same time assume that this experience is representative, that it is telling us something about the world, human beings, or life in general. The duality is caught up in the question, "What is the text about?" One range of answers has to do with content: "It's about this man who falls in love with a woman and gives up everything to pursue her." The other range of answers (and these are the kind that tend to be valued in English education) has to do with more general concerns: "It's about the all-consuming nature of love," or "It's about the destructive nature of passion," depending on the detail of the story as shown. As this example suggests, the work of close definition of the general concept is done through the particulars of the representation (although it can also at times be done more directly through overt statement, particularly with earlier novelists). To simplify, as the representation becomes more precise or more complex, so too does the concept. Both *Othello* and *Antony and Cleopatra* could be said to be about the destructive nature of passion, but the particular development of the drama means that both the passion and the destruction are very different in each case, and we see the world in very different ways.

Material/Numinous

Its particularity suggests that the aesthetic has to do with the embodied.[2] The kind of knowledge that the aesthetic brings is not a matter of airy thought but of (the representation of) physical, material things. Against the philosophical, which tends to privilege abstract intellect, the aesthetic makes a strong claim for the importance of the material and of knowledge gained through engagement with material reality. However, there is also a persistent strain in the aesthetic that relates it to the numinous, to things immaterial and immanent. There are two major manifestations of this. One stems from the artist's creation of an imaginative reality: however potent the representation, it is *not* the material reality it represents. It is for this that Shakespeare and many before and after him have likened the poet to the madman (and the lover):

> The lunatic, the lover, and the poet,
> Are of imagination all compact . . .
> The poet's eye, in a fine frenzy rolling,
> Doth glance from heaven to earth, from earth to heaven;
> And, as imagination bodies forth
> The forms of things unknown, the poet's pen
> Turns them to shapes, and gives to airy nothing
> A local habitation and a name.

A MIDSUMMER NIGHT'S DREAM, V.I.7–17

The other manifestation stems from the generalising force of art, its propensity to confer a sense of grand meaning on the material it presents. There is thus often a revelatory force in the representation, and so a belief that the artist is not concerned with just the actual but with looking at the deeper energies and forces implicitly at play. This is perhaps most obvious with the Romantic poets (Blake, Wordsworth) or perhaps with works of "magic realism" (Marquez, Borges), but even a solidly realist work like *On the Waterfront,* say, creates a sense of major forces at play underpinning the material conflict, the sense that more is at stake than just this story about the power of unions and one man's involvement with them.

Emotional/Intellectual

It is generally recognized that the aesthetic is bound up with emotions, but it is almost as regularly acknowledged as a product of the intellect. The emotional aspect is the more apparent. While working towards intellectual engagement with major concepts affecting our lives (e.g., the destructive nature of passion), an aesthetic text will move us to these perceptions primarily by emotional means, not by rational, argumentative ones. Aesthetic texts often (although not always) work by encouraging us empathetically to experience events that lead us to particular conclusions. The reliance on empathy does not mean, however, that there is no intellectual engagement. It is a fundamental mark of the aesthetic that however emotionally carried away we may be, there remains an appraising, evaluating objective element operating alongside the emotional experience. At its simplest level, we never believe that what we are seeing is actuality, but rather know that it has been created for some purpose, and we process the text with that purpose in mind. Even if the purpose of the text is to make us cry, as in a sentimental tearjerker, because of the aesthetic text's tendency towards universalising the represented experience, there is an element of conceptualising about the implications and so a move to intellectualisation. This may not be very profound intellectual engagement, but the nature of the engagement is fundamentally different from the emotional engagement we would feel if we were actually living the events, because we register the shaping and so abstract meaning from it. In "real life," the process is almost exactly the reverse: we register the events and try to make them meaningful by imposing a shape on them.

The emotion created by the work is not necessarily empathetic but can be produced by a recognition of meaningful and pleasurable shaping. Some works involve us emotionally through their ability to structure experience (e.g., by counterpointing two elements, such as plot strands or metaphors, that give different perspectives, or simply by producing a particularly striking formal structure that is powerful in itself.) In these cases the intellectual element is even easier to identify, since the power of the text depends on our ability to recognize pattern and take meaning from it.

To insist that the emotional engagement with artistic works has an element of intellectual engagement embedded within it is not to deny the emotional power of such works, but rather to particularize it. The power of the aesthetic to carry one away emotionally is fundamental to its attraction and its force. This privileging of emotion has led to the deep suspicion that has been felt towards the aesthetic through the centuries: reason and logic are safer guides than the emotions, and the powerful work of art can lead to acquiescence in ideas that one might find logically suspect. This tendency is, of course, why the aesthetic is treated with such suspicion in critical versions of literacy, which is the fundamental problem being addressed in this book.

Inspiration/Control

A parallel opposition comes in conceptualising the creation of the work. One line of rhetoric sees the artist as inspired, as carried away by deep forces within or outside herself or himself, becoming little more than the channel through which these impulses can be externalised. The artist is a sleepwalker, instinctively producing greatness. Another line of rhetoric stresses the craft of art, the hard work in finding the right word, the exact curve within the painting, the unexpected but exactly right keyshift. This opposition often comes close to the emotional/intellectual one, the artist being seen as either carried away by emotions and pouring out the art from an overflowing soul, or seen as exercising higher intellectual qualities, mastering emotion by subjecting it to formal control. Although most artists presumably would acknowledge the importance of both dimensions, a legacy of this distinction can be seen in some of the debates that go on about writing pedagogy, particularly those ten to fifteen years ago in Australia between the advocates of the process writing and genre approaches. The battle lines were drawn up between those who believed that good student writing came from allowing the students to work intuitively on their own self-determined projects, and those who believed in the fundamental importance of having the students learn and practise the linguistic and structural features of the text-type. Good (aesthetic) writing unquestionably requires both personal motivation and knowledge of genre.

Individual/Traditional

The view that art springs from inspiration gives the artist a particular heroic status. She or he is a unique individual with talents beyond those of the ordinary person. Art is thus seen as intensely individualist, as expressive of the unique individual personality.

A widely held twentieth-century variant of this belief is the psychologised view of art as the projection of the artist's psychological preoccupations, usually indeed of their psychopathology. Whether the artist is seen as super being or as psychological misfit, what matters in this view is the uniqueness of the creator, and her or his ability to tap profound inner sources. Art, however, is also seen as a matter of tradition. Indeed, there is a common theme of the art of a culture being its highest expression, being the thing that defines the culture. Every artist draws on those who come before her or him. Every artist works with (or against) the forms that she or he has inherited. Again, there is not necessarily any deep contradiction between the two views, but there is a tension. Harold Bloom, in *The Anxiety of Influence* (1997), has suggested that this tension is a central dynamic in art, that every new artist misreads and reacts against those that have come before.

Content/Form

Implicit in a number of the points of tension already mentioned is the content/form dyad. In the ideal work of art, it is often felt, there is a perfect match of content and form. The form has become expressively unified with the content; the content has found its natural (however strenuously worked-for) form. However, there are works in which the content is played against the form (e.g. *The Osbournes*), and there are works in which form is almost all that matters (e.g., abstract geometrical art such as that by Rothko, some concrete poems). It is probably true that it is a sign we have moved into the realm of the aesthetic when we notice the form. We will return to this in a moment.

If we move away from oppositions (although we will see that there are still tensions aplenty), there are two other terms that we need to consider in relation to the aesthetic: beauty and pleasure.

Beauty

The aesthetic has a long history of relationship with the beautiful. Indeed, there is a temptation to make beauty a necessary condition of the aesthetic, particularly if one accepts as synonyms for *beauty* the *transcendental* and the *sublime* (terms that are geared to moving attention away from the physical to the intellectual or spiritual). It is this connection that led Keats famously to equate Truth and Beauty and to see them as sufficient and absolute knowledge for this world.

However, things that are aesthetic are not necessarily beautiful in the common understanding of the term. One has only to mention the blinding of Gloucester or Blake's vision of London to make the point. There are various strategies used to get out of this dilemma. One is to argue that the work as a whole is beautiful by asserting that in the end it produces a meaningful pattern that transcends any momentary ugliness that is part of the pattern. Such an argument stresses the redemptive power of Cordelia in *King Lear,* or argues in terms of the cathartic effect of fear and pity. Another strategy is to argue what one may call the Keatsian line, that the work is revelatory of truth, and so in the end affirms beauty (however terrible). Another is to see the beauty in the artistic form and control: the evident control over the shaping of the material is in itself a thing of beauty, however ugly the vision it is painting. Whether one always wants to or should want to make such moves as these is obviously a matter of debate. Trying to accommodate such texts to a notion of beauty could well be seen to weaken much that is most powerful in them.

And yet, most would agree that there is something there in aesthetic texts for which the word *beauty* is being used as a convenient label. It is a kind of intensity, a sense that what we are seeing is saturated with significance and calls forth a heightened perception beyond what one expects in day-to-day existence. This intensity is attractive in itself because it provides us with heightened experience. It moves us, and so we want to involve ourselves with the things that are displaying the quality.[3]

Pleasure

Pleasure is an equally problematical term, although obviously again gesturing towards something that is basic to the aesthetic. Mentioning the blinding of Gloucester as a limit case once more raises the problem: what can possibly be found pleasurable in witnessing this vile and violent act? The word *pleasure* is obviously inadequate in its common meanings, although the complex understanding of pleasure that one finds in psychological writings could perhaps cover the phenomenon, since it allows for a core of potential pleasure in revulsion and negativity. If *beauty* as a feature of the aesthetic work needs to be glossed by *intensity*, then pleasure needs to be glossed by some term such as *engagement*, which can suggest the degree of response without necessarily implying that its nature is benign.

In our consideration of the aesthetic so far, we have been blurring the question of where this thing might be located. It is now necessary to turn to this question and think about the aesthetic as a process.

The Aesthetic as Process

Part of the reason why the aesthetic is so hard to define is that it is so hard to locate, or rather, it is located across a process involving various elements, and there is no way to determine which aspect is most important. It will also look different depending on which element we concentrate on. Commonly the aesthetic entails a creator, the work created, and an audience.[4] Thus, if we take something that most people would recognize as involving the aesthetic, like Keats's "Ode to a Nightingale," we have the poet John Keats, who has embodied (imagined) experience in a linguistic text, a poem, that it is reasonable to assume he expects his readers to see as having a significant aesthetic element; there is the text itself, which has certain features (stanza form, metaphor, a particular range of discourse) that are indications it is an aesthetic object; and then there is the audience—we come along and read the poem, activating our strategies for responding aesthetically, noting and appreciating (or not) the aesthetic aspects of this work. Quite clearly, all three elements are crucial, and we cannot locate the aesthetic in any one of them without taking the other two into account.

There is a temptation, in common with most recent theory, to bracket off the creator/artist figure, working on the argument that her or his intention is irrelevant except insofar as it is manifested in the work itself.[5] However, if we did this, we would be limiting ourselves to a concern with reception and would only be interested in the aesthetic decoding of texts. As long as writing is taking place in classrooms, we have to take an interest in the processes by which experience and ideas are turned into aesthetic works. On the other hand, it certainly is arguable that the creator is the most dispensable of the three elements. It is possible for us to take aesthetic pleasure in naturally occurring phenomena (waves crashing on the rocks, ranks of snow-capped mountains at sunset, a panorama of pastoral plains, even the song of a nightingale itself), and in these cases there has been no artist figure at all (unless one wants to argue that an artistically inclined God created these things for our aesthetic contemplation and pleasure, or that a nightingale is a conscious artist creating its melody).[6]

Often there is also in theoretical work a suspicion of the third element in the aesthetic process, the audience, since individual taste is so notoriously erratic. "Beauty is in the eye of the beholder," we are told, and one person's overwhelming artistic experience can be another's load of sentimental crap. Theoreticians tend to feel that anything so subjective as an individual response must be a very shaky foundation on which to build a secure conception of a phenomenon. However, again in educational terms, the student audience is of central concern, and how the aesthetic object affects them is primary material for educational work; developing the ability to work with the aesthetic text is the primary educational objective in many circumstances, so it is not possible to take this particular purist theoretical line here either.

So, we will have to consider all three elements in the process, and the relationship between them, if we want to develop an understanding of the aesthetic. However, given the uncertainty surrounding both the creator and the audience, it is perhaps advisable for us to start off by concentrating on that middle term, the aesthetic work itself.

The Aesthetic Work

In looking at a work, we need to consider both form and content to identify the aesthetic. One of the qualities of the aesthetic, as we have already seen, has always been considered its melding of the two—form and content joined together to make a uniquely expressive whole—but it is useful for our purposes, at least at the beginning, to treat them separately.

There are often certain obvious formal features in a text that mark it as available for aesthetic reactions, and perhaps even as *requiring* an aesthetic reaction from audiences. Even before we read a word of "Ode to a Nightingale," the layout of the lines on the page has alerted us that this is a poem and therefore is to be read with a certain mindset. Thus, when we do start reading, we are alert for, and responsive to, such things as the repetition of sounds in rhyme ("pains . . . drains") and alliteration ("with beaded bubbles winking at the brim"), or the imitative use of sound in onomatopoeia ("the murmurous haunt of flies on summer eves") or the deployment of expressive rhythms ("fade far away, dissolve, and quite forget . . .").

With aesthetic texts, one is often conscious that the language is being used in uncommon and uncommonly intense ways. This can involve the use of a particular range of language, a particular style or discourse. One would not expect, wandering along an English street or even standing in an English wood in the early nineteenth century, to hear a nightingale addressed as "light-winged Dryad." Indeed, one would not expect to hear a nightingale addressed at all. Very particular discourse conventions are operating here that involve a range of heightened language, with reference to mythological figures (Bacchus, Ruth) and sites (Lethe, Hippocrene), archaic or "made-up" words ("darkling," "murmurous"), a heavy use of metaphor ("as though of hemlock I had drunk"), and personification ("mid-May's eldest child").

Of course, the discourse in aesthetic works can be very ordinary, mimetic of everyday speech, so the aesthetic is not necessarily bound up with heightened language. Still, there is a sense of heightened significance achieved by the shaping of the work. In the Keats poem, there is a clear pattern of "base situation—imaginative journey—return to base" established. In narratives, events succeed one another in a significant order, often building up a pattern of cause and effect, or patterns of likeness or dissimilarity bring themselves to our attention. There may be parallel incidents or meaningful juxtapositions of which we can scarcely avoid taking note if we are concerned to make maximum meaning out of the text. Our expectations of certain patterns are played with, and (ideally) we are led to a point where, at the end, we see the principle on which the text has been organized, even if it is one of randomness.

The crucial element that activates aesthetic expectations in any work seems to be a sense that "composition" has taken place, that the material has been purposefully (if not necessarily consciously) laid out in this form for the audience, that space and time have been organised with care to produce certain effects, and (frequently) that the kind of language used is itself meaningful. One can, of course, be aware of such things in non-"creative" texts, but, as mentioned before, when this is noticed, the perception is moving into the realm of the aesthetic, whatever the initial purpose of the text or the content being handled.

The content is also important, not for what is represented but for how it is represented. There is no particular range of material that is aesthetic, nor anything that cannot be subsumed within an aesthetic text. It is a matter of how the material is seen. Our mapping of the aesthetic suggests some things that are likely features of the aesthetic text. It will tend to deal with the representation of particular experience rather than overtly with generalities. It is likely to have an emotional element, both in that it is likely to show us someone experiencing emotion and in that it will try to draw forth an emotional reaction from us. Beyond that, it is hard to generalize very much at all.

If the aesthetic is a particular way of knowing, then, in the end, how the content is seen, understood, and presented is what matters. One cannot think of any material that is aesthetic in itself: that most aesthetic of flowers, the lily, may be irredeemably prosaic in a botany textbook. (Even here, one can play the rather postmodern game of receding mirrors and imagine a description of a lily in a botany book being a text embedded in a novel. We will come back to this later, when we come to the reader, since, of course, one would read the botany textbook material differently in this context, and so it suggests just how much the aesthetic is a matter of reading practices.)

Once we start thinking about how the material is represented and seen, we move away from a concern with the text itself and start thinking about the other two elements in the aesthetic process, the artist/producer and the audience.

The Artist

Artists come in all shapes and sizes and, more significantly, in all predispositions, temperaments, and ranges of concerns. The stereotypes range from the lily-carrying, ultra-sensitive fin-de-siècle aesthete to the hard-drinking, passionately intense, loft-dwelling rebel. It is not possible to say anything about the kind of person who produces art (although some things might be said about the nature of creativity),[7] and so all we can consider here is what artists do.

What artists do, one might say, is produce aesthetic artefacts. If the aesthetic is a way of knowing the world, then they come to know an aspect of the (possible) world through embodying it aesthetically, and in embodying it, they make it available for us as their audience. To produce an aesthetic artefact one must have some material on which to work (which can be experienced, imagined, found, or otherwise acquired) and the propensity to work with this material aesthetically, which is both a mental disposition and a matter of having the technical skills to achieve the aesthetic outcomes one has set oneself.

The relationship of artists to their source material is an endlessly fascinating topic and has enabled libraries to be filled with scholarly works, as well as shopfuls of more popular biographical (and autobiographical) texts to be written. There is no point in denying that artists often do make works out of their own experience, while it is equally important to insist that the experience is inevitably transformed in the aesthetic making. What actually happened becomes irrelevant. One can certainly imagine that Keats was feeling depressed one night when he heard a nightingale singing, and the nightingale's song set him thinking about escaping the world, the fragility of human happiness, mortality, and so on, but that experience (if it ever happened) has undoubtedly turned into something quite different as the poem developed and the aesthetic imagination produced new elements and perspectives. The notion of the artist's personal emotional experience being the source of the work and guarantor of artistic truth and worth has a long history: Sir Philip Sidney, at the beginning of *Astrophel and Stella* (c. 1591), presents himself as tormented, trying to find the right words for his experience, until finally

"Fool," said my Muse to me, "look in thy heart, and write!"

(SONNET 1, L. 14)

And he did. But it is worth noting that when he looked in his heart he found a sequence of perfectly formed Petrarchan sonnets, some one hundred and eight of them, all fourteen lines long, with a complicated rhyme scheme, using classic Petrarchan metaphors. If it were just a matter of discovering the text in our heart and transcribing it, the process of writing would actually not be very interesting. It is the way the material transforms itself through the creative process, becomes richer or clearer or funnier or more complex—in other words, reveals to us more possibilities by being known through the aesthetic—that makes writing a significant thing.

To claim for the artist a special kind and degree of (aesthetic) knowledge is problematic in many ways. While Shelley famously extolled poets as the "unacknowledged legislators of the world," there is rightly a great suspicion these days of assuming that artists are somehow more intelligent and knowledgeable than the ordinary run of people: there is indeed plenty of evidence that they can be quite stupid when asked questions in interviews or when they decide to give us their opinion on politics or even art. However, in terms of the aesthetic way of knowing, one can at least credit the good artist with knowing the world well in that particular way while they are operating in the aesthetic domain. When they move into the intellectual domain or the interpersonal domain, they can be very limited, even with subjects on which they may be aesthetically profound.

So far we have been looking at "great" artists. What about the student as artist? If education is about developing human potential and about giving students the tools to know and operate in their world, then obviously it is important that they have experience and develop skills in producing aesthetic artefacts, knowing the world through that creative experience, as well as knowing it through creating other kinds of text. Producing aesthetic works is no more natural than producing a CV or a critical essay (telling students to "look into their hearts and write" is not likely to be highly productive), and so students need to be scaffolded into the aesthetic way of thinking and given the necessary tools to succeed in producing aesthetic texts.

The experience of writing texts and the experience of reading them are complementary. However, we should note that the relationship between what the artist thinks she or he has created, the actual features of the aesthetic text, and the experience a reader takes from that text is deeply problematic. According to one ideal, the text would perfectly embody the author's vision, and the reader would experience that vision with total fidelity. That, of course, never happens. In particular, readers take what they will (and can) from texts. This openness and flexibility is an ideal from another perspective. It is to the reader we now turn.

The Reader

The author has created a text that she or he expects to be read aesthetically. The text has features that are characteristic of the aesthetic. All this becomes significant only if a reader comes along who recognizes the signals and so undertakes a particular kind of reading of the text.

How much the aesthetic is a product of reading was suggested above by the speculation about what happens if a section of a botany book about lilies is introduced into a novel. Once it is embedded within the aesthetic text, it is read differently. The following short poem by Robert Lowell (1974, p. 141) is a far more graphic example:

Women, Children, Babies, Cows, Cats

'It was at My Lai or Sonmy or something,
it was this afternoon. . . . We had these orders,
we had all night to think about it—
we was to burn and kill, then there'd be nothing
standing, women, children, babies, cows, cats. . . .
As soon as we hopped the choppers, we started shooting.
I remember . . . as we was coming up upon one area
In Pinkville, a man with a gun . . . running—this lady. . .
Lieutenant LaGuerre said, "Shoot her." I said,
"You shoot her, I don't want to shoot no lady."
She had one foot in the door. . . . When I turned her,
There was this little one-month-year-old baby
I thought was her gun. It kind of cracked me up.'

The poem is by Robert Lowell, but every word of it is taken from a soldier's testimony at the hearing into the My Lai massacre during the Vietnam War. It is a "found poem." Thinking about how we read these (same) words differently when we see them set out as a poem published in a book of poetry can give us some insight into the features of aesthetic reading: we become more aware of the language (i.e., the form) and what it is telling us; we become interested in the speaker as "character" and read what kind of person he is from his words; we focus on the events as emotional experience and the impact they had on the speaker; we open ourselves to the text as affective experience; we think and feel beyond what we are shown in the text and contemplate its implications and its general significance; and we read the poem as a purposeful statement (we have no doubt about Lowell's attitude, even though he hasn't written a single word of his own).

This all, of course, accords with the elements we have mapped as characteristic of the aesthetic, and the signalling that this is a poem has activated us to look for them. In a very profound way, it is in one's perception that the aesthetic lies.

Such perception is heavily influenced culturally. Sir Philip Sidney's readers, back in the sixteenth century, undoubtedly had quite different expectations of poetry and what poetry did. They expected different kinds of meanings and so made different sense of poetry than we do in the twenty-first century. They would probably not see "Women, Children, Babies, Cows, Cats" (or perhaps any of Lowell's poems) as poems at all. Most twenty-first century readers would probably recognize a sonnet from *Astrophel and Stella* as a poem but, without a feat of historical imagination, might have considerable trouble reading it as meaningful, emotionally interesting, or in any way engaging.

Even at the level of formal elements, perception of significance and beauty is culturally bound. It may be true that some basic ingredients such as repetition and contrast are basic elements in the texts that all cultures perceive as aesthetic; however, the ability to perceive and take pleasure in these elements within particular texts is largely determined by the culture in which they are being produced and how compatible its understandings are with those of the culture in which they are being read. To experience the aesthetic is not a natural ability but shows a considerable degree of cultural sophistication, a point easily shown since the forms of the aesthetic are so culturally specific. To understand and appreciate an Aboriginal dot painting is very different from understanding and appreciating *King Lear* or *The Simpsons,* which is not to say that we are incapable of appreciating all three, and even that our appreciation of each of the three may be enhanced by our knowledge of the others.

There is also a strong element of the personal in aesthetic appreciation. The concept of "taste" is frequently addressed in the philosophical writings on aesthetics, but in the end it remains largely a mystery. It is reductive to argue that it is purely a product of social determination: there is no doubt that individuals can respond very differently to the same artefact, even if they have more or less equivalent cultural knowledge and equivalent ability to read it. There is no point in trying to avoid the personal element. We all have our individual dispositions that dispose us to like or not like certain things. One can speculate on a particular person's taste and what predisposes them to make the judgments they do, but in the end this tends to become a rather boring pop-psychology game. All that one can do if one is concerned to make the pleasure of the work available to someone else (e.g., one's students) is to try to persuade them to see the work differently, to see elements with which they might engage.

There are, of course, many kinds of aesthetic experience. Once one starts looking for the aesthetic, one sees it everywhere. This leads to the three final concerns that must be addressed here: what are the limits of the aesthetic, where does the notion of value come in, and, related to that, what is the relationship of the aesthetic to ideology?

The Limits of the Aesthetic

If aesthetic reading is triggered by particular formal features and is characterized by affective engagement with the textual material, then the aesthetic is clearly not limited to artistic works like poems and plays. If we become conscious of the "quality" of writing in a newspaper article, then we are beginning to treat the text as aesthetic; if we take pleasure in the cleverness or design quality in an advertisement, we are responding aesthetically. Speeches, feature articles, and critical works all often have elements of the aesthetic in them, some particularly strongly, although we would not necessarily think of the genre as essentially aesthetic.

Not that we can claim that any text that produces an emotional effect is aesthetic. Although Lowell has made that part of the My Lai trial transcript available to us for poetic contemplation, it would be a callous and inappropriate distortion to claim that the newspaper report of, say, a political atrocity, which may be intensely moving, is aesthetic, not because the aesthetic is necessarily of less value than the political, but because the kind of attention involved is not the kind called for in the circumstances. If Lowell had published his poem the day after the words had been spoken in the trial, he may well have been charged with being heartless and opportunistic, and perhaps rightly so (although it could still have been read as an aesthetic text). Since there is an element of intellectual contemplation in the generalising move we make with the aesthetic, there needs to be at least some distance from the actuality. However, in cases where one feels that a text has been structured formally to produce certain kinds of emotional responses in the audience, then this is an aesthetic experience, although not necessarily a valued or profound one.

Which brings us to the matter of value.

Value

In much talk about the aesthetic, there is often a particular evaluation implied. The aesthetic is assumed to be a good thing, and aesthetic works are given a high value. It is actually a case like "art" or "literature," where the term is often used to exclude by definition works that the speaker judges as having no value. However, just as with art and literature, even those who run such a line must acknowledge that there are bad examples of the aesthetic. A strong presence of the aesthetic does not necessarily make a work good: any anthology of pre-Raphaelite poetry would confirm this statement.

As we have seen, the aesthetic is very much a matter of reading practices, and there can be an element of the aesthetic in all kinds of text, since all kinds of texts can be made available for aesthetic reading. Certainly, all works that are created imaginatively to engage the recipients either through experiences represented or through formal structuring can be considered aesthetic. They can also be considered bad or good, worthwhile or not. There can be good and bad advertisements, just as there can be good and bad poems. However, it is worth insisting that to judge something on aesthetic terms might not necessarily produce the same evaluation as judging it on political or philosophical terms.

The criteria on which we make value judgments on the aesthetic are enormously complex, variable, and frequently subjective, as we will see in more detail in Chapter 5. It is virtually impossible to say anything general about them, although it is perhaps possible to separate out three different (deeply related) elements on which we make judgments: the form, the affective experience, and the content. It is possible to see that these are separable because we can sometimes be positive about one of them while being less positive about the other two. We can be impressed by the mastery of form in a work, but we might claim that, while formally interesting or perfect, it is "cold" or "doesn't have very much to say." Similarly we can be greatly moved by a work, have tears pouring down our cheeks, but in the end think that it is not very well done or rather shallow. (This happens regularly with sentimental movies.) We can also be really interested in the subject matter of a movie, or think that it is intellectually saying important things, while remaining unmoved and wishing it were technically more accomplished.

More significantly, we can think that a work is technically accomplished but not approve of the ends towards which the accomplishment is directed. The works of the Nazi filmmaker Leni Riefenstahl are often cited as an example of this, but we can find examples closer to home in many advertisements, for example, where we actually admire and are caught up in the cleverness or the beauty of the image but do not (or did not) want to buy the product. In the same way we can be quite deeply moved by a work, while being implacably opposed to the values it espouses. Romantic movies can be a case in point, where we really want the hero and heroine to get together while not approving of the gender assumptions on which that romantic scenario is based, or an action movie where we get excited by the hero's ingenuity and prowess in evading and incidentally killing his pursuers, whereas we do not actually approve of the message that problems can be solved by violence.

We have moved here from talking about value to talking about values—that is, about the ideology of aesthetic texts. To round off our discussion of the aesthetic, we do need to say something about its relationship to ideology, since ideology is a central concept in socially critical versions of literacy and therefore is vital to the argument of this book.

Values/Ideology

Ideology is a notoriously complex topic, and the word is used in many different ways.[8] The simplest definition would be that an ideology is a socially significant system of values. It is a system in that it is not just a single belief, but a configuration of beliefs that shape in a substantial way how the people holding those beliefs operate in the social world. It is socially significant in that it is not just a single person's private system but must at least be shared by enough people for it to be acknowledged (even if only by rejection) in the social structure. The term *ideology* can have either a negative charge or a neutral one: it is rarely used positively. For our purposes, we will use the term neutrally, and we will follow much recent thinking about ideology in seeing it as largely conveyed through representations—including, very powerfully, textual representations—that lead us to see the world in certain ways. (This idea will be explored further in the next two chapters.)

If the aesthetic is a way of knowing, then it is inevitably and inextricably bound up with ideology. There are two ways in which this is so. First, in making us see the world in particular ways, it draws our attention to and makes us value certain things, such as emotion, individual experience. Second, by involving us affectively, it creates attitudes and orients us into reacting positively or negatively towards the actions, ideas, or attitudes represented in the text. We are positioned by the text into seeing and valuing in particular ways what it shows. Thus the aesthetic element of the text is not simply a detachable cover there to make the content more attractive and the message more palatable—it is an integral part of the content and the message, and a very powerful part. The aesthetic can create intense experience that, as we have seen, encompasses both the emotional and the intellectual/rational: it is apprehended rather than comprehended. Critical versions of literacy are essentially rationalist: they are predicated on the belief that showing analytically how the text is limited and tendentious will undercut its ideological power. They generally fail to see that the textual power is not just a matter of intellectual commitment: the affective commitment is just as powerful, and just as ideologically implicated. And it is not easily undercut by rational analysis, if one wants to undercut it. There are two questions here: how does one defuse the power of the aesthetic with its ideological positioning; and should one want to defuse the power of the aesthetic anyway?

In order to work towards dealing with these questions, we first need to consider further the ways in which the aesthetic is a social phenomenon and so embodies social values.

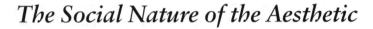

The Social Nature of the Aesthetic

The contention that the aesthetic is a social phenomenon might strike one as a reductive (and even perhaps surprising) statement, or, alternatively, it might seem to be so obvious as not to need saying. The first reaction would arise from a perception of the aesthetic as having to do with expressive emotion and personal response (which are frequently seen as operating in a purely private realm), while the second would arise from an understanding that art is a form of communication, and communication is inevitably a social phenomenon. The latter emphasis on the communicative social nature of the aesthetic becomes particularly clear if the focus is on verbal art, on the aesthetic use of language. Critical literacy is built on the concept that language usage is contextual and social, and so it is important for us to investigate the notion of the aesthetic as social communication.

Language as Social Communication

Language is inherently social. If there were no society, there would be no need for language: we would just know things. (This is not to deny the significance of language as an instrument of thought, and there can be no doubt that the mental manipulation of linguistic symbols has enabled great conceptual advances for humanity.) For language to achieve its purpose there must be a community of at least two people with something that needs communicating. And the two people must agree on certain rules and conventions, such as that the sound *food* represents a possibility of what the animal one of them has just noticed at the water hole might become. We are, of course, talking here about language as a semiotic system: a system of signs. Language is rule-governed behaviour. It can work only if systematically shared conventions are established for making meaning. Rules and conventions are a matter of social negotiation and social practice.

Since communication is purposeful, the meaning of any act of communication is governed by the context in which it occurs. The simple denotational meaning of the words is filled out by an understanding of what they mean socially. *Food* in the context mentioned above means something like "There is a cow at the waterhole, and so we have to get our weapons and creep up on it, kill it, and eat it. This will satisfy our hunger." This particular meaning depends on the fact that the people in this community are carnivores, that they have developed at least a primitive technology in weapons, and that they have some basic hunting strategies. They may have even discovered fire, and if our two people are male, and one of them turns to a female nearby and says "Food," it could mean something like "Start a fire: there'll be meat so you can cook a roast dinner for us." This would imply that gender roles have been assigned, and there is a power differential already in place: the men hunt, the women dependently (and dependably) cook.

In other words, ideology, if not always present in every example of language use, is never far away, and once any sort of power differentiation is present in society, this will be reflected in the language. Language will be used to enforce and reinforce the social roles. Even the word *Food* in this context could have profound ideological meaning, if this social group has developed a religious awareness of which animals can be eaten and which animals are sacred. The word in this case could mean "Thank God, at last a cow! Deer are holy to us, but they've been hogging the waterhole and not letting any animals we can eat get close." There are few things more ideological than religion, and our hunter can embody immense ideological understanding in a single word.

Of course a single-word utterance is language at its simplest: the kinds of texts that we are concerned with—aesthetic texts—display a much more complex use of language, and indeed some of them show language at its most sophisticated. However, since they are fundamentally acts of communication, they are social, and they work semiotically; that is, they rely on the reader's knowledge of the codes—the rules and conventions—they are using. They are also ideological, since human beings, as social animals, can scarcely speak without implying values and beliefs.

The question can be raised whether aesthetic texts work only semiotically or whether we need to allow that the aesthetic cannot be explained purely as a semiotic phenomenon. Semiotics is a discipline obsessed with system. Its ultimate dream with any text would be to explain completely how it generates its meaning, finding a signifier (a formal element) within the text that produced any signified (meaning content) a reader might take from it. It is a dream that will never be achieved, as poststructuralists have taught us, because language is inherently unstable and meanings slip and slide around under the surface forms. There is always excess of meaning in a text, an overflow of possibilities, something unsystematic and out of control. Texts can always be recontextualised, and thus new meanings can be found in them. Aesthetic texts in particular tend to be multivalent (i.e., give multiple meanings). They also work on us affectively, which ultimately might be explained semiotically, with textual features triggering off certain emotions, but the complexity of individual affective response must cast some doubt on this possibility. All these things make interpretation inevitable (and English studies possible). Nevertheless, texts do have specific meanings, they do work with (or against) a shared understanding of basic conventions, and so there is a great deal we can say about them in semiotic terms before acknowledging that not everything can be caught in the semiotic net.

If we turn from our monosyllabic hunters and think about, say, Shakespeare's Sonnet 18—"Shall I compare thee to a summer's day?"—we can see many gains over "Food." This is highly organised language that comes from a very sophisticated culture. It is language that has been shaped for use in a specialised field, not the language that one imagines people using when hunting or cooking. Language, by this time, has been carved up into different ranges that are used by different people in different circumstances. These ranges of language provide the vocabulary, the ways of talking needed to establish group identification or deal with the particular field, and they also "write in" the kind of attitudes that go along with the field. We normally these days call them *discourses*.

We also note that the language is shaped in a specialised textual structure. It has been divided up into stretches of more or less equal length; we have rhymes; the ideas don't come randomly, but there is a development. It seems to have been shaped for its particular purpose, and if we look around it in the book in which we found it, we discover that there are a lot of poems with this shape. And if we look in general at the writing of the time, we discover thousands more of them. We, of course, say that these similarly shaped texts belong to a genre.

Both discourses and genres embody shared understandings between the producers of texts and those who are being addressed. As social life and the language that reflects, facilitates, and shapes it become more complex, there is greater need to organise language in a way that helps the listener sort through the possible meanings of any utterance or text and enables the purpose to be achieved more economically and efficiently. Discourse does this by grouping together the language that is needed for working and talking in a particular field of endeavour. People operating within that discourse, both the speakers and the hearers, have particular expectations of the language to be used and put on a particular mindset that involves the working assumptions and characteristic conceptual strategies of the field. A genre, on the other hand, gives a particular shape to a text, so that one knows the arrangement of material to expect and so can organise the material as it comes. A text-producer can play against the expectations of discourse or genre, of course, but they are dependent on those expectations even when they do so. A genre will often imply a particular discourse, so the two concepts fit well together, but let us first look at them separately in more detail.

Discourse

A discourse, as implied above, is a commonly accepted way of speaking or writing about a particular area of experience. It can be defined by its subject matter (e.g., the discourse of education, the discourse of romantic love) or by the particular social community that uses it (the discourse of black urban youth, the discourse of Elizabethan sonneteers). Usually there are aspects of both content and community: a particular range of content interests talked about by people in a particular group, the group being defined by the shared interests. The range of language used within a particular discourse not only gives people a way of operating successfully in that field, but in doing so it defines what is accepted as the common knowledge, attitudes, and beliefs of people who are working in the area: it defines their particular way of seeing the world. In fact, the discursive practices constitute the field, make it come into being. It is to this that Michel Foucault, from whom much of the current thinking about discourses stems, was referring when he said, in a famous, rather sybilline statement, that discourses "are practices that systematically form the objects of which they speak" (1972, p. 49).

Discourse is a useful concept, but not one we need to get purist about. One could attempt a lexicon and grammar of a particular discourse, but it would be so patently an arid exercise that it seems rarely to have been attempted. Foucault tends to speak about "discursive practices," "discursive fields," or "discursive formations," all of which suggest that discourses are not tight canisters of language, but that the boundaries are flexible and permeable. Discourses operate at greater and lesser degrees of generality, and there are discourses within discourses. For example, the discourse of Marxist criticism is a subset of literary criticism, and in itself it could be split into different fields depending on whether it is working from a classic Marxist base, from a Soviet Realist base, or from an Althusserian one. Alternatively, the discourse of Marxist literary criticism might be seen as a subset of Marxist discourse, and the discursive field might be perceived differently if it were approached in that way.

The important point to make is that we are always operating within some discourse. If we seem not to be, it is because the discourse is our everyday one, embodying our common understandings of ordinary existence. James Paul Gee (1990) makes the useful distinction between primary and secondary discourses. Primary discourses are those of "people like us." They seem as natural as the air we breathe because they offer no resistance to commonplace understandings. They are our "default mode" of discourse. Secondary discourses are those that we take on in special circumstances, when we are part of a particular group of people with our own insider language, or when we are dealing with a particular subject area. We move between discourses seamlessly, even laying them on top of each other in a single sentence. It is only rarely that we are aware of a gear shift from one to the other, or a clash between two we are using, which attests to how naturalised they are in our ways of thinking and doing things.

Aesthetic works are built up out of discourses. Sometimes, they are specialised literary discourses, as in a Shakespearean sonnet; at other times the works give representations of discourses, both primary and secondary, found in "real life." Narrative works, in particular, whether novels, films, TV series, or plays, frequently depend on showing us particular discourses in action, often clashing with each other, certainly supplementing each other to give a sense of the breadth of the world being depicted. It is this representational use of discourses that we will look at first, before going on to examine more specialist literary discourses.

Gee's notion of primary and secondary discourses might be usefully adapted in thinking about novels. It is certainly not always the case, but the narrator generally provides the primary discourse, and the significance of other, secondary discourses is established by their distance from the primary discourse. This can be less true if it is a first-person narration, but even then there is a tendency for the narration to set the discursive norm. Let us take Harper Lee's *To Kill a Mockingbird*. This is a first-person narration, but not from a character narrating while involved in the thick of the action. Scout is immediately established as looking back at the events from an adult distance:

> When he was nearly thirteen, my brother Jem got his arm badly broken at the elbow. When it healed, and Jem's fears of never being able to play football were assuaged, he was seldom self-conscious about his injury. His left arm was somewhat shorter than his right; when he stood or walked, the back of his hand was at right angles to his body, his thumb parallel to his thigh. He couldn't have cared less, so long as he could pass and punt.
>
> When enough years had gone by to enable us to look back on them, we sometimes discussed the events leading to this accident. (1960, p. 9)

During the novel, the events are often focalised through the con-sciousness of the young Scout, but we never lose the possibility and underpinning of this mature, sensible, generally good-humoured voice.

As said above, every discourse implies beliefs and values, even though it might seem neutral, as primary discourses such as the narrating Scout's are wont to do. Without labouring the analysis too much, we can see that already a whole ideology is being built up, particularly around family and gender. The brother/sister relationship is obviously important and enduring enough for them to get together in later life and look back on their childhood without any bitterness. Stronger in the passage, however, is the gender construction: the physically active boy who gets his arm broken and seems to care more about playing football than the pain. Certainly he cares more about football than his physical appearance. There is a warm, slightly ironic tone playing around: boys are like that! We know very clearly the kind of world we are in: a world of solid mainstream family val-ues is being constructed discursively.

This primary discourse is contrasted with an array of other "secondary" discourses. Mikhail Bakhtin has written:

> The novel can be defined as a diversity of social speech types (sometimes even diversity of languages) and a diversity of individual voices, artistically organized. The internal stratifi-cation of any single national language into social dialects, characteristic group behaviour, professional jargons, generic languages, languages of generations and age groups, tenden-tious languages, languages of the authorities, of various cir-cles and of passing fashions, languages that serve the specific sociopolitical purposes of the day, even of the hour (each day has its own slogan, its own vocabulary, its own emphases)— the internal stratification present in every language at any given moment of its historical existence is the indispensable prerequisite for the novel as a genre. (1994, p. 114)

He could simply have said (if he had been writing post-Foucault) that the novel depends on a diversity of discourses. In *To Kill a Mockingbird*, we get, for example: the discourse of the young Jem, confirming his impetuous boyish energy—

"Scout, I'm tellin' you for the last time, shut your trap or go home—I declare to the lord you're gettin' more like a girl every day!" (1960, p. 57)

—which seems to be largely indicated by a propensity to mild slang and "dropping the g" on present participles, and that confirms that boys are indeed "like that" and, as such, very much to be preferred to girls; the discourse of the trashy Ewells—

"Well, I was sayin' Mayella was screamin' fit to beat Jesus. . . . Mayella was raisin' this holy racket so I dropped m'load and run as fast as I could but I run into th' fence, but when I got distangled I run up to th' window and I seen—" Mr Ewell's face grew scarlet. He stood up and pointed his finger at Tom Robinson. "—I seen that black nigger yonder ruttin' on my Mayella!" (1960, p. 176)

—which is marked not only by nonstandard English such as Jem could never dream of, but by slang based on blasphemy, and everything brought to physical animal terms ("ruttin'"); then there is the discourse of the honourable black person—

"Mr Finch, I tried. I tried to 'thout bein' ugly to her. I didn't wanta be ugly, I didn't wanta push her or nothin'." (1960, p. 199)

—with an innate, but almost inarticulate, sense of human dignity, gentleness, and rightness (Scout comments, "It occurred to me that in their own way, Tom Robinson's manners were as good as Atticus's" (p. 199); and Atticus, who never "drops g's," and whose discourse is marked by a calm, humane gravity, even in domestic conversation—

"You can't do that, Scout," Atticus said. "Sometimes it's better to bend the law a little in special cases. In your case, the law remains rigid. So to school you must go." (1960, p. 36)

—which has the authority of abstractions, judiciousness, inversions, and perfect grammar. These are just a few of the many discourses interacting in the novel. It is important to insist that it is not just a matter of characters having individualising voices.

Each of the characters comes with his or her own discourse, and these discourses import a range of different social values.

The discourses are not only those of the different characters from their different social classes, but we have what we might call institutional discourses as well, playing across the narrative and character discourses. They are most obviously marked by specialised vocabulary. There are discourses of schooling (treated ironically):

> The remainder of my schooldays were no more auspicious than the first. Indeed they were an endless Project that slowly evolved into a Unit, in which miles of construction paper and wax crayon were expended by the State of Alabama in its well-meaning but fruitless efforts to teach me Group Dynamics. (1960, p. 38)

discourses of religion (also treated ironically):

> He warned his flock against the evils of heady brews, gambling, and strange women. Bootleggers caused enough trouble in the Quarters, but women were worse. Again, as I had often met it in my own church, I was confronted with the Impurity of Women doctrine that seemed to preoccupy all clergymen. (1960, p. 125)

and, much more seriously, discourses of the law, which in Atticus's big speech to the jury can move from technical legal matters:

> "[The state] has relied instead upon the testimony of two witnesses whose evidence has not only been called into serious question on cross-examination, but has been flatly contradicted by the defendant." (1960, p. 207)

to a passionately ethical humanist discourse that is the book's valued alternative to the ironically treated religious discourses:

> "But this is a truth that applies to the human race and to no particular race of men. There is not a person in this courtroom who has never told a lie, who has never done an immoral thing." (1960, p. 209)

and can even surprisingly encompass serious (if rather reactionary) educational comment:

> "The most ridiculous example I can think of is that the people who run public education promote the stupid and idle along with the industrious—because all men are created equal, educators will gravely tell you, the children left behind suffer terrible feelings of inferiority." (1960, p. 209)

Atticus's courtroom speech is so much the moral centre of the book because it does provide the positive reference point around which all the institutional and ethical discourses can be organised, the evaluations supported by the grave and serious tones of the idealised Atticus character discourse. As Bakhtin suggests, it is the artistic organization of the array of discourses that is fundamental to any novel.

The organization of the discourses *is* aesthetic, and it is also, inevitably, ideological. It is aesthetic in that the discourses are arranged in a way that engages the reader emotionally and intellectually in a splendidly realised evocation of a particular reality that also focuses significant conceptual concerns. The organization is ideological because the clash of the different discourses is the clash of worldviews and the clash of moral and ethical values. Through the aesthetic shaping, we are led to value some particular discourses more than others, even particular aspects of particular discourses. There are a number of things contributing to this. First, there is the primacy of the narrative voice of the older Scout and the kind of discourse it uses. It sets a framework of values in which and through which we can place the other discourses activated in the novel. It is, of course, no accident, that although it focalises the action through the young Scout and so appropriates her character voice at times, the character voice it comes closest to in its "neutral" mode is Atticus's. He is the character who has the same mature, affectionate, and good-humouredly ironic perception. Then there is the pattern of contrasts in the novel that positions us within a particular network of moral valuations: the poor but responsible Cunninghams are early contrasted with the poor but irresponsible Ewells, just as the Ewells are contrasted with the righteous and respectful black folk. There is also, of course, the actual story, which leaves no doubt about where our sympathies are to be aligned and about whose value system we should support. The book moves inexorably to a particular outcome that draws us in to the values implicit in that outcome; the triumph of liberal humanist/Christian equity and generosity over prejudice and selfishness and even over institutional law.

In some ways the contrasting discourses in *To Kill a Mockingbird* make it easy to analyse the social and ideological implications of the text, because one can contrast the discourses with each other so readily. It is harder when the discourse is much more homogenous. The characters in *Friends,* for example, all talk much the same language, and it is so much the language of a desired fantasyland of inner-urban lifestyle that it is hard to step back and see it as a particular discourse that is aesthetically deployed and that brings with it very particular social values. Students find it particularly difficult to distance themselves sufficiently with works such as this, to see the sorts of values that the program is promoting. Not that one would want them to reject it—on the whole, it's benign enough—but the problem for teachers is that the show seems so straightforward and the surface so impenetrable that it is hard to work with it and develop analytical strategies.

If we take a characteristic, albeit famous, episode and look at it closely, we can soon see the way the discourse is working. The episode is "The One Where Everybody Finds Out" (Lembeck, 1999). What they find out about is that Monica and Chandler are "doing it." The other strand in the program is that Ross wants the flat that the "ugly naked guy" across the street is vacating, and he goes to considerable lengths to procure it. If we want to analyse the discourse of the program, the first question to ask is, rather primly, what are the areas of interest these people have? The (rather unprim) answer is, of course, sex, and the related areas of attractive (indeed seductive) appearance and (more distantly) material possession. The phrase "doing it" is repeated in the program as a kind of leitmotif, the centre of the discourse of sex, until it gives way to a discourse of love (we will look later at the moment when this happens). There is, however, a range of other phrases used: being "with a guy," "hitting on me." One of the best comic moments is actually when Phoebe, playing at being attracted to Chandler, says how she is looking forward to having "sexual intercourse" with him, and the sudden shifting of the discourse from the expected young singles range of euphemisms to the blunt professional/academic kind of naming gets a huge shocked laugh on the audience laugh track. Personal attractiveness is a premium value in this world, but it is an attractiveness to do with sex. A lot of this is created through Chandler's not being the sexy kind of attractive—"foxy"—but being "charming in a sexless kind of way." When Monica acknowledges that Phoebe does seem to be coming on to him, she almost immediately realizes that Phoebe knows about their relationship and is trying to "freak [them] out." Chandler is momentarily a little reluctant to give up the possibility that he is a sexy kind of attractive: "O.K. But what about, you know, my pinchable butt, and my bulging biceps . . . She knows!" (Self-delusion is so difficult sometimes!) The crime of the "ugly naked guy" in the apartment across the street is not his nakedness but his ugliness. It would have been quite different if he had been "hunky naked guy"! The show is notable for a particular "attitude," and the attitude (with attendant values) is carried by the discourse.

Friends and *To Kill a Mockingbird* are aesthetic texts that are mimetic in their use of discourses: that is, they imitate and present for our aesthetic engagement the ways in which discourses might be used in the world. There are, however, purely literary discourses, as we noted when looking at Keats's "Ode to a Nightingale" in the last chapter. These tend, historically, to be most used in poetry. Poetry is a mode of writing that, in general, is marked by its distance from everyday language. This is as true of folk ballads as it is of Shakespearean verse. It is as true of Wordsworth and Coleridge's poetry (in spite of their claim to be speaking the language of ordinary people) as it is of Alexander Pope or Allen Ginsberg. Thus it is more likely that we will find specialist literary discourses in poetry, language such as no one ever spoke in everyday circumstances, unless "being poetic."

Let us take the Shakespeare sonnet mentioned before:

Shall I compare thee to a summer's day?
Thou art more lovely and more temperate.
Rough winds do shake the darling buds of May,
And summer's lease hath all too short a date.
Sometime too hot the eye of heaven shines,
And often is his gold complexion dimmed;
And every fair from fair sometime declines,
By chance, or nature's changing course untrimmed;
But thy eternal summer shall not fade,
Nor lose possession of that fair thou ow'st,
Nor shall Death brag thou wand'rest in his shade,
When in eternal lines to time thou grow'st.
    So long as men can breathe or eyes can see,
    So long lives this, and this gives life to thee.

(SONNET 18)

This is a very specialised discourse. It is originally taken over with the poetic form (which we will discuss later) from Italian models, most notably the sonnets of Petrarch, but behind that is the literary tradition of the troubadours and writers of romances, the tradition of *amour courtois*—courtly love. So, for Shakespeare, this discourse would come with connotations of exclusivity: it is an elite discourse, implying a world of refinement in action and feeling. While undoubtedly thoroughly naturalised in England by this time, it would also still have retained an undertone of the exotic continental, of a kind of worldly consciousness beyond the reach of ordinary people. So, even before thinking about what is said, the discourse is deeply ideological in that its use inscribes class.

This particular discourse is obviously very powerful: it lasted for centuries, and we can still see many elements of it persisting in a superficially transformed state in modern discourses of love. The way such a discourse establishes itself is obviously bound up with the myths, the fantasies of the society. It is a social construct, but rather than relating to the actuality of society as lived, it relates to an ideal form of relationship, a dream the society has of how life might appear if lived with aesthetic intensity. One can imagine a society where this particular form held no power whatsoever, but for readers at the beginning of the twenty-first century, there is still enough potency in this myth for the poem to engage and hold most of us.

A discourse has a number of different aspects. It is marked by a particular range of language related to what is being talked about, but it also involves two other things: a range of characteristic strategies for building texts (e.g., the use of metaphor), and a conceptual framework that is assumed between poet and reader as true. A clear indication that such a framework is operating here is that the speaker of the poem nowhere says that he loves the person being addressed, but, of course, the discourse is so clearly one that is used in love poems that there cannot be a moment of doubt.

There are a number of strands in the conceptual framework of this particular discourse:

♦ the relationship of love and physical beauty
♦ the connection of love and beauty with Nature
♦ the notion of love as eternal
♦ the persistence of art (*Ars longa, vita brevis*)

Not one of these ideas in itself stands up to logical scrutiny, and as a collection they are particularly dubious and contradictory. They are not necessarily connected either, but they have become so in the discourse and certainly seem powerfully so when we experience them in the poem. The discourse has become so naturalised, and is perhaps so desired, that we do not notice the fallacies—we elide the discontinuities.

But, of course, it is the aesthetic deployment of the discourse that makes the poem so powerful, and so powerfully ideological. The intensity of aesthetic realisation engages us thoroughly. The poem weaves a textual web that enfolds us in the discourse, implicates us, as the expected terms fall into place. There are particular, discursively favoured, textual strategies used here. The poem has a fairly tight argumentative structure, but rather than a rational development, the argument is set up almost entirely through aesthetic means, most notably metaphor. The initial question proposes the issue to be addressed, and the argument is subsequently conducted in terms of the natural, seasonal metaphor, first of all through the qualifications that apply to Nature and then positively through the assertion of the beloved's immortality. This goes on until the eleventh line, when the second string of images of mutability and mortality surfaces dominantly, with Death being overcome by "immortal lines." The shift here is again achieved through metaphor: the metaphors in asserting the comparative limitations of the natural world have introduced the notion of decline and decay, but that has not actually been explicitly set up as a problem. The shift to the assertion of immortality through poetry thus requires an associative leap. In this poem, the involvement in following through the argumentative structure is an involvement with a metaphoric pattern being built up, not a purely, or even predominantly, logical pattern.

There are further ways in which the metaphors are working to engage us intensely in the discourse. There is no necessary connection between love-producing personal beauty and Nature—this is part of the discourse, the ideology—but the metaphoric procedures continually work to bring the two together and so make us experience the discourse as emotionally logical. The natural images that are defining the beloved's beauty are, in fact, often humanised, so that it is as if the human becomes a metaphor for the natural phenomenon as well as vice versa, such as in the line about the sun, "And often is his gold complexion dimmed," where the beautiful friend is made so strikingly present through the metaphor of the sun's "complexion." This creates textually the link between the beauty of the friend and a kind of ideal nature that is validating the highly ideological belief that the connection between love and beauty is a natural phenomenon.

The discourse is, to repeat, a social construct and profoundly ideological. Shakespeare, needless to say, utilizes the aesthetic discourse with tremendous impact, so that we experience it as something intensely personal, almost newly discovered, and that makes the ideology all the more powerful.

Genre

The poem is in a very specific genre too. Genre, like discourse, has been a much-debated concept, but we do not need to let the debates detain us here. We can simply say that a genre is a particular category of text. Genres are defined structurally: they may be defined by their mode (poetry, film, drama), or by the rules on which they structure the language within the mode (sonnet, haiku, ode), or by their shaping, often narrative, of the material depicted (romantic comedy, film noir, courtroom drama), or by the intended outcome on the audience (comedy, tragedy, horror story). A text will often be defined simultaneously on a number of these axes. It is clear from this that the term is often used very loosely, and there can be genres within genres. Again, we need not be purist about this and will find it most productive to use the word flexibly.

Genres, like discourses, are generated for particular social purposes. As Anne Cranny-Francis has written:

> Genres work by convention and those conventions are social constructs; they operate by social assent, not individual choice (in the same way that the red/orange/green configuration of traffic lights is a social construct, not a matter of individual interpretation). These conventions are themselves subject to social pressures and social mediation. (1990, p. 17)

They are a contract, a set of common understandings between an artist and her or his audience, that governs the expectations with which the audience comes to the text. Their purpose is to structure reality, and indeed such a generic structuring is impossible for any artist to avoid:

> Every significant genre is a complex system of means and methods for the conscious control and finalization of reality. . . . The process of seeing and conceptualizing reality must not be severed from the process of embodying it in the forms of a particular genre. . . . The artist must learn to see reality with the eyes of the genre. (Bakhtin, 1994, pp. 178–79)

Because each genre structures reality in a particular way, genres inevitably determine what is considered significant and what values attach to what is shown.

> Each genre is only able to control certain definite aspects of reality. Each genre possesses definite principles of selection, definite forms for seeing and conceptualising reality, and a definite scope and depth of penetration. (p. 177)

They are thus inevitably ideological.

If one thinks about comparatively simple genres like sitcoms, film noir, adventure video games, romantic comedies, or disaster movies, it is not hard to see that there are starkly different value systems underlying each of them. A genre is a way of seeing the world, of comprehending how the world operates, and of understanding what human beings are like. The heroine of a romance, a film noir, and a video game, for example, are likely to be very different creatures, scarcely recognisable as the same species. This suggests how profoundly ideological genres are. They create a set of expectations about what the world is like, what matters and what does not, and how people should behave. They often confirm us in the grand narratives of our culture: the narrative of romance leading to matrimony, of individual heroism as the saving force, of social transgression being punished in the end.

One indication of how ideologically implicated genres are is how they evolve as societal beliefs evolve. Sitcoms provide a clear example of this. Until the 1990s, sitcoms were basically about families, even the ones that were aiming gently to subvert the genre, such as *Roseanne*. These days, while there are still some family ones, sitcoms are more likely to be, like *Friends*, about a group of people in some specific living environment or workplace. Nuclear families are no longer seen as the most attractive ideal: even those engaged in them would prefer in their fantasies to be with a group of friends living in an apartment building in New York. The family sitcoms that there are, such as *Malcolm in the Middle*, now have a very different value system, subversive of traditional family values. Perhaps the ultimate nail in the coffin of the traditional family sitcom (if nails were needed after *The Simpsons*) is *The Osbournes*, where we have a real (and really weird) family presented as if they were inhabiting *Father Knows*

Best. Scepticism about the dominant ideology of the nuclear family has become the new dominant ideology around the beginning of the twenty-first century in much of the urban West, and sitcoms participate in this shift unerringly.

If we look at the genre of the Elizabethan sonnet, we can see two ways in which the genre is ideological. The first has already been hinted at in talking about the tradition of the Italian sonnet and courtly love from which it comes. The sonnet form itself brings expectations of a particular kind of love. It is no accident that when Shakespeare came to write his major play about tragic romantic young love, there is an Italian setting, and he starts off the play with a sonnet:

> Two households, both alike in dignity
> In fair Verona where we lay our scene . . .

> (*ROMEO AND JULIET*, PROLOGUE, 1–2)

He has his two lovers first address each other in sonnet form:

> If I profane with my unworthiest hand
> This holy shrine, the gentle sin is this . . .

> (I.v.93–94)

And he even finishes with a truncated sonnet in the Prince's final speech: "A glooming peace this morning with it brings . . ." (V.iii.305). The sonnet form here has the function that might be taken by a major theme song on the soundtrack of a movie: once we recognise the sonnet form (if we are Elizabethan), we know what emotional world we are inhabiting, and intense love is somewhere around.

Why this particular form of fourteen lines has evolved and taken on these meanings is much harder to say, and one can only speculate. Perhaps there has been a certain arbitrariness about it (and, of course, the Elizabethan sonnet form is not the same as the Italian sonnet form, the three quatrains with final couplet having a quite different effect from the more complicated Italian rhyme scheme). Poetic form, unlike the form of, say, a business letter, has evolved in ways that are felt to give pleasure in themselves, rather than for any functional purpose. It is a test for the poet to create a poem that follows the rules and communicates without straining. In one sense, a tight poetic form, such as this, is giving a message about the importance of control, of focusing the emotion through formalising it. Beyond that, this form invites a view of love as essentially set about by problems, since fundamental to the form is a contrastive or oppositional shift, either at the ninth line or at the move into the couplet. Even in the gloriously affirmative Sonnet 18, there is the pivotal contrast between the natural decline of every living thing and the eternal glory of love and the beloved. The closing couplet also generally comes as a final assertion of a viewpoint that the poem has been concerned to achieve. The complications of the situation are spelled out in the quatrains; the couplet inevitably comes as a comparatively straightforward simplification of the ideas, and so has the force of an expected summation: this is what we have been working towards. (In fact, the final couplet is often the weakest part of Shakespeare's sonnets, since it does seem so often to be merely a rather simplistic assertion: this does not mean that it is not emphasising the values underlying the poem, of course.)

The ideological function of generic structure becomes clearer when we move away from lyrical to dramatic or narrative texts. The TV sitcom is a very tightly controlled genre, with the action needing to be completed (usually) in twenty-five minutes running time, and with all the regular characters being given a chance to display their comic character quirks. There is usually an initiating premise of some kind of tension between what various of the characters want or how they understand a situation, and this is followed through until there is resolution, usually based on the characters playing out their personalities or by an assertion of the underlying unity of the group. There will often be subsidiary plotlines running that are linked in narrative terms or thematically to the main plotline.

The episode of *Friends* we were discussing obviously operates within this generic framework. There is the central game-playing based on who knows what about Monica and Chandler's relationship, and the two camps entering into competition to get back at the other for the lack of openness in not telling what was going on or what they knew. There is the subplot of Ross wanting to take over the lease on the "ugly naked guy's" apartment, which leads to Phoebe finding out about Chandler and Monica, but which also provides a kind of thematic link as Ross enters the fierce competition for the apartment and wins through pretence.

In terms of ideology, how the final closure is achieved carries the greatest impact, because any narrative/dramatic genre will set up questions or problems that will (normally) be resolved at the end. In the next chapter, we will consider further how closure is attained and will look at how it works on us. In the meantime, suffice to say that the way in which closure is achieved will be critical in positioning us ideologically. In this episode of *Friends,* the crucial moment comes when Phoebe and Chandler are reluctantly going through with their charade of wanting to have sex with each other. Chandler is increasingly uncomfortable in his dilemma that he does not want to be doing this, but he knows how competitive Monica is, and how she will not like it if he is the first to break. Finally it gets too much for him, and he cedes defeat, crying out that he can't go on because he loves Monica. Monica rushes in, there are mutual protestations of love, Monica and Chandler embrace, the audience sighs, and Phoebe articulates the significance of the moment: "I thought you guys were doing it: I didn't know you were in love." The message is clear: love is what matters, and it makes irrelevant such things as competitiveness or concealing information from friends (a sentiment with which one would generally not disagree). Ross gets the apartment, but at some cost to his dignity by having his friends see him joining the ugly naked guy in his nakedness, the payoff of apartment against dignity on the whole not being an unreasonable one. The aesthetic resolution of the comic situation in the program is an ideological affirmation of what really matters, and how much.

The generic conventions of a novel are much more complex than those of a TV sitcom, and indeed there are many different genres contained in the overarching genre of the novel. However, there are some fundamental ways in which we are conditioned to read by our expectations of the genre. We have already seen how the characters in *To Kill a Mockingbird* are placed in relation to each other, often in oppositional pairs, and our generic expectations lead us to note and take the meaning from this patterning.

In the end, with most novels, we expect all the elements to be purposeful, and purposeful in particular ways that are governed by the genre. So, when the mystery of Boo Radley is set up in the first pages of *To Kill a Mockingbird*, we know that by the end of the book he will have played a significant part, the only question being what that part will be. He could turn out bad, but he is presented so much as the victim early on, and the signs of his presence—putting the various items in the hollow in the tree for Scout and Jem—are so pathetic, that we expect a positive outcome that will bring him out into the world and to at least a limited redemption. When the justice system fails, and Tom Robinson is sent to jail, we know that this cannot be the end of the matter. In another kind of novel, one concerned primarily with the unfairness of the justice system, it might have been left at that, so we would be confronted with the massive injustice, but this novel clearly does not have such a polemical political purpose, and so we expect the imbalance created by the injustice to be redressed. When Tom Robinson is killed in jail and so any kind of legal reparation is not possible, we know generically that the only way our expectation of justice can be reached is outside the law, with a higher kind of justice intervening, which it does. The narrative of Bob Ewell's evil in the end turning on itself to set up the conditions for his death is common in such novels. In a different kind of adventure story, we would expect the hero to overcome him and openly avenge the injustice: in this kind of quasi-philosophical novel, the revenge must come about more or less naturally, as evidence of a greater justice beyond the Law. The fact that Boo Radley is instrumental in it and that it occasions his emergence from pitiful seclusion, anticipated by the reader from the beginning, draws the novel together all the more tightly. All of these expectations come from our understanding of the genre that we have built up from other stories, whether through reading novels, seeing them on film, or just hearing people tell stories shaped in this way.

Again we can ask the question, how much is the aesthetic fundamental to these processes of establishing ideological values within particular genres? The answer is that the genres are aesthetic genres, and so they work aesthetically. There are many non-aesthetic genres, genres of discussion and argument, for example, that work by other discursive means. But these genres work aesthetically in the ways we have looked at: they represent a particular action in which we see general significance. Indeed, it is probably at least partly through the fact that the individual work is operating within a genre that we do see the action represented as representative and generalisable: we have heard stories like this before, and so the text seems to draw on a fundamental pattern of human experience that has been established in the genre. The aesthetic requires the establishment of concepts through emotional means, and aesthetic genres have been shaped to produce particular affect, whether it be the quiet pleasures of the lyric or the shattering experience of tragedy. They also foreground to some extent the sheer act of shaping the material into the form, while at the same time calling for a maximum amount of inventiveness and individuality within those parameters. The aesthetic shaping is fundamental to the meaning and thus is inevitably bound up with the ideology.

To return to the original contention, the aesthetic is inevitably social because it depends on conventions shared between those producing aesthetic texts and those responding to them. The match between writer and reader is almost never perfect, and we would not want it to be. We are very differently positioned in social terms from Shakespeare and Harper Lee, and even from the producers of *Friends,* or rather, we are positioned differently than their texts, and it is that different positioning, the fact that we can bring other discourses to bear, that allows us to be critical, that allows us to see the limitations and strengths of the particular discourses that are being displayed in the work. This is not just a matter of bringing a personal response to bear, because the personal is (largely) constructed through discourses, and so we are always positioned within some discourse or other, or in a number of discourses simultaneously. Reading aesthetic texts is a personal thing, but the personal is not divorced from the social: it is largely constructed by it. How texts play a part in this process of constructing the personal will be the subject of the next chapter.

Engaging the Aesthetic Subject

O ne of the favourite marketing statements on the backs of novels, whether a quotation from a reviewer or a publisher's claim, is the one that says reading the book will change your life. It is partly a testament to the desire for a transforming experience that will irradiate our generally problematic and ambiguous lives with certain meaning, but it is also a testament to the power of writing—imaginative experience—to make us see the world differently, change our way of thinking, indeed change ourselves.

The power of artistic representation, indeed any kind of representation, to do this is something few would contest, although the major life-changing works don't come along very often. However, it is one of the fundamental tenets of poststructuralist thought (and of critical literacy) that texts, representations, are continually changing our lives—often imperceptibly, if incrementally—but changing them nonetheless. Poststructuralism in some of its inflections can thus provide a strong theorisation of what is happening in that subtle interplay between text and reader that changes the reader's way of seeing the world. Critical literacy has taken up this theorisation and attempts to intervene in the work of texts changing us in unwanted ways, but it often does so without a subtle enough awareness of the complexity of the process, and certainly without an awareness of what can be lost.

Subjectivity

To understand what is going on in poststructuralist terms, we need to look at the concept of subjectivity (defined as "the way we experience our 'selves'"), and in particular, we need to examine "the discursive construction of subjectivity" (how our experiencing selves are constructed through our participation in discourse).[1] This can be an immensely difficult topic, but the basic concepts are not in the end particularly hard to grasp.

Any text assumes that it is addressed to a particular kind of person, a person who has certain attitudes, certain knowledge that can be assumed as given, and certain beliefs about the world. We can relate this to the notion of the implied reader (see, for example, Chatman, 1978; Iser, 1974). Any novel, for example, implies an ideal reader who will be operating with the knowledge and attitudes that are assumed in the text, and who will go along accepting totally the text's way of seeing the world. (We may have trouble accepting such an uncritical reader as "ideal," but that's another story.) Similarly, if we are speaking (i.e., producing an oral text), we work on an assumption of shared understandings with our listeners. We leave much unspoken, assuming that our listeners will fill in the gaps. Of course, the pattern of assumptions in texts of the same kind is similar: the same range of language with its load of attitudes and beliefs is used. This is where the notion of discourse comes in, as discussed in the previous chapter. Texts are constituted out of discourses: it is by writing within a particular discourse that the implicit framework of assumptions is activated in the listeners/readers.

In some ways, the explanation so far is comparatively unproblematic: few would deny that texts make assumptions about their readers or that texts activate discourses that carry with them frameworks of assumptions. It would also probably be generally accepted that texts (and discourses) have power and sometimes can make us see the world in certain ways, that is, that they can turn us into the kind of person they are assuming—their ideal reader—for the time we are reading that text. They put us into a certain "subject position." Mostly in thinking of this phenomenon, people will see the taking on of the subject position as something that is superimposed on a preexistent self. We take on the subject position, and then afterwards we go back into neutral—the default mode of our identity—when we have finished reading. In this case, it might be accepted that the default mode is not the same after as before—it may well be modified by what we have read—but basically that is a kind of overlay to the underlying identity. Poststructuralist thinking does not accept this easy assumption.

Poststructuralism asks the radical question: what if there is no underlying identity, but rather, what we are is simply the sum of all the subject positions we have taken, all the discourses we have produced or received? What if our sense of ourselves—our subjectivity—is simply built up by our participation in a range of discourses that give us our knowledge, attitudes, and beliefs? To put it in more technical terms, what if our subjectivity is built up discursively? Rather than being born with a particular identity, the person we are might well be the result of this "discursive construction of subjectivity"?

There are two assumptions behind this idea that need to be spelled out:

- ◆ Everything in the world is textual. This does not deny that there are natural phenomena, such as rocks, but this notion assumes that a human being can never have access to an unmediated natural world. We always know the world through discourse. We see a rock, and we "read" it as a rock, and we read it differently as a rock if we are operating at that moment as a romantic poet, a cyclist, or a geologist. Our learning from the moment of birth is of discourses, ways to read the world.

- ◆ Subjectivity is not singular but multiple. We are capable of participating in a great variety of discourse communities and of taking on a great variety of subject positions, and we do not flip cleanly from one to the next, with only one discourse active at any time. Rather, the subject positions are overlaid one on another; some are more powerful, some less, some active, some dormant. We cannot integrate them into a coherent whole. Contradictory ones will co-exist, and when that happens, we may find ourselves quite happily holding irreconcilable attitudes at the same time: a Goth can be a Sunday School teacher, a lawyer can be into S and M. Rather than simplifying the conception of human identity, the theory of multiple subjectivities helps explain our complexity.

The theory of the discursive construction of subjectivity is central to socially critical versions of literacy, because it gives an explanation of how texts transmit ideology and why, if we are to make judgments about the ideology of texts, it needs to be done by developing critical reading practices. The discussion here has been built on the notion that texts make assumptions about our attitudes and beliefs, that they are made of discourses that embody particular ways of seeing the world. In other words, they carry particular ideologies that are not explicit but part of the implicit framework of assumptions within the text. And a text assumes that framework in its reader. More than that, by calling the reader into the particular subject position, texts are activating those attitudes and beliefs in the reader, making the reader feel them as her or his own, giving the reader the experience of seeing the world in this particular way. In fact, since human beings are constructed through their participation in discourses, the texts are making the ideology an implicit part of what the reader is. This is why the most powerfully ideological texts are usually not the ones that explicitly state ideological positions—these can be resisted through logical discourses—but ones that represent the world attractively as it would be if we believed certain things (e.g., most advertisements). We are unwittingly seduced into wanting the world to be that way.

So, to return to our starting point, the claim that a novel can change your life is no empty boast: novels (and sitcoms, and advertisements, and clothes, and sunsets, and supermarkets, and all the other texts we read daily) are constantly changing our lives, turning us into different people.

Textual Engagement and Desire

Of course, it is not as simple as that. We do not just accept what each text says, become its ideal reader, and take up the implied subject position with its attendant ideology. We accept, modify, or reject what it says. Total acceptance or rejection is rare, so it is mostly *modify*; we modify by bringing to bear the perspectives of other discourses. We are not blank pages on which ideology imprints itself. Most people today are street-smart sceptics, as likely to reject textual assumptions as accept them (although we must acknowledge that the discourse of scepticism is as much a discourse and as ideologically blinding as any other, and perhaps even more seductive).

Although any text we read is concerned to make us see what it is saying as worth saying and concerned to get into our minds and modify what we have previously thought, to do that it must engage us, and the level of our engagement is subject to many factors and often seems irreducibly personal. Some texts seem to conquer the world—everyone loves them—and you feel a kind of guilt if you cannot go along with the almost universal euphoria, but you find them limited and boring. Other texts seem to be very much specialised tastes, and if you alone seem to be strongly engaged by a text, you greet with relief as evidence of your own sanity any other person who seems to have become involved with it as deeply as you.

The psychology of textual engagement has actually not been much studied, probably because in the end what makes a particular person engage with a particular text is so complex, multifaceted, and deeply buried in the unconscious as to be practically unknowable. It clearly has much to do with our desires and the degree to which a text conforms to and feeds them, but the shapes of desires are extraordinarily complex because only the most superficial of our desires are fed by the pleasant and escapist: it is possible that our more profound desires are fed by the difficult, the horrific, the intellectually challenging, the subversive. Thanatos is at least as powerful as Eros and as much a basis of imagination and, paradoxically, creativity.

It is worth our spending a little time looking at the concept of desire since it is obviously a nexus where several of the key concepts with which we are concerned interact. As we have just noted, desire is related to engagement: if a text is to engage us, at some level we must desire that engagement and desire what the text has to offer. More specifically in relation to the aesthetic, in Chapter 2 it was argued that *engagement* was how the key concept of *pleasure* needs to be understood if it is to cover the range of phenomena that the term *pleasure* refers to in the aesthetic domain. Pleasure is, of course, intrinsically related to desire. It arises from the fulfilment of our desires, from being able to act in a desired way. Aesthetic texts are centrally concerned to offer us pleasure, and if we desire the pleasure, we become engaged, thus moving into the subject position such texts construct. More than that, because we desire the engagement and the pleasure, we feel ourselves as actively engaged in engaging. We feel that the move to engagement comes from something deep in our being, and so we often have little sense that the text is working to put us into subject position; rather, we seem to be actively recognising in the text what we are. Thus desire is crucial in understanding engagement, pleasure, and the whole process of the discursive-aesthetic construction of subjectivity.

Desire is a concept that has been discussed a great deal in recent times, although it would certainly not be true to suggest that we have come much closer to understanding it. There are two main streams of thought in recent theorisations: one is most associated with the name of Lacan, the other with those of Deleuze and Guattari. In many ways they are antithetical to each other, but both provide very potent images of how desire is constituted. It is perhaps true to say that the power of their accounts is a poetic power, its potency dependent on sheer suggestive force, rather than on any scientific evidence or even the weight of personal introspection. If one wanted to talk in literary terms, it could be said that Lacan's account is inherently tragic, Deleuze and Guattari's not exactly comic, but inherently optimistic.

Lacan's conception of desire is based on loss and absence: many a scholar writing in English has been tempted by the pun "Lac(k)an."[2] The psychic world as delineated by Lacan is a shadowy one of lack, instability, and yearning. In his rereading of Freud's theory of the Oedipus complex, the moment of crisis when the child realizes that the world is not just a place of gratification, but a place of restrictions and responsibilities, becomes for Lacan, in one significant aspect, a crisis of signification.[3] Lacan sees the child as passing through the "mirror stage," a time when the world seems to be reflecting back at her or him a pleasingly complete and integrated image that the child can recognise as herself or himself. This is not necessarily a literal mirror but is a matter of the way the whole world addresses the child (the way caregivers speak to the child, the possessions she or he has, and so on). However, the crisis comes when the child has to recognise that these external things are not itself but signifiers, symbolic stand-ins for the self, and so its sense of its own reality is, in fact, dependent on things external to itself. It has been misrecognising these external things as the self. The child realizes it is not the centre of the world, but part of a larger order in which it is but a small element. At the same time as it is coming to this realisation, it is being inducted into language and is learning that words are signifiers that do not necessarily give access to the things signified. Language promises to give access to meaning but always contains the possibility of being just hollow, empty. Signifiers potentially float unattached over the depths of signifieds. The child is plunged into a state of crisis from which it emerges by submitting to the symbolic order of language (with all its inherent emptiness) and being a good citizen (with all its attendant limitations and frustrations), but unconsciously it is still yearning for the fullness and integration of that time when it thought itself central to the world, when the inner world and outer world were unified as the self. Thus, at the core of its being is a sense of lack and a restless (largely unconscious) searching for that lost sense of fullness, and it is this restless searching that is desire.

That is an extraordinarily simplified account of what Lacan is saying, leaving out, apart from anything else, the whole realm of the parallel development in gender and sexuality that is going on, but one can see that it does provide a view of why we become so involved in texts. We desire texts because they potentially reflect back to us that sense of fullness, of our being addressed as the centre of a meaningful, "full" world. In texts, we are given a world where everything is significant, and they address us as the consciousness in which this whole world can be held. Rather than "losing ourselves" in an imaginative world when we read, we actually feel as if we are finding ourselves—the true selves with fullness of being that have been lost in our subjugation to the symbolic order.

Deleuze and Guattari see things very differently.[4] They reject the very notion that desire is a force stemming from absence and lack and is therefore bound up with negativity and compensation. Desire to them is a productive, creative energy, part of the constant "becoming" that is all life. Desire is the desire for connection. There is a drive in all living things to connect, to create new "assemblages" that are productive in themselves. So, if we apply what they are saying to reading, a human capacity for reading connects with texts and, in so doing, creates new forms of life and energy. It is important for Deleuze and Guattari that this is not seen as simply something that a preexisting person experiences, that we read something and add that to our store of experiences, or take from it knowledge to add to our repertoire. The creation of new assemblages is not confined, controlled, or limited in this way: the creative energy is not anchored in or controlled by the constituent items. We might subsequently take these new assemblages and try to make sense of them by imposing a pattern and limits that we call our identity or our personal experiences. But for Deleuze and Guattari, the very essence of the "desiring machines"—this drive to connect and create productive assemblages—is that they are uncontrolled, productive of unexpected energies, and inherently disruptive of any attempt at imposing a logical pattern or order.

It is worth insisting that the theorisations of desire by Lacan and by Deleuze and Guattari are not an either/or opposition: both powerfully show something of the overall working of desire (as do other theories—desire is an enormously complex phenomenon). When we consider how texts answer to our desires and we become involved with them, it is perhaps easiest to think in terms of Lacan and the ways in which the texts are making up for what we lack, but it is also important to acknowledge that this is only one possible theorisation. It is also possible that texts are providing material for us to work on productively, that we engage with texts not because they make up for a lack in our lives, but because they allow us to generate more exciting and pleasurable thoughts and feelings. In fact, we do not need to adduce Deleuze and Guattari for models of this, since Roland Barthes gives a particular version of the same thing in his *The Pleasure of the Text* (1990) with his ecstatic, erotic, positively orgasmic vision of reading as an active making of meaning that is productive of pleasure, a process that is indeed pleasurable in itself because of its freewheeling escape from the constraints any textual material might try to impose. We will come back to these productive pleasures more directly in Chapter 8.

The two different ways of looking at desire offered by Lacan on the one hand and by Deleuze and Guattari on the other are useful here because they are suggestive of two rather different emphases when working with texts in the classroom. One would see engagement as coming from our recognising in the text a vision of a fuller, more coherent world than the one in which we live, and we find this attractive and enriching; the other view sees engagement as coming from texts extending us, drawing us into a kind of creative activity, releasing energy and creating new forms. One leads to textual work that is concerned with emotional engagement, sympathetic projection into the textual world; the other leads to textual work that is more improvisatory around the textual materials. Both kinds of work are valuable ones to foster, both are active and creative, both draw on the reserves of the imagination.[5]

Let us now turn to look at some of the ways in which texts engage us through engaging our desire through textual form and through offering us affective experience. We will also consider the kinds of personal investments we make in texts.

Desire and Textual Form

Long before Lacan or Deleuze and Guattari were ever heard of, Kenneth Burke had recognised the significance of desire in literature, not just in terms of engagement but actually as the basis of literary form:

> *Form* in literature is an arousing and fulfilment of desires. A work has form in so far as one part of it leads a reader to anticipate another part, to be gratified by the sequence. (1953, p. 24)

This is a good starting point for our investigation, since it provides at least an initial explanatory thesis on how textual form works on the reader. For one thing, it sees form not simply as a textual feature but as something that exists only insofar as it is created within and by the reader. The reader is aroused, put into a state of desiring suspense, by some future development that the work promises: later, that promise is gratifyingly fulfilled, and the reader feels satisfied by this formal closure. We need, however, to look more closely at how exactly these promises are made, and at how (and why) we are gratified by the sequence created. We also need to examine how this process positions us to accept certain beliefs—that is, how the subject position into which we are drawn is implicated in ideology.

Let us take a very simple example of narrative structuring: the prophecy. If, in real life, someone prophesies that a baby will grow up to kill his father and marry his mother, we might feel a little uncomfortable, but we (probably rightly) assume the person is crazy, and we would be most surprised indeed if the event came to pass: in a literary text, we have no doubt that it will happen. When the witches hail Macbeth as one "that shalt be King hereafter," we would be amazed if hereafter he were *not* king. In Burke's terms, that part of the text leads us to anticipate the other part where the prophecy is fulfilled.

Our expectation that the prophecy will be fulfilled is not based on experience: any reader of horoscopes knows that prophecies rarely come to pass. Our expectation is based on literary convention, but also on a desire to see the unexpected and outlandish happen. To prophesy that a crown prince will become king or that a young man will marry a nice girl someday is so predictable as to be scarcely a prophecy at all (even if both are becoming rather less predictable in recent times). But marrying your mother or becoming king if you are a minor thane "stands not within the prospect of belief." Attention is thrown not onto what will happen but onto how it will happen, and our experience of the form of the narrative will be governed by seeing the steps fall into place that lead to the (un)expected outcome.

Alternatively, the prophecy will be seen to be fulfilled in an unexpected way: again Macbeth provides the example by managing to get himself killed by a man not "of woman born," Macduff having been "from his mother's womb / Untimely ripped." Not to fulfil a prophecy can work only where there is some superordinate move to overcome the expectation and take us into a different realm beyond ordinary fatedness. The most sublime example of this is Calderon de la Barca's *La Vida es Sueño* (*Life Is a Dream*). The portents at Segismundo's birth all show that he will grow up to be a cruel, amoral tyrant who will do violence to the king, his father, but Segismundo finally asserts a human moral power to overcome the violent impulses within him that would bring the prophecy to pass, thus outstripping our tragic expectations.

It is easy to see how the structuring through prophecies implicates us in ideology. With *Macbeth*, we expect that the witches' initial prophecies will be fulfilled, but the very fact they come from witches tells us that their fulfilment is not likely to be morally positive or beneficial. We are thus alerted to be aware of the moral weakness exposed in Macbeth and so positioned in an ideological framework in which he must be judged. By the time of the Act IV prophecies, we realise that, in fact, they could not be literally true in the way Macbeth is reading them, and so we are positioned to be aware of his self-deluding immersion in evil and to believe that in the end it will be self-defeating. Again our expectations are fulfilled, and their fulfilment works to lock us (at least within the terms of the play) into accepting a view of the world as ultimately providential and just.

Form is all about expectations, and probably the most powerful force creating expectations in our reading/viewing is genre. Genres, as we saw in the previous chapter, are groupings of texts that are similar to each other in form, content, and intended effect. If we take a simple genre like the pulp romance, then we can see that there is a very limited set of rules in each of those three areas—form, content, and effect—for creating a text within the genre, and thus a limited (if powerful) set of desires activated in the reader. The form has to include an initial meeting of the hero and heroine where they may feel mutually attracted (but don't show it), growing attraction, a complication (often a misunderstanding about the hero's relationship with another woman), and then a resolution in which the lovers come together. The content is all to do with emotions, personal dilemmas, and the vagaries of relationships. The intended effect is for us to escape into a world where the mundane complexity and possible unsatisfactoriness of ordinary relationships can be forgotten. The genre plays on our desire in all three areas: we desire the happy outcome, we desire the emotional display, and we desire the escape into this world of intense and simple emotions.

Genre is fundamental in shaping all our reading. In the highly unusual circumstance that we start on a text not knowing what its genre is (every book has its cover, every DVD has its box), our first consideration, as soon as we start reading, is to establish the genre, because, as discussed in the previous chapter, the genre is a set of expectations that allows us to make sense of the text. Genre is always ideologically implicated. The narrative shape of particular genres promotes particular values: the heroine gets her man in a romance by sticking to her values of fidelity to emotion; the modern detective solves the case by sticking to (usually) his values of sardonic objectivity and personal control. We as readers are positioned within these values, if we are reading from within the genre, in two ways. The first is through desiring the completion of the generic structure. We get onto the train of the particular genre, and we want the payoff of reaching the final destination: love avowed, crime solved. That affective desire for the emotional completion of the journey locks us into the values that permit the emotional payoff. Secondly, since the genre calls us to make implicit connections, fill in those things that the author doesn't need to explain, we are imaginatively called into the world of the text, become creators of that world, and so participate in its implicit values. We will return to this in a moment.

So far, we have been almost exclusively discussing plot elements and how their structuring works on us as readers/viewers and how we make sense of them, but there are purely formal elements that we need to consider, such as various aspects of poetic form. A theorisation of form as the creation and fulfilment of desire works with poetry too. Rhythm, for example, depends on a desire, set up by repetition of the metrical beat, for a regularity (coupled with variation) that we find involving and pleasurable. We feel pleasure in the way it catches us up and leads us into a kind of bodily engagement with the text. Later, in Chapter 7, it will be argued that there is a bodily component to our reading of all texts. Here it is only necessary to note that rhythm works in two ways. One is to fulfil the desire for repetitive metrical regularity, which operates to engage us in the text and gives its onward movement inevitability. The other is through the shaping of the natural speech rhythm above the metrical beat, which provides us with a sense of a speaking voice and intensifies the expressiveness, fulfilling our desire for intense meaning and feeling. In thinking of the realization of meaning and feeling in this way, we are at the point where form becomes experience.

Poetic forms also give pleasure through the creation and fulfilment of desire. When we launch ourselves into a Shakespeare sonnet, for example, if we are experienced readers of Elizabethan sonnets, we have a mental map of where we are about to go. There will be three quatrains that ring changes on the central theme, with perhaps some reversal at line nine, and then there will be a final couplet that sums up, opens up a counter perspective that qualifies what came earlier, or makes an assertion about what has been said. We know this lies ahead of us, and so we move from one landmark in the structure to the next, mentally organising the material accordingly, particularly alert at the points where the argument can shift to see what will happen. Looser poetic forms bring their own demands on the reader, who is concerned to see how the laying out of the content across the form adds to the experience, particularly in terms of how it articulates the shifts in what is being said as the work builds up. When complex stanza forms work, as in the best of Keats or Donne, there is a kind of inevitable fusion between the experience and the formal embodiment. Indeed, the form of any text not only works to show the reader a particular structuring of experience but also is there to embody and communicate experientially what is represented in the text.

Investing in Texts

Texts work in many ways to engage us imaginatively, but it could also be said that we become engaged with texts because they make *us* work. We want texts to give us intense experiences, we want them to make sense, and these desires mean that we are all the time working to fill out actively and imaginatively what is implied in the words and form, working to create the experience. This investment of our intellectual and imaginative energy in itself tends to make us committed to texts, just because we have given so much to them. In Deleuze and Guattari's terms, there is a drive for us to become part of the assemblage that is the reading of the text. The text calls us in, and we join our productive energies with those of the text, thus creating something new in which we have a strong personal investment.

The kind of investment is different with different kinds of texts. Popular texts, in simple genres, for example, tend to leave a great deal of space for readers to fill in the fantasy details, so that the readers' projections are necessary to fill out the text. With texts that we consider to be more "high art," we work hard to get meaning, and so we become involved through the level of intellectual and imaginative commitment we are called on to invest.

This active working to fill out the text is productive not only of textual meaning but also of our subjectivity. We produce certain conceptual and emotional understandings out of the discourses we have at our call—the discourses that the text activates (those out of which it is constructed and those that it draws out in response from us)—and so we implicate ourselves in the way of thinking and being that is the foundation of the discourse. Discourses do not just impose themselves and their attendant ideology on us: we work to position ourselves in them in order to make meaning of texts, and so we are complicit in producing our subjectivity.

It is useful to think of this in terms of what some structuralist and poststructuralist writers call "naturalising" the text (see, for example, Culler, 1975). Any reader works very hard to make sense of elements in a text, to make them seem "natural" and in accord with our experience of the world. Experienced readers have a whole range of strategies to generate meaning when they come across seemingly incongruous elements. If, in a story about relationship breakdown, the narrator tells us, "And so they fell asleep, secure in their king-size bed, in their perfect apartment, in their ideal relationship," we immediately think, "She is being ironic." If we are told in an argument scene, "Jason was just a mouse, and Justin a very large, lithe, voracious cat," we do not imagine that Jason and Justin have suddenly, unexpectedly, metamorphosed into feline and rodent, but we naturalise what is said as being metaphoric.

This, of course, does not only happen locally; more significantly, it happens over the stretch of large works. We are always concerned to make sense of a work, to make it cohere. We desire that all elements should be meaningful, and by "meaningful" we usually mean "internally coherent," and so when we see an element whose function or significance is not immediately apparent, we work very hard to naturalise it, to find a way to make it belong. We look for thematic significance or for symbolic significance, or we employ one of the many other strategies we have for making sense of texts. We do the same in life, but in life we are more ready to accept (of necessity) that things happen at random, that events may not have any deep significance. In works of art, we do not accept this, which is why the plaintive cry "But it really happened like that" cuts no ice when an aspiring author is responding to criticism of the plotting of her or his work.

There are various things we look for. If there are parallel plots running in a work, we search for the payoff of a meaningful refraction of the main action in the subplot, either through contrast or through a strengthening of the significance of the main action. As always, we value works where this is put to unexpected use. After centuries of plays and operas in which the relationship of the heroic lovers was comically refracted in their servants, Beaumarchais in *The Barber of Seville* and *The Marriage of Figaro* created powerfully revolutionary works—although they seem tame enough nowadays when we come with a different structure of expectations—by endowing the servants with as much individuality and, on the whole, rather stronger ethics than the noble characters.

We can naturalise a work with many plot strands as showing us a panorama of a particular society. George Eliot in *Middlemarch* has often been justly celebrated for doing this, but many other authors—Thomas Mann, Jackie Collins, Alessandro Manzoni, for example—in their very different ways, give us panoramic views. With this sort of panoramic structuring, we often achieve the desired coherence by understanding the largely unconnected actions thematically, as giving us a broad view of a particular world. Several of the films of Robert Altman, such as *Short Cuts,* are examples of this, where a number of seemingly unrelated stories happening simultaneously are woven together. If any text remains stubbornly incoherent, we even have recourse to saying that it is a text *about* incoherence, and naturalising it that way.

The way in which such mental structuring of a text's material operates to implicate the reader/viewer in ideology is not hard to see. A reader wants coherence from a work, a sense that it has been meaningfully shaped. If the work seems to consist of disparate threads in narrative terms, then a reader will work hard to find consistency on another level, such as the thematic or the metaphoric. The act of reading will become a hypothesising about how the work hangs together, a desire that becomes an expectation as we lock onto the structuring theme, that becomes a satisfaction as our hypothesis proves to be true and subsequent episodes fall into place by expanding and elaborating on the theme. Again there is the pattern of our being positioned (or positioning ourselves) in a particular expectation, the fulfilment of which aligns us affectively with the ideology implicit (or explicit) in the thematic ordering.

Our investment in texts through filling out the form and searching for coherence is highly significant, but our more obvious investment in texts is affective. When we talk about the impact of a work on us, we more often locate that impact in the experience rendered (and in our related experience of the text). A text matters to us because of what it says and shows, and our major investment is in working with the text to make real to ourselves the experience represented. This is particularly significant for our purposes here, since critical literacy is often centrally concerned with representations and analysing the ideology inscribed in them, but it has not been particularly concerned with the affective element in our response (except to deplore it) and certainly has not generally addressed the question of what makes us desire to engage with represented experience.

Desire and Represented Experience

At one level, it hardly needs to be argued that we are engaged by the representations of experience that texts give. It is self-evidently true. It is perhaps almost as self-evident that the reason we become engaged is because the texts meet a desire we have for broadening our range of perception and experience, or a desire for reaffirmation and renewal, working through afresh what we already know. Again one can see this as the working of a Lacanian desire: there is a feeling of lack and emptiness, a restlessness within the self that we consume the text in the hope of satisfying. Alternatively, we can see it as a productive desiring force, as would Deleuze and Guattari: we desire to create a new (or renewed) sense of being, to generate endlessly new possibilities or infinite variations on old possibilities for ourselves.

There are different kinds and levels of engagement with the represented content, and these position us in different ways or perhaps arise from the different ways we are positioned in relation to the textual material. In common thinking, engagement with a novel or film is often seen in terms of characters and our empathy with them. It is true that we are often closely aligned with particular characters as we move through the experience of a text. These tend to be the characters to whose thoughts we have greatest access and the characters we care about most. The "meaning" of the text is felt to reside in what happens to them and how they respond to it and deal with it. There are, however, complexities here. There are some texts, such as the Harry Potter series, or *Seinfeld,* or *Great Expectations,* where the central character is comparatively bland and is there more to provide an entrée into an alternative world peopled by other more vivid and rather extreme characters. Few children when asked will say that Harry is their favourite character in *Harry Potter*: Ron gets most of the votes. There are also texts where we are kept at a distance from the main characters. In *Wuthering Heights,* we have access to Nelly Dean's and Lockwood's thoughts a great deal, but we care little about them compared with how we feel about Catherine and Heathcliff, whose thoughts we have no direct access to, except when they memorably articulate them.

It is worth stressing that characters in novels are the product of a particular narrative and particular situations: they are quite unlike real people in that they always come with a meaning attached (see Misson, 1996). A character, created out of ruthlessly significant details, can give us the sense of an extraordinarily complex personality, but it is the product of a particular view about people and about how people should, or do, or might, act. Characters are significant within the total structure of the text. Catherine and Heathcliff have significance only because they exist in a narrative that gives a particular value to their transgression and transcendence of the bleak reality in which they exist. It is meaningless to extract them from that narrative and talk about them as if they lived in Jane Austen's world, or Anne Tyler's. Which is not to say that we must accept the narrative's evaluation, nor that we cannot read against the grain of the text and take alternative meanings from the narrative in which they are involved.

If characters always come with a meaning attached, then our sympathy or empathy involves us with those meanings. We do not necessarily take on the values of the character, but rather we engage with the attitude towards the character implicit in the work. The meaning attached can often be that this character is not particularly or wholly admirable: Shakespeare's Falstaff and Milton's Satan are both extraordinarily strong characters with whom we become very involved, but the meaning attached to them is that many of the qualities represented in them are not admirable, despite the attractiveness. (Of course, in both cases, how we should respond to them is a major point of critical contention, but that in itself suggests the complexity of our relationship with fictional characters.)

In spite of the importance of characters, it is probably true to say that our engagement with texts is to do with story and situation, rather than just characters. This has been implied in talking about characters always coming with a meaning attached. Our involvement with a text is rarely just about identifying with a particular character; rather, it is about becoming involved in particular situations or narrative actions that focus particular dilemmas or issues for us. Often it is a matter of understanding what is going on for each of the people involved in a way that they do not understand themselves, and seeing the complexity of human relations and interactions crystallised for us in moments of crisis. If we were witness to such situations in "real life," we would each make sense of them using the particular frameworks—discourses—we have for understanding human behaviour and the way the world operates. In texts, we do something similar, except for one very crucial difference: the creator of the text has inevitably shaped the situation to show it to us in a certain way, through her or his favoured discourses, and that shaping implies certain values about what matters in the situation and what matters in the world. Again, stories and situations come with meanings attached, meanings that we might accept or reject, but meanings with which we have to engage if we are involved in the text. The discourse of the text creates a way of seeing the world and is working to call us into the subject position implied, at least for as long as we are engaged with it.

Engagement with texts is thus about perception, about entering a specific perceptual world. Whether playing a Lara Croft video game, watching *Fawlty Towers,* or listening to *Tristan und Isolde,* we are submerged in an internally coherent world where everything is seen in a particular way. It is that sense of meaningfulness that is so attractive, as long as the meaning is sufficiently in alignment with our previous sense of the world for us to be inclined to accept it. It is not necessarily a matter of the multiplicity of the world being simplified through the discourses activated. The way of perceiving things might be more complex than any with which we have previously engaged, in which case the attraction might be the greater capacity it gives for us to process complex phenomena. On the other hand, we might resist such complexity. (We will look at the whole issue of aligning ourselves with or resisting the ideology of texts in the next chapter.)

It is easy enough to see why we become engaged with texts that represent positive experiences, that overwhelm us with a sense of glowing beauty and unalloyed pleasure. But why are so many of the texts with which we become most deeply engaged ones that deal with negative experiences? Emotional trauma, natural disaster, supernatural terror, crime, violence, relationship breakdown—the list could go on for a very long time. One answer was suggested earlier—that many of our desires stem from a fascination with the dark and difficult—and this is undoubtedly so. However, it is worth pressing a bit further and considering some of the ways in which we are engaged by negative experience.

In one sense, every narrative text at least has to represent some negative experience. If we see the structure of simple narrative as orientation–complication–resolution, then the complication must be a negative move away from the stable situation established in the orientation phase. Any narrative that was purely positive—where things just kept on getting better and better and better—would be boring, not to mention sickeningly sentimental. (One remembers in *The Simpsons* when violence was banned from Itchy and Scratchy cartoons, and all they could do was be nice to each other: all the Springfield kids actually turned off their TVs and went outside to play.) The function of the negative element if it is only in the complication stage is to provide the crucible out of which the revised affirmation of the resolution stage can emerge. Elizabeth and Darcy must go through many vicissitudes arising from pride and prejudice before they can find happiness together. If we are generically sure that the outcome is going to be good, as we are in most traditional comedies, for example, then the negative is piquant contrast, a dallying with the unkind forces that in a just world will be overcome.

There are many texts, however, in which the negative forces are not so easily overcome, and our engagement with the texts is all the stronger for that. It is true that in most texts there is some kind of resolution where the immediate destructive forces have played themselves out—the crime has been solved, the world-threatening crisis is over, the monster is dead, the family has irretrievably broken apart—but there is a kind of exhaustion and focus on the loss rather than triumph and resolution, particularly in those works we call tragedies.

Why do we put ourselves through these negative textual experiences? The question becomes particularly acute the more extreme (and perhaps gratuitous) the negative element becomes, as in horror films and novels. Supernatural horror is a particularly interesting phenomenon because most consumers of it, working within their everyday discourses, would profess themselves to be nonbelievers in supernatural phenomena. Thus we have two questions: why do people put themselves through the torture of the horror text, and why is it torture anyway, if people don't believe such things could actually happen?

The response to the second question is probably, "Well, they might!" In other words, it is to do with imaginative projection. We are willing to enter the imaginative world in which a ski resort hotel is peopled by malign ghosts, and a small boy is pitted against them (and against his own father) with his psychic power, called here "the shining." The answer to the first question—why do we so compulsively read a book like Stephen King's *The Shining*?—almost certainly has to do with our desire for intense emotional experience. The very fact that this intensity of emotion is something we are not likely to experience as we sit in our living room or at our office desk is what attracts us. There is a very willing suspension of disbelief (for those into the genre), because the payoff is a feeling of being affectively engaged in ways and at an intensity that would rarely occur "naturally."

Which is why *Oedipus the King* has been so widely admired through the centuries, in spite of the fact, as we noted, that the prophecy that is the source of the action would not be given much credence these days. Which is why *King Lear* remains the supreme example of a text that engages because it progressively disrupts all our expectations of social justice and then, shatteringly, of natural justice in the world. Which is why, when the Countess intercedes in the finale of Mozart's *The Marriage of Figaro* and the Count pleads for forgiveness, we can scarcely stop the tears. Which is why, in *ER*, when a happy couple with the mother in labour comes into a busy understaffed hospital, and hours later the baby is born but the mother is dead, we are emotionally shocked and drained. In all these, and thousands and thousands of other cases, we are made to feel emotions and see the world in ways that we perhaps suspect we have the potential for attaining but have rarely been called on to activate.

Which can be dangerous. All of these texts are transmitting a particular view of the world; all of them are making claims about what matters in human experience and how we ought to be responding to those things. They are created out of discourses that embody particular belief systems; these discourses are becoming part of our subjectivity. Not only do the intense affective (and intellectual) experiences produced by the texts have inscribed in them particular ideologies, but it is often the coherence that the ideology provides that is the very source of the emotional power. How do we respond? How should we respond? The question of the dynamics of our alignment and resistance with texts will be taken up in the next chapter.

The Dynamics of Alignment and Resistance

[The work] cannot be reduced to the reality of the text or to the subjectivity of the reader, and it is from this virtuality that it derives its dynamism. As the reader passes through the various perspectives offered by the text and relates the different views and patterns to one another he sets the work in motion, and so sets himself in motion too.
WOLFGANG ISER, *The Act of Reading*

These dynamics between texts and readers are the subject of this chapter. We have seen in the previous two chapters how thoroughly imbued with culture are the forms, structuring, and discourses of a text. So too are readers' responses to these, involving elements of the text (both its form and its content), cultural understandings and positioning, and personal dispositions. All of these aspects contribute to readers' emotional and cognitive alignments or disaffections. And we have seen how readers' desires are engaged by aspects of a text's form and the promises that it offers of engagement and intensity of thought and feeling. It is now time to explore in more detail the shifting, interconnected patterns of ideological and aesthetic alignment and resistance that readers experience as they respond to the complex configurations of texts.

(An aligned—compliant or complicit—reading of a text is one that takes up the reading position that the text offers and finds aesthetic and ideological satisfactions there; a resistant reading rejects this positioning and its satisfactions.)

Conditioning Readings

Our responses to a text may be schooled or unschooled. Unschooled readings cannot be purely "natural," if by that is meant a simply personal, spontaneous, autonomous response. All our reading is framed in one way or another, and it has always been learned. A number of factors beyond the text, in the culture and its institutions and practices, shape our responses. We are always "pre-occupied" by our families, the media, and the subcultures in which we participate, each with their knowledges, values, and beliefs. Those unschooled readings can, of course, involve various degrees and combinations of complicity and resistance. One's response to a text could involve a "natural" resistance as a feminist, for instance, without benefit of any schooling in feminist critical literary theory.

In any culture, there are norms of interpretation that influence our responses, whatever the degree of alignment or resistance. For example, there are accepted views about what is realistic, and how it is to be valued. The incursion of the supernatural in the "magical realism" tales of Marquez or the coincidental patterning in a Dickens plot may offend those who have more rigidly prosaic notions of "normal" causality in socially realistic novels. (They may, however, be quite accepting of Gandalf's wizardry or Spiderman's climbing feats, given the rules that operate in fantasy or science fiction genres.) This is one instance in which knowledge of the culturally specific conventions can encourage conventionalised ways of understanding. These norms can govern the way we perceive and understand our perceptions, though their hold is not absolute, and can shift, as we do, across time and discourses and texts.

However individual they may be, we have learned our expectations and desires, our satisfactions, our disappointments or boredoms within our culture. And they are often expressed within the social. Hence we should not overlook the contingencies of the circumstances in which we encounter and discuss texts—skimming a hypertext poem in a crowded student computer lab, going to a movie with a crowd of cynical friends, or talking about the latest prize-winning novel at a book club. The situations in which we encounter texts or report on such encounters condition our responses, which may of course shift if we revisit the text in another context.

Those reading practices that are schooled are more deliberately taught by means of the teacher's arguments for and demonstrations of a particular reading of a text. Or they may be elicited by various forms of classroom activity. These schooled readings are more programmatic and work towards consistent and stable interpretations of the studied texts. They may tend towards a more compliant or more resistant reading. In more traditional curricula, students are instructed to look for particular elements of the text in order to infer the motivations of characters, patterns of imagery, themes, and the like. They are taught to fit these together into a coherent package of interpretations and to find satisfaction in this construct, aligned as it is with the meanings the text invites us to make. In critical literacy classrooms, by contrast, students are taught to look for contradictions and incoherences and to find satisfaction in catching the text out as it falls apart. In either case, teachers hope that their students will apply these learned practices beyond the classroom walls.

This chapter discusses such unschooled and schooled responses, across the range from aligned to resistant. First, however, it will be useful to consider an instance of a taught critical literacy reading to enable us to consider the implications for the aesthetic dimension of such reading.

Critical Resistance—An Exemplary Instance

Critical literacy writers and teachers have taken up the idea that our reading practices are culturally conditioned. This leads them to want to account for the politics of texts and make generalisations about what reading does or should entail. They refuse as a myth the notion that any reader's response can be purely "personal" and emphasise rather how we read by means of all the social, cultural, and political factors that shape those responses. Within such a scheme it is hardly possible to account for the particularities and peculiarities of an individual reader's negotiations with a text.

In this view, texts are potentially guilty until proven inno-cent, and all texts are partial and political. Sometimes student readers are encouraged to take up one of three positions: "with" (a reading in accordance with the dominant or preferred mean-ing), "across" (an alternative but not ideologically oppositional reading), or "against" a text or portions of it (an ideologically oppositional reading) (Moon, 2001; Pope, 1995).

When critical literacy teachers pursue resistant readings (i.e., readings "against" the text) with their students, their strategies are often underpinned by a number of questions, which may or may not be explicitly asked (adapted from Lankshear, 1994, and Luke, O'Brien, & Comber, 1994): Where does this text come from? What kind of text is this? What social and cultural func-tions does this text serve? How does this text construct a version of reality and knowledge, and what is left out of this story? How does the text represent the reader and set up a position for read-ing, and what other positions might there be for reading? How does this text set up its authority and encourage your belief, and how might its authority be deconstructed and challenged, where its ethical stance is at odds with the reader's?

Consider for a moment a characteristic approach to resistant reading. This comes from *Studying Literature,* a widely pro-moted Australian textbook for senior secondary students that aims to induct them into critical poststructural theories (Moon, 1990). After an introduction challenging the traditional valua-tions of "literature," students are shown how texts are cultural artefacts, how readings are constructed, and how they might interrogate dominant or conventional readings of a text. They are then offered a series of exercises designed to help them chal-lenge representations of gender in literary texts. Among a range of poems and fictional stories for discussion is John Donne's "A Valediction: Forbidding Mourning." Students are directed to identify the series of comparisons that structure the poem (the lovers are like a pair of compasses, like gold beaten thin, like the motions of the heavenly bodies). Then they are told:

> Four centuries of critical study have assumed that the speaker of this poem is a male, yet nothing in the poem says it must be so. Part of the reason has to do with a tendency to equate the

speaker of a text with its author—in this case, a man. Another reason for the assumption is that the poem supports a series of gender stereotypes when read in this way. (Moon, 1990, p. 59)

By analysing the comparisons students are directed to identify which character is mobile, which static, which emotional, which rational, who speaks and who listens, and so on. Then they are asked:

Do these aspects of the poem prevent you from reading it as the speech of a woman? Do they at least make it harder to construct such a reading? How would such a reading—that is, reading it as the speech of a woman to a man—differ from a traditional, patriarchal reading? How might readings of the man's and woman's behaviour and motives be changed? (p. 59)

Note how quickly the discussion moves from the comparisons of lover and beloved to a critique of gendered oppositions within patriarchy.[1] Certainly it is legitimate to identify these elements. Indeed, to a modern reader they may be quite evident anyway and even distracting, though there is little point in blaming Donne for not being a feminist. But it is also regrettable if there is no space for students or their teachers to also explore and enjoy the wit and daring of those comparisons, drawn as they are from discourses of astronomy, geography, geometry, and religion.

The gendered reading offered in this textbook is explicitly set in opposition to a compliant, or "dominant," reading of the poem, according to which "'Valediction' proceeds by a series of arresting yet beautifully integrated comparisons" (Moon, 1990, p. 58). This reading is rejected by being dismissed, rather than being offered as a real alternative with which students are to engage seriously. They are not given an opportunity to imagine what this compliant reading involves: to imagine what a pure and noble love is being celebrated here, in which the partners can part with dignified restraint, and to understand the satisfactions of a world in which men act and women are, in which men speak and desire and women are spoken of in terms of desire. This is necessary if readers are to appreciate what they are being asked to assent to.

This is not to advocate a completely compliant reading, one that denies any uneasiness or wry recognition of the implications in the metaphor of the beloved as the fixed, stay-at-home point. It is precisely *not* to advocate any single reading. Incidentally, a compliant reading does not have to precede a resistant one. Many students today are "naturally" resistant readers of such a poem, and part of a teacher's role may be to help them take up a more aligned reading, at least for a time.

Many readers today may experience both forms of recognition and response. This can lead to ambivalence: the threads of one's aesthetic response to the poem's rhetoric and imagery and imaginative assent to these may be interwoven with the strands of one's critique of the gendered relations so beautifully presented in the poem. At some point, and for some readers especially, such critique can outweigh the pleasure. But it need not lead to a denial of pleasure.

There is no suggestion in *Studying Literature* that reading is anything other than an intellectual exercise of catching texts in the act of purveying suspect ideologies or concealing the unpalatable realities that underlie the dominant values and beliefs of a culture. The realities of response, however, are far more complicated than this practice of resistant reading would suggest. As we have seen in previous chapters, our engagements with any texts involve pleasure and desire (why else would we bother to read?) as well as (at times) displeasure, disengagement, even enragement. Our affective responses contribute to the patterning of our alignments and resistances, as do our cognitive engagements. And we respond in both ways to the formal structuring of texts and the content that is represented. These cognitive and affective negotiations with texts are many-layered, shifting, ambivalent, or contradictory, simultaneously aligned with some aspects of a text and resistant to others, or indeed the same aspects. And these kaleidoscopic patterns may shift not only during but also after reading. Given the contribution of all of these factors, it is not surprising that it is in fact so hard to pin down and neatly label any of our responses to a whole text or even to parts of it.

Some Provisos

Before we begin exploring these complexities, a few points need to be made about the limits of such an attempt. For a start, whenever one tries to get at what a reader does in reading, one inevitably tells a story about it. The account can never be the same as the experience. Nor is it possible ultimately to disentangle the text from the reading, or to distinguish what can be read in the text from what can be read into it. Then too there is a risk of a reading by Misson or Morgan being offered as *the* reading and an expectation that all sensitive readers will have had the same experience. Moreover, the texts mentioned below may not work for all readers by way of illustration of the range of alignments and resistances. Certainly many readers who have similar educations and experience with texts, and who have similar affiliations with particular groups and their ideologies, will respond in similar ways. But some of our dispositions and preferences are deeply personal, even idiosyncratic. Moreover, not all aspects of our responses are accessible even to ourselves; some lie buried deep within the recesses of our "under-minds."

Barthes once famously proclaimed the death of the author and celebrated the birth of the reader, but we need to proclaim the death of the reader too, at least as a singular, stable entity. No reader is always the same. This goes beyond the obvious point that our preferences and needs change over time, as anyone knows who has ever returned to a favourite childhood book and tried in vain to reactivate its magic. In the previous chapter it was argued that we take up a negotiated position in a number of discourses and hence are multiple as subjects. And since any text is woven out of various discourses, any reader will engage with each of its discourses, variously, from his or her sometimes changeable subject position. Readers, like texts, are multifaceted, like the surfaces of a prism. And we can be changed by our reading.

Between Alignment and Resistance

Given these factors, all that can be done here is to explore a suggestive array of responses, attempt to account for some of their complexity, and in this way be reminded of their unpredictable dynamics. In what follows, we consider in turn the various factors that lead readers to respond with degrees of dissonance from or alignment with the text. These can be mapped on a continuum.

There may be complete affective and cognitive satisfaction with the text's formal features and its content. There may be alignment with its content and ideologies but dissatisfaction with elements of its form. There may be willing assent to a text's aesthetic and affective structuring but not to its content. And at the far end of the continuum there may be rejection of both aesthetic and ideological aspects of a text. Or—to complicate these positions—there may be an unresolvable ambivalence: contradictory responses may be held simultaneously.

Before we come to some examples of this range, we need to recall that texts are "dynamic happenings" (Iser, 1978). When we talk of the form of a text, we must remember that in reading *form* means the gradual structuring of our understanding and responses; the text is an unfolding event in the reader's mind. And though we may project a gestalt of the text during reading, it is only afterwards, looking backwards, that we can really conceptualise it as a whole and as a completed experience—or so we think (it is, of course, still a partial construct). But even afterwards the text can continue to unfold dynamically for us, as we continue to review, sift, re-evaluate, restructure, and find new patterns and points of significance.

That "unfolding" or "structuring" is not necessarily smooth and consistent: uncertainties, impasses, interim resolutions, hypotheses, realisations, corrections, and complications succeed one another in the course of our reading a text of any length. With those shifts can come changes in affective response. And we may read backwards as well as forwards (even without flipping back through the pages or rewinding the video): a seemingly unimportant detail may take on new significance in the light of later information. The classic case of this is the clues in a Christie detective novel, though it can occur in any text.

Then there are postmodern texts—those of Barthelme, or Coover, for instance—that deliberately play with our responses, unsettling and even undermining any secure stance. (Coover's short story "The Babysitter" is an often anthologised instance of a radically ambiguous text. A series of interwoven fragments offer various versions of what happens, or could happen, when the babysitter minds the children while the parents are out at a party. These are imaginatively realised, even if only as fantasies—

is the babysitter raped by her boyfriend and his mate? seduced by the children's father? murdered? These and other possibilities are played out in brief segments whose tone ranges from farce to horror. Our responses therefore also oscillate, as we entertain these alternatives.) Hypertext fictions, such as Michael Joyce's "classic" hyperfiction *afternoon* (1990), are another form of text whose uncertainties are built in to the multilinear possibilities of their unfolding. Very different readings and alignments depend on which links a reader chooses, and therefore depend on which fragments of the text are accessed and in which order, and whether the reader is able to reach deeply buried nodes (Yellowlees Douglas, 2000).

The dynamics of our reading correspond to the multiplicity of the text—its capacity for generating a range of meanings and emphases. No one reading can encompass all that an aesthetic text has to offer, and indeed, this sense of its inexhaustible potential can be a source of satisfaction to readers.

Bearing these points in mind, let us now explore that continuum mentioned above. When readers read a text that completely satisfies them, it means that they have been able to respond fully and freely in ways that it invites them to. It means they sense that its form is a just and proper crafting of the content and leads them on towards emotional and intellectual satisfactions. They find themselves in sympathy with the worldview being represented in it, or they find it enlarges their view. Having consented to be managed by the text in this way, readers take delight in all that it has to offer. And so they feel replete as readers who have been enabled to have their desires evoked and satisfied, perhaps in new or intensified ways, and who have been shown a world whose ideas resonate with or extend their ideas of how things are or can be. As they sense the congruence of the form that realises its world, their ideological alignment matches their aesthetic engagement with the text.

Even in such cases, as they read they may find themselves making little assessments, queries, and demurrals. (Is this episode really doing the work it should? Is that metaphor fully worked out? Is this character's viewpoint the only one worth inhabiting?) This work of evaluation can itself be pleasurable. Indeed, such acts of discrimination need not interfere with readers' alignment or engagement with texts that generally delight them but may in fact enhance their enjoyment, when they bring these intellectual and aesthetic capacities to bear on their reading.

Other texts may strike some readers as worthy—the content wins their assent—but the writing fails to move. There may be several reasons for this. Readers may think that the content has been handled in a technically inept manner. Or they may find that the form does not accord with the content, or the rhetoric of the language is too strident. For whatever reasons, they simply fail to be swept up in the work aesthetically and affectively and even intellectually, however closely aligned they may be ideologically.

Particular readers—older perhaps, or more cynical—can respond in this way to some novels for adolescents These are the kinds of stories that take a "problem" characteristic of the target audience (being bullied, living in a dysfunctional family, being cast as the misfit at school, nursing an unlikely ambition, and the like) and show how the protagonist, after a number of obstacles, triumphs at last. It all seems too pat somehow, the triumph too neatly contrived, its therapeutic designs on readers too palpable. In such cases, the fact that the text has failed to win readers' intellectual assent or their belief, however sympathetically inclined they may be, interferes with their engagement of other kinds.

Sometimes subcultural groups take up forms that readers who have more literary sophistication find limiting, such as ballads. When such readers hear or read these texts, they are in no doubt about the genuineness of the writer's feeling or the worth of the cause being espoused, but they may be distracted by the clumsiness of the writing when channelled into heavily metrical lines marked by assertive rhymes. The effect can be lamentably lame for readers who come to it with different tastes formed in other contexts. They may have great good will towards the individual, their group, and their cause, and these preexisting sympathies will lead them to feel sympathy for the emotion being represented, but this has not been evoked by the aesthetic element in the text. They may try to set aside their aesthetic disappointment, but a dissonance remains: the head and heart are aligned, but the aesthetic fails to engage and move.

In other cases, the form may not be overfamiliar but on the contrary is so remote as to be alien. Readers who have grown up knowing the satisfactions of cause-and-effect narratives in the European tradition may be puzzled by traditional Indigenous tales that seem incoherent or shapeless or even meaningless. Such readers may take the trouble to learn about what gives these tales their meaning (features of the terrain, for instance, in Aboriginal Dreaming stories). They may try to set aside their desire for strong narrative linearity and plotted development. Yet both form and content may remain so strange as to impair readers' capacity to derive aesthetic enjoyment, however well intentioned they are. It should be said, of course, that quite the same is undoubtedly true for members of Indigenous cultures when they encounter the restrictively causal narratives of mainstream Western culture. In such cases the alignment of one's sympathies and values is impeded by one's aesthetic puzzlement.

Then there are texts with which readers do not concur ideologically, or which seem unworthy in some way, but which move or please nonetheless. A trivial example is a politically incorrect joke. If its lampooning seems mild and its targets are not victimised, and if the situation in which it is told is "safe" (we are among friends who also share our enlightened attitudes), hearers may set aside their scruples for a moment and listen along for the sake of the punch line and the exquisite timing of its comic surprise.

Action movies are another instance. If viewers stand back and consider the nature of the world represented there, it is a nasty place in which harm lurks round every corner, physical violence gets positive results, and bystanders and lesser characters are expendable. This is not how many of us see our world, nor do we value the casual brutality depicted here. But if viewers accept this world for the time (after all, it's vividly and realistically present to their eyes), they get the payoff: a ride on a roller coaster of anticipation, suspense, fear, followed by momentary relaxation before the next wave, each wave becoming faster and more intense, until the final climax, after which the hero(ine) walks away, wounded perhaps but undefeated. In such cases, though viewers may take pleasure in the stylish treatment of the action, it's the forward drive of the events that matters, when they make the narrative's questions their own: How will the protagonist escape from this latest tight corner? How will the villains finally be overcome?

Later, or at moments during the film, viewers may register some disquiet about the world represented here and the values it espouses. But they have also known the exhilarations of participating imaginatively in such a world.

So it is too with stories of supernatural horror. In one's everyday life one may certainly not believe in incursions from another world but may entertain the possibility in order to be entertained, and terrified, despite one's scepticism. When readers are persuaded, through a narrator's focalisation or the suturing of gazes in a movie, to identify with the character to whom the horrifying things are happening, they know and feel the reality of the supernatural events. They invite the opportunity to rehearse extreme feelings by participating in the emotional traumas of the characters. In such cases, they may take pleasure in being horrified, wincing as they watch through their hands.

Readers may also give acquiescence to older texts that still have power to move even though they have different ideologies. One's republican sentiment need not prevent one from watching *Macbeth* and sensing the rightness of the end with its restoration of a legitimate monarchy and with it a reordering of nature. One can feel the desire for such an encompassing order even as one dismisses it as impossible, perhaps in a sense undesirable. And though most of us today find it difficult to stomach Dickens's pious, meekly modest heroines (an Agnes, a Little Dorrit, a Nell), some of us may be moved momentarily, despite our twenty-first-century scorn, by their quiet endurance in suffering. Even when we recognise how Dickens is manipulating and exploiting our feelings, even when we know our responses are sentimental, and we resent it, we can still get swept up in our feelings for the characters and the poignancy of the situations in which they are involved. We can be both engaged and critical readers.

When the form and substance, the ideological and aesthetic elements of a text, fail to satisfy, the result is boredom or disengagement, disapproval, or even rage. Readers may find a text trivial; they may think it offers too easy satisfactions of the desires it sets up; they may find its form too neatly contrived or too shapeless, its language too lax and self-indulgent, heavy-handed or bombastic, or its values repugnant. There are many sources of disaffection and disapproval. Readers may not even be able to put their finger on all the sources of their disappointment: "I just couldn't get into it," one says with a shrug; another makes a wry mouth: "It simply wasn't my cup of tea." And they move on to another text, if they are optimistic readers with an expectation that pleasures and satisfactions certainly await them in their next encounter.

More interesting for this chapter's argument about the dynamics of response are those points in readers' encounters with texts when their responses are contradictory: ambivalent, conflicted, simultaneously aligned and resistant. We have seen how some aspects of a text engage us while others do not. But at times it can be hard to come to a single response to the same element of a text. Some members of an audience can see the argumentative and climactic narrative logic of Nora's slamming the door as she leaves her children and husband inside the "doll's house," in the play of the same name. She must first find herself or be no use to anyone else either. But they may still be unable to accept the necessity or rightness of her leaving her children. (In this case, of course, the play encourages such intellectual and ethical conflict, in order to generate debate.)

In other cases we may get deeply engaged with, even revel in, what we find repugnant, such as those texts that depict disruptions to the social or natural order. Supernatural horror stories depend on such disruptions and on our fascinated engagement with them. But there are plenty of other texts that work in similar ways. In Shakespeare's *Henry IV, Part 1,* for instance, we know very well that Prince Hal must give up his life of revelry and his carousing companions in order to become a mature, worthy monarch. But we are much more engaged by that master of misrule, Falstaff, who is so much more exhilarating a character. The play leads us to value the former; at the same time, it asks us to know the attractions of the latter that are to be rejected.

Oedipus the King is an instance of a slightly different kind. We know how terrible the transgressions of parricide and incest are, how offensive to the moral order on which society depends. As we get caught up in the story, our desires are aligned with the ethical imperative to cleanse Thebes of its pollution and the drive of the narrative towards finding and punishing the pollutant. But as our sympathies with Oedipus are also engaged, our desires pull us in the opposite direction. We anticipate the denouement and can see the deliverance it will bring to Thebes, and yet we dread that fulfilment, for the destruction it will bring to its king. We are deeply moved for the man we must condemn and whose downfall we must also desire for the health of the social and natural order. Our ambivalence remains.

In yet other cases, where a text, or a passage within it, is woven out of several discourses, readers may find themselves in sympathy with one and not with another, and yet be unable to disentangle the threads of their response, because of the way the discourses are working together in the text. For instance, *To Kill a Mockingbird* may seem plausible in its depiction of the complexities of class and race relations in the time and place of its setting. And as we saw in Chapter 3, the imbricated discourses of family, religion, race, and the law invite one's alignments. Readers may well be moved by the unjust tragedy of a Tom Robinson, disgusted by the mean and brutal self-interest of Bob Ewell, inspired by the wise counsel and abiding sense of justice that Atticus demonstrates. And yet even as on one level one becomes engaged with the working out in the story of those discourses of family, law, and religion and finds its denouement richly satisfying, one may also see how those same discourses pull together to secure a particular set of race relations. Patriarchy, family, law, and religion encourage white benevolence and black dependence. The novel's discourses coincide here, and collide.

All these examples of patterns of alignment or resistance may have given a rather too tidy impression, as if any reader's response can be predictably located along the spectrum. To correct this, let us look at an example of how two readers—Wendy Morgan and Ray Misson—with similar education and similar experience of and orientation to literary texts, read the same text.[2] As we shall see, the responses are surprisingly divergent in some respects.

Two Readings

The text in question is Shakespeare's Sonnet 18 (the sonnet that was discussed in Chapter 3). Here is the poem again:

Shall I compare thee to a summer's day?
Thou art more lovely and more temperate.
Rough winds do shake the darling buds of May,
And summer's lease hath all too short a date.
Sometime too hot the eye of heaven shines,
And often is his gold complexion dimmed;
And every fair from fair sometime declines,
By chance, or nature's changing course untrimmed;
But thy eternal summer shall not fade,
Nor lose possession of that fair thou ow'st,
Nor shall Death brag thou wand'rest in his shade,
When in eternal lines to time thou grow'st.
    So long as men can breathe or eyes can see,
    So long lives this, and this gives life to thee.

Reading 1 (Morgan)

When I think about my reading, it's a hearing rather than a saying. Rather curiously, I haven't chosen to become "I" with the speaker. I don't identify with the poet-creator whose work has power over death. Instead, I've identified dramatically with the beloved; I've taken up as my reading position the one who's being addressed as "thee." To slip into that position came so naturally, as I read the poem again after a gap of thirty years, that I didn't question it until later. It now strikes me as rather odd, and my first explanation is undoubtedly far too simple: that my reading position may say much about how I was learning to perform my gender in New Zealand in the 1960s, when I first read the poem. And it may say much about how persistent a first, studious reading can be, if it's not reexamined.

How I've inserted myself into the drama of the poem has certainly affected how I've experienced its aesthetic. Let me retrace my steps briefly, to show how my sense of the poem's beauty (its intensity) and my pleasure (my engagement) are shaped by the way I'm enfolded in the poem.

For me those first two quatrains build up a picture of the pathos of universal decay. As I glimpse this vision I feel a longing that beauty shouldn't be obliterated. The more I let those quatrains work on me to create that desire (it's also a desire to enjoy that yearning and pity), the more I feel the assurance of lines 9 to 14. Since I've been identifying with the beloved, that pathos affects me the more directly. But can my desire for escape from mutability be so completely satisfied? Suppose I register that the words "So long as . . . eyes can see" refer to me as one of those later generations of seeing readers. (This requires me to make a shift of reading position—as happens often enough within the gestalt of any text.) When I'm recalled to my reading self, I'm distinguished from the beloved. Not yet "translated" into poetry, I still yearn for that ultimate satisfaction of living on in eternal summer.

When I disengage from my reading, as a middle-aged woman touched by feminism, I most certainly do not want to be rescued from time by an egotistical poet. But while I'm in the space of the poem I know that desire: it becomes mine as I take up the subject position and subjectivity that the poem's emotional structuring and form offer. It may be easier to take up that position of the beloved because he's addressed directly and described only by means of those comparisons. But the very ease with which I can insert myself is also the source of some unease: how empty that self is whose bright blurriness I inhabit for a while. I feel a similar ambivalence about the poem's final demonstration of triumph over time and change. I'm not sure if I feel more reassurance and relief or dislike of the speaker's self-congratulation. Or perhaps, it now occurs to me, this is no more than the witty turning of a convention, and thus a rhetorical conceit rather than personal conceitedness. How much I feel the triumph of the final couplet probably depends on how far I'm prepared to give consent to that social valuation of art.

Reading 2 (Misson)

I'm rather disconcerted by Wendy's way of reading the poem. In spite of some minor points of difference, we both agree about "the meaning" of the poem, we both admire it enormously and generally agree in our accounts of how it's working, and yet when Wendy and I started to talk about the poem, a huge chasm opened up. We were obviously reading the poem very differently, not on any linguistic or even critical level, nor in the general area of the affect of the poem, but in the way we were inserting ourselves into the drama that the poem enacts. The difference is in the stance we take. I identify with the speaker, Wendy with the addressee. I relate to the "I," she relates to the "thee."

A number of possible reasons present themselves. It might be because I could never imagine anyone thinking me the remotest bit like a summer's day, let alone "more lovely and more temperate." It might be a gendered positioning, the male seeing himself as the active speaker, the female the passive listener. It could be because of my (rather minor) drama background, and so a propensity to take on a character rather than hearing a writer speak to me. Or perhaps it's because I got to know this poem really well when I was teaching the sonnets and performed this poem in the lecture. It came at a crucial point in the first of the lectures, in that I planned it as the revelation to the students that the major relationship in the sonnets was a homo-erotic one. I therefore wanted to project the experience of the poem as overwhelmingly, radiantly positive, to force the students to grapple with any heterosexist feelings they might have. (And there were personal reasons operating there too that, at the time, weren't totally brought to my consciousness.) The poem has come to me to be very much my performance of the poem, how I hear it and voice it. Even this may make a difference to my reading. If the poem has a kind of physical, material presence, that presence depends partly on the voice: "so long as men can breathe. . . ." Because of my own internalised vocal range, I perform the poem to myself in terms of it, even if I can't necessarily realise that reading in a performance.

I can, of course, argue why my way of reading the poem is the better one—which, of course, it is, since one's own reading is always the better one, as Stanley Fish argues (1980), because it wouldn't be one's reading if one thought another reading was better. I might note, for example, that

Wendy tends to stress the mutability more strongly than I do, whereas I see that as largely the dark shadow that acts as foil to the glory of physical beauty and art. I'd say that the beautiful friend is so much a cipher, an idealised object, that it's not easy to identify with him, but then, one could equally well argue that the emptiness of the figure is an open invitation to insert oneself in his place. I'd argue that the emotional centre of the poem is the way the speaker feels about the young man, and that the very essence of it is the way the emotion outstrips and re-creates the object, but then it could be argued that this emotional centre can equally validly be approached through being addressed in these terms as through speaking them.

It is important to note that this alignment with the speaker or addressee is only one strand in our response to the text and our ways of engaging with it. Identification is often not simply a matter of choosing one of the actors in the drama and immersing oneself absolutely in that particular positioning, but of connecting to the whole situation. We can become extraordinarily involved in fictional situations without identifying with any person in them, or while not identifying with the person through whom the textual experience is focussed. To take a very simple and obvious example, a love scene might be managed totally from the woman's point of view, but a man can still find it arousing. So too readers will relate to the total experience of a sonnet like this and identify with the whole situation as well as inserting themselves into it imaginatively in more particular ways. Thus identifications are multiple and complex and do not result in a single predictable alignment.

The two responses demonstrated here are obviously products of highly complicated personal and contextual factors, and prior positionings, as well as the circumstances of the immediate encounter with the text. As we saw in Chapter 3, the text is undoubtedly working to position readers in certain ways, but how we take up those invitations is very variable and unpredictable, and not all of them will be communicable. For instance, just how any reader visualises the "darling buds of May" (or September) and imagines their being shaken will depend on his or her memories of having seen something of the kind, and the emotional colouration associated with those memories will be some of the very personal threads in the texturing of desire and satisfaction.

It would, of course, be impossible to identify all the subtleties of responses to any one text in the classroom, let alone trace them to their sources. But it is possible for a teacher to acknowledge the various and variable nature of responses, and rather than cajoling students towards the same reading advocated by the teacher, whether with or against the grain of the text, to work productively with that multiplicity. (This idea will be taken up further in Chapters 8 and 9.)

The few examples discussed in this chapter have been intended to show something of the complexities of response, across the spectra, from aesthetic engagement to disengagement and from ideological alignment to resistance. We now turn to consider briefly the implications of this for English classrooms.

The Dynamics of Schooled Response

As noted previously, in critical literacy a resistant reading is one based on ideological critique. Teachers sometimes assume that students are "naturally" prone to be complicit readers, or have learned to be so by their previous schooling, and need to be trained to see the ideological shaping of texts: they must be shown why and how to resist the partial, interested, and even pernicious representations on offer in texts. However, the case of resistance is rather more complicated. Readers may be inclined on first reading to be resistant to aspects of a text's form and meaning but may come, after further study, to a more positively appreciative understanding. "Natural" or "schooled" alignment or resistance can be aroused towards the aesthetic aspects of texts and their capacity to affect us emotionally, as well as towards the content and the values espoused. That is why the aesthetic must be taken into account if English teachers are to undertake a comprehensive critical literacy agenda.

In different countries, under different curricula and assessment regimes, students are coached into developing diverse specific capacities according to the response modes privileged by their teachers and systems. In each case, different "procedural displays" of response (Bloome, 1985) will be required. While a number of teachers have gone beyond the embarrassed attempts of the now old New Critics to excommunicate readers with all their "vague states of emotional disturbance" (Wimsatt, 1954, p. 91), some residual anxiety may remain about readers going off in the wrong direction if their responses are not properly managed. With the best of intentions, and assuming that what matters is "what the text has to say to us," some teachers try to coach a class towards the one, authorised reading before the students have had any opportunity to engage with the text themselves. Even where a teacher invites class members to present their developing responses to a text as they are reading it, his or her questions and commentary often nudge students towards a gestalt interpretation that really depends on the teacher having read to the end and developed an understanding derived from hindsight. The students' tentative, contingent responses are thus formalised and hardened into a single interpretation.

The implication of this argument is not to fetishise students' "own" responses: these are, of course, always learned and conditioned by culture. It is to recognise that teachers may direct students' readings towards the one holistic interpretation and not legitimise the dynamic shifts and interplay of response along a continuum between alignment and resistance. However, even when students are encouraged to air their diverse views in the course of discussion, when it comes to summative written responses, teachers and students expect to move to considered, logical, evaluative statements and away from their more immediate, inchoate, and emotional responses. And they are certainly not encouraged to be shifting, ambivalent, or undecided.

It can be said that textbooks like the one discussed at the beginning of this chapter do quite equivalent work, in directing readers to the one ideologically critical stance being advocated, even though this is specifically *not* "what the text has to say to us" but what we say in speaking back to the text. Poststructuralist theorists, however, have enabled us to characterise the text as a problematic representation with multiple, possibly contradictory readings that can be activated. The point is not simply to coerce students to substitute one "correct," resistant reading for another, more aligned reading, but to set the text and its readings in play. Nor is it just a matter of getting students to adopt different "frames" for reading—for example, by taking up a role-played position as a feminist or a member of an ethnic minority or working-class group or whatever. Nor is the point simply to set the kind of analytical exercises exemplified earlier in this chapter. Although such activities can be useful in getting students to denaturalise their own reading assumptions, ideologies, and preferences, they will not help students explore the multifariousness of their own sometimes shifting alignments and resistances.

Teachers can help here. Every text is capable of many different realisations; no one reading can exhaust all its potential. We need to welcome the plenitude as well as the instability of the text, while also recognising that texts and reading practices nudge readers towards particular readings. Reading is both a generative and a disciplined enterprise. It is important for us as teachers to acknowledge and value the complexity and dynamism of our own responses to a range of texts, including responses that are "incorrect" in some way. It makes for much more interesting work in classrooms to pluralise readings and see how they play out. This means being explicit, as far as one can, about the sources of and reasons for one's preferences. It means teasing out the affective and cognitive grounds, the aesthetic and ideological ones, and allowing for interplay among these. (These and other suggestions for working with the aesthetic and the critical are explored further in Chapter 9.)

As this chapter has attempted to suggest, any reader's reading generates complex cognitive and affective negotiations, and these are both dependent on the social and the subjective. In the next three chapters we go beyond the arguments offered so far in the book, which have emphasised the ways in which the aesthetic is a sociocultural phenomenon. We now turn to re-evaluate the aesthetic by considering the ways in which the aesthetic exceeds and even disrupts the framework of sociocultural conceptions of literacy.

What's the Use of the Aesthetic?

Much of this book up till now has been concerned with showing how the aesthetic is socially situated, how it puts us into
particular subject positions, and how it is ideologically implicated.
If all that one were concerned about in life (or English education)
were not becoming ideologically subject to texts, then one would
have every right to be suspicious of the pleasure and beauty that
the aesthetic offers. However, the aesthetic, as we have also seen in
the first half of the book, is a powerful mode of human knowing
and can give us intense and engaging experiences that we find
enormously valuable. It is now time to turn to investigating this
element more fully and to ask, "What's the use of the aesthetic?"

It is a not uncommon belief that the aesthetic has no use at
all, at least in the sense that it is not utilitarian. On the one hand,
this has led to its being decried as a waste of precious time that
could be used for meeting other rational and functional goals.
Dickens has given us the apotheosis of this attitude in the figure
of Thomas Gradgrind in *Hard Times,* who one day, on hearing
his daughter say, "I wonder," castigated her with the words
"Louisa, never wonder!":

> There was a library in Coketown to which general access was
> easy. Mr Gradgrind greatly tormented his mind about what
> the people read in this library. . . . It was a disheartening cir-
> cumstance, but a melancholy fact, that . . . these readers per-
> sisted in wondering. They wondered about human nature,
> human passions, human hopes and fears, the struggles, tri-
> umphs and defeats, the cares and joys and sorrows, the lives
> and deaths, of common men and women! . . . They took De
> Foe to their bosoms, instead of Euclid, and seemed to be on
> the whole more comforted by Goldsmith than by Cocker. Mr
> Gradgrind was for ever working, in print and out of print, at
> this eccentric sum, and he never could make out how it
> yielded this unaccountable result. (1854/1983, p. 41)

On the other hand, there are those who have gloried in the sheer uselessness of the aesthetic, in the fact that it is an escape from the rational and utilitarian. Oscar Wilde famously declared at the end of the preface to *The Picture of Dorian Gray* (1891/1974, p. 139):

> We can forgive a man for making a useful thing as long as he does not admire it. The only excuse for making a useless thing is that one admires it intensely.
> All art is quite useless.

However, most people would see the aesthetic as at least marginally useful. The reasons for this fall into three categories, all of which are activated to different extents at different times when arguments are mounted for studying literature in schools. The aesthetic can be seen to be useful in terms of giving us access to "truth," in terms of personal development, or in terms of entertainment. We will look at each of these in turn, not just to see how well they stand up to scrutiny, but to consider how they might be rethought in terms compatible with a poststructuralist framework such as that to which critical literacy subscribes.

The Aesthetic and Truth

One of the most famous (or notorious) statements about the aesthetic is that made by Keats's Grecian Urn:

> 'Beauty is truth, truth beauty,'—that is all
> Ye know on earth, and all ye need to know.[1]
>
> ("ODE ON A GRECIAN URN," LL. 49–50)

The statement is generally greeted with a degree of scepticism, and it would hardly be possible to mount an argument for its literal truth, except perhaps by a radical redefinition of "truth" and "beauty." Even then, there would be some doubt as to whether this really is the sum of all necessary human knowledge. And yet, the lasting power of the statement suggests that it has struck a chord for many people, and perhaps still does, although rather than seeing truth as related to "beauty," we are increasingly likely to think of it as related to its opposite these days. We are more often concerned, along with Michael Moore, with exposing the "awful truth" than with pondering the truth of the beautiful.

Truth and beauty are two elements of a famous triad, and the third one is undoubtedly lurking around Keats's statement too. From Pythagoras through Plato and beyond, beauty was linked with truth and goodness: the ideal of education, for example, was to inculcate the true, the beautiful, and the good, and so classic education had to be concerned with the intellectual, the aesthetic, and the ethical realms (see Gardner, 1999). What is of significance for us is not that they are covered in disparate disciplines, but that, as Keats attests, they are felt to be so strongly articulated with each other. There is a strangely persistent belief that beauty is a guarantee of truth and goodness, that there is a natural order, a Providence, that ensures that that which is beautiful must be authentic and moral. Such a belief, of course, is highly seductive, because we are attracted to the beautiful (in a way that we perhaps are not necessarily attracted to the true or the good), and so it would be very convenient if there were no rational or ethical reason to reject it.

Although we can all think of many examples where the beautiful is guarantee of neither truth nor goodness, the persistence of the belief makes it worth investigating to see if there is any grain of truth in it. First of all, a reminder that in Chapter 2 it was argued that the essential function of the aesthetic is that it is a way of knowing, and also that it was argued that we need to redefine beauty as intensity, that the term points to "a sense that what we are seeing is saturated with significance and calls forth a heightened perception beyond what one expects in day-to-day existence." This intensity can be the result of harmonious formal patterning, of an intense concentration on what is pleasant, but it can equally well be, at the other extreme, a "terrible beauty," born out of the disruptive and emotionally difficult.

If we think of beauty in this way, then the traditional connection between it and truth becomes at least a little more comprehensible. It works on a model of the writer engaging intensely with some aspect of experience, coming to know it in this particularly penetrating way through transforming it into the aesthetic text being created. It works on a model of readers coming to the text and, in reading it, being convinced that this indeed is a version of experience that corresponds to how we might see the world, and that the text reveals something that is a genuinely interesting, personally extending perspective on reality. The problem, of course, is that all this is so subjective: both the reader and the writer might be wrong. In particular, they might be in the grip of a particular ideology that leads them both to find such a construction of reality pleasing and convincing, whereas the rest of us are less impressed.

It is very easy (indeed, seemingly natural) to think one's own reading of a text to be what the text is *really* saying. The kind of criticism stemming from F. R. Leavis and the New Critics in the middle of the last century, which is still behind some of the critical practice in schools and elsewhere, is deeply flawed because of this. Leavis, in particular, assumed that great literature embodied a set of "universal" values that turned out to be remarkably like his own. The New Critics were concerned to isolate the text as an artefact to be contemplated directly and objectively. One was not to fall into the trap of thinking that the text meant what the author intended (the intentional fallacy), or that it meant what its effect was on the reader (the affective fallacy). How one might actually gain access to a text without being a reader who comes with a particular subjectivity was never considered a problem worth confronting. This suggested that there was a single (inevitably very complex) meaning in the poem that criticism was concerned to discover. Leavis also believed this: the title of one of his books was taken from a phrase of T. S. Eliot's in which he spoke of the study of literature as "the common pursuit of true judgment"—that is, *one* ultimate judgment that the judgments we haltingly make along the way are steps towards. His work is almost comically peppered with statements of incredulity that anyone could be so intellectually and morally deficient as to read a work differently than he does.

Although Leavis would probably have scorned thinking about it in these terms, his whole approach to literature was predicated on the belief that the beautiful (i.e., literature of which he approved) was inevitably revelatory of the true and the good. He saw a deep relationship between the writer's art and the profundity of her or his thought:

What is manifested in the organization that commands such a variety of resource and method with such seeming ease, so that they work together to serve a complex significance, is a remarkable intellectual grasp: the novelist's imaginative grasp is at the same time that. (1964, p. 162)

and a deep connection between art and the moral:

Every detail, character, and incident has its significant bearing on the themes and motives. . . . The magnificence referred to above addresses the senses, or the sensuous imagination; the pattern is one of moral significances. (1962, p. 211)

For all that Leavis's legacy is scorned these days, this assumption that the moral quality and the aesthetic quality of a book are inextricable from each other still persists in much general thinking about literature. Obvious exceptions prove that there is no necessary connection between the two, as discussed in Chapters 2 and 5, but there does seem to be some level of correlation, and so it is worth testing a little further why they do seem so aligned by taking a case where there is general agreement that there is a decline in quality within a work, and seeing whether (or how) the decline is apparent in both the moral and the aesthetic quality.

Mark Twain's *The Adventures of Huckleberry Finn* (1884/1985) provides an interesting case to consider in this respect. Most readers find the last section of the book, set at Phelps's Farm, a terrible disappointment. After the magnificent, crucial moment when Huck decides, "All right, then I'll *go* to Hell" (p. 283) and determines to free Jim, once Tom Sawyer reappears, we seem to be reading a different book, with Tom "staging" Jim's escape in the most lurid traditions culled from his adventure reading. There is not space here, and it probably is not necessary anyway, to demonstrate that the quality of the writing is poorer, both verbally and in terms of the narrative, even in simply keeping up the reader's engagement with what is going on. Beyond that, to sound like Leavis for a moment, there can be little doubt that the failure here is not just artistic but manifests itself in terms of veracity and morality as well.

Leaving aside for the moment the very fundamental and difficult question of what we might mean by "truth" in regard to artistic works, it is at least possible to say that the section is not very convincing. Basically, we find it hard to believe that this could really happen. The problem is not that the action is based on Tom's romantic-heroic code culled from his reading of adventure stories; the problem is that one cannot for a moment believe that he could get away with doing what he does in any world we would care to imagine. One can see that Twain is trying to make him a mini American Don Quixote, and the central dynamic, as in Cervantes' work, is created by setting the romantic action against a mundane domestic setting, but whereas Don Quixote's folly is constantly being shown up as just that when the world doesn't accommodate him—a windmill is still a windmill, a serving girl remains a serving girl—Tom happily rereads the world, and there seem to be no negative consequences. Rather, we seem to be meant to find him and everything he does cute and engaging. Even his wounding is not presented as a consequence, but as another case of how entertaining Tom is in his commitment to romantic adventure: "We was all as glad as we could be, but Tom was the gladdest of all, because he had a bullet in the calf of his leg" (p. 348). It is almost impossible to accept the "truth" of such an unqualifiedly positive reaction to a bullet wound, but that is just symptomatic of the kind of unreal reactions in which we are expected to acquiesce throughout this section.

Bound up with that is a weakness in terms of ethics. Few readers today could fail to be appalled at the treatment handed out to Jim. The book has centred on the growing friendship and interdependence of Huck and Jim, on Huck's instinctive goodness leading him constantly to recognising Jim's humanity, this playing against his socialised sense of "niggers" as basically non-human. ("Good gracious! Anybody hurt?" "No'm. Killed a nigger" [p. 291].) It is in fact one of the least convincing aspects of the final section that the Huck we have come to know would be complicit with Tom in his treatment of Jim, not just because of his personal attachment to him, but because of his natural sense, that we have come to expect and respect, of what is right. Tom's revelation that Jim had in fact been freed, and that Tom was planning to compensate him for the agonies he has unnecessarily put him through by "pay(ing) him for his lost time" (p. 368), seems to make matters worse, because it makes what Jim suffered totally pointless: it wasn't even a misguided and misconducted attempt to achieve a valuable and necessary outcome. Huck's decision to save Jim is made in intensely ethical terms, although Huck, of course, sees it as an inherently immoral decision: the way that the attempt to free him is played out in the novel bears no relation to the values asserted there, and so the novel through this sequence becomes ethically incoherent.

So, in this case, or more to the point, in this reading of this case, we do not seem to be able to separate out the artistic weakness from the failure to convince us that the story might conceivably be true and from the inability to maintain ethical consistency. This is not always so, as we saw in Chapter 5, but it is often true that a serious weakness in one area does contaminate or affect our sense of the whole representation and lead us to an overall negative evaluation.

Huckleberry Finn has, of course, been a much-disputed text in other ways, particularly in relation to its status as a school text. The novel reads to many as a great statement against racial discrimination. For these people, it is almost incomprehensible that it should be banned by some school districts in the United States for its racism.[2] (It almost produces a Leavis-like reaction, "If they were *really* reading the novel, they could not think this!"[3]) And yet, of course, again reading from a particular position, the charge has some point. The thing that people have found most racist is the novel's use of the word *nigger*. One can perhaps not charge Mark Twain with insensitivity over this: it clearly was less problematic at the time (postslavery) he was writing than it is today, and he was writing a story set some forty years before (preabolition), when the word presumably was even more acceptable. Besides, it could be argued that the word is not used approvingly or even neutrally in the novel: it is so insistently repeated that it becomes a kind of verbal lightning rod, drawing in and becoming charged with all the social energies of racism against which the novel is speaking. However, we cannot simply ignore the modern impact of the word: as novelist David Bradley puts it, "'Nigger' is offensive not because it was said by literary characters in 1845 but because it was *meant* by literal Americans in 1995" (quoted in Arac, 1997, p. 85). Thus the instability of language, combined with the different ethical and political positioning of readers more than a hundred years after the book was written, has meant that, for many people, the book is deeply problematic ethically, even though they might recognise that Twain had good intentions and that the book is brilliant in many ways.

The stronger charge of racism against the novel, and the one that is more likely to be mounted in a critical literacy classroom since analysis of representations is a standard strategy, is that Jim often seems like a stereotype: superstitious, childlike, dependent on Huck, not very bright. Even in some of the great set pieces of the novel where Huck's feelings are educated by an awareness of Jim's humanity, Jim himself can seem rather limited. The "trash" speech when Huck has played the cruel joke on him after the night in the fog is undeniably powerful, but it depends on Jim's description of his mourning at the supposed loss of Huck, and so in the end depends on an overly sentimental image of the good and faithful black carer. The story of his deaf daughter is also very moving, but again the dominant mode is sentiment. Sentiment can carry a lot of force, but in the end it simplifies human emotion. Jim not only seems secondary to Huck, providing opportunities for Huck's development, but he seems to be simpler as a human being because he is black, and that is racist.

Of course, any of these readings that claim weaknesses in the book are *only* readings. No less a critic (and moralist) than T. S. Eliot, for example, defended the book's ending (see Eliot, 1950/1991, p. 48). The variability of response is very much the point. We cannot expect a single reading; there is no single "true judgment" to pursue. Poststructuralism has made us dubious of any claims to a single, stable meaning in a text, let alone to claims of absolute truth. We have never been further away from accepting a statement such as "Beauty is truth, truth beauty."

Roland Barthes is a central figure in signalling this shift, or at least in popularising it. Barthes argued that the standard mid-twentieth-century practice of reading is predicated on the notion of the author standing behind the text, establishing a meaning that it is the job of the reader to intuit. The author is the authority: a reading is good or less good as it corresponds to what the author (often unconsciously) wanted to show.[4] Barthes argues that we should get away from this notion. Once the text goes out into the world, the author is dead:

> We now know that a text is not a line of words releasing a single 'theological' meaning (the 'message' of the Author-God) but a multi-dimensional space in which a variety of writings, none of them original, blend and clash. (1977, p. 146)

He reminds us that "etymologically, the text is a tissue, a woven fabric" (p. 159), and that

> In the multiplicity of writing, everything is to be *disentangled,* nothing *deciphered;* the structure can be followed, 'run' (like the thread of a stocking) at every point and at every level, but there is nothing beneath: the space of writing is to be ranged over, not pierced. (p. 147)

The threads come together in the reader's mind, not the author's: the reader's patterning of them is what matters.

Thus, if we think about *Huckleberry Finn,* we can see that it is perfectly possible to highlight the thread of the representation of Jim as a black person and to find the book wanting, even racist. It is equally possible to pick on the thread (as most people do) of the developing relationship between Huck and Jim and see the book as a triumphant assertion of a common humanity beyond racism, a strong statement of an anti-racist position. Both views are perfectly defensible. One could equally read the book as a terrifyingly accurate critique of the violence and rapacity of American society, with its exploitation of black people being only one aspect of its ultimate contempt for human decency and human life, whether it be in the form of a drunken father, criminals dividing up the spoils, feuding families, a contemptuously arrogant Colonel, conmen playing tricks, or even a boy misled by his adventure reading. Or one could read it as a book about the demands made by this society's way of doing masculinity, or as a book about the economic basis of class structure and class values. There are endless possibilities.

If there is no single meaning in a work, but a work is just a space wherein a reader can play and follow through whatever line of meaning seems interesting, and if there are no such things as ultimate truths—"all we know on earth, and all we need to know"—then the claims made for literature in terms of being revelatory of truth would seem to fall apart. In fact, that is not the case.

Poststructuralism is often misunderstood. It is sometimes claimed that it is saying that anything can mean anything, and that everything is of equal value. While there may have been the (rather) odd person here or there who has made such claims, this certainly is not the general view. To say that all language is unstable and indeterminate is not to say that it is an empty receptacle into which any meaning can be poured at the whim of the reader: a rose is still a rose (or something metaphorically related, e.g., a ceiling rose, an English beauty) and not a tub of Kentucky Fried Chicken. To say that there are no absolute truths is not to say that nothing is true, or that one thing cannot be truer than another, or rather, that the truth of some things matters more than the truth of others. The fact that the news will be on television tonight at 7.00 p.m. is undoubtedly true (if there isn't a sports telecast that's running overtime): the fact that people, both military and civilian, are being killed in a war zone (as we may see on the news) is just as true, but matters rather more. To say that there is no absolute standard of value and all value is relative does not mean that we are unable to value things. We may enjoy reading both Jackie Collins and George Eliot, but in the end we who regularly read such a range of novels in the first part of the twenty-first century would probably say that *Middlemarch* is a greater book than *Hollywood Wives*. The fact that in centuries to come, the relative valuing might be different—George Eliot could be seen as psychologically naïve and moralistic whereas Jackie Collins could be considered a brilliantly subtle social satirist—does not make our current sense of their relative value any less relevant or meaningful to us.

When we say that a work of art is "true," we usually mean that it makes us accept that what we are being shown is a convincing representation of a world and action in it that we can at least imagine. It goes deeper than that, however. We are usually also implying that it shows us something with a clarity and intensity that reveals aspects of the situation that seem essential to us, or makes us think of it in a way in which we had never quite thought of it before. Works of art are not valuable because they

are clear glass onto the world: works of art are valuable because
they frame the world, and in doing so add to our understanding.
They make us see things differently. In this way they make us see
"truth," not *the* truth, but truth nonetheless.

If *Huckleberry Finn* does not give us "the truth," it is nevertheless not a lie. It gives us *some* truth (quite a lot, actually). It
allows us, through its aesthetic shaping, to know some things
that we would not, *could* not, know otherwise. If we take the
Grangerford sequence, for example, we can see how it is shaped
around a powerful contrast. The Grangerfords seem to Huck an
ideal family. They are civil, civilised, glowingly dressed in white.
Their house is ordered, beautiful, bountiful. The family accept
Huck with a wonderful generosity and make him feel as if he
belongs. But within the midst of all this bright life there is mor-
bidity and violence. We first get an inkling of this with the wonderful passage on the late Emmeline Grangerford, artist and
poet, in what must surely be a candidate for the funniest couple
of pages in literature. Emmeline's mind runs on death. If the
impression one gets of the Grangerford household is shiningly
bright, Emmeline's pictures are "different from any pictures I
ever see before: blacker, mostly, than is common" (p. 160). Death
is her inspiration, and it is her business, even down to life-and-
death competition with the undertaker:

> The undertaker never got in ahead of Emmeline but once,
> and then she hung fire on a rhyme for the dead person's
> name, which was Whistler. She warn't ever the same after
> that; she never complained, but she kind of pined away and
> did not live long. (1884/1985, p. 162)

Far worse, of course, than Emmeline's morbid sentimental preoccupation is the irrational violence of the feud with the Shep-
herdsons. No one knows what started it, but it is the ruling
passion of their lives, a massively destructive passion with
tragic consequences:

> When I got down out of the tree, I crept along down the river
> bank a piece, and found the two bodies laying in the edge of
> the water, and tugged at them till I got them ashore; then I

covered up their faces, and got away as quick as I could. I cried a little when I was covering up Buck's face, for he was mighty good to me. (1884/1985, p. 175)

The shaping of the experience tells us something significant about the society and perhaps about human beings in general, how a refined culture, experienced in depth—it would be wrong to think of the Grangerfords' civilised qualities as just a veneer—can coexist with the morbid, the violent, and the irrational that it would seem to have overcome but has only suppressed.

This is only one reading of the section, of course, and what is shown in this reading is perhaps not something that is universally true, but it is a truth nevertheless, and quite profound in its way. It is certainly profoundly experienced as we read the novel.

This, however, does not really answer that objection, raised earlier, that both the writer and the reader may be in the grip of an ideology that makes them think this moving and profound, but that other people find quite unacceptable. Of course, it goes without saying that the reader and the writer *are* in the grip of an ideology, because everyone always is. The question is not whether this shapes and limits the truth of what is being written and read, because it obviously does. Nor is the question whether or not it matters, because it clearly does matter if someone is taking for a natural and absolute truth something that is constructed and partial. The question is whether the limits of the truth, the fact that it is constructed and partial, are recognised, even as its power is acknowledged and felt. To recognise a truth as partial is not to reject it, but to acknowledge its limitations.

So one of the uses of the aesthetic is that it allows us to know the world in ways that we could not know it otherwise. This knowledge is provisional and contingent, but then so is all knowledge, or all knowledge beyond the bluntly factual that matters. Our awareness of the provisional nature of truths makes us examine more carefully the ones with which we are presented, but it also perhaps makes us value even more strongly those that remain meaningful.

The Aesthetic and Individual Development

The second kind of answer to the question of what might be the possible use of the aesthetic is couched in developmental terms and is implicit in the discussion of the "truth" of literature. If a text gives us some new perspective on the world, then to that extent we have developed. The aesthetic allows us to have a broader range of intense experience and so come to know the world better. We are thus turned into different, and hopefully more comprehensive, human beings. In most ways, no one would argue with this account. The area of argument comes in considering exactly how this process works, and whether it is as inevitably positive and benign as it sounds.

There is a persistent mystique about high art in the public imagination, a belief that the mere contact with it must be good for you. This is no longer a belief that is much articulated in academic circles, although it can still be found latent here and there.[5] However, the notion that reading Shakespeare, for example, makes you more intelligent and more moral has had a long life and is not dead yet in newspaper articles and letters to the editor complaining about the watering down of school curricula. Most such arguments seem to be thinking in terms of "personal growth," which works on a horticultural model. The student is the plant, and Shakespeare is the fertiliser. If great works are applied in sufficient quantity, the student seedling will turn into a wonderfully sensitive and mature adult. If young people just read the classics, they will realise (in all senses of the term) their true humanity.

The personal growth model has come in for a great deal of criticism because it is predicated on a belief in an essential self and on the notion of a natural propensity to perfectibility, the belief that our development is organically towards some ideal of what a human should be. The problem is that it naturalises the processes of identity construction and fails to recognise that development is not always positive or linear but can be erratic and not always in desirable directions. Poststructuralist views of how subjectivity is constructed, such as we examined in Chapter 4, are much more sober in their outlook and suggest that human beings are more various (indeed contradictory) and mutable than the classic developmental model suggests.

But accepting the poststructuralist anti-essentialist view of the discursive construction of identity does not mean rejecting the notion that the aesthetic is important developmentally. In many ways, it not only explains why aesthetic texts are important but intensifies their significance. If we are constructed multiply through the different subject positions we can occupy, our subjectivity being constructed by the discourses we command (or that command us) and the texts we read and write, then the aesthetic discourses and texts become not just fertiliser but a crucial constitutive part of what we are.

Engaging with a text can allow us to extend our existential repertoire; it adds to our range of possible subjectivities; it allows us to rehearse other ways of being. When we read *Huckleberry Finn* sympathetically, we understand—we have felt—a whole range of thinking and feeling that we never knew before. We understand the paradisal nature of the rhythm of days spent in harmony with the river—"you feel mighty free and easy and comfortable on a raft" (p. 176):

> Two or three days and nights went by; I reckon I might say they swum by, they slid along so quiet and smooth and lovely . . . Next we slid into the river and had a swim, so as to freshen up and cool off; then we set down on the sandy bottom where the water was about knee deep, and watched the daylight come. Not a sound anywheres—perfectly still—just like the whole world was asleep, only sometimes the bullfrogs a-cluttering, maybe. (1884/1985, p. 177)

We undergo the torture when this paradisal state is corrupted by the advent of the King and the Duke, and endure the frustration of their continued presence. As desperately as Huck and Jim, we want to be rid of them, but we also feel with Huck when he has his last glimpse of them, tarred and feathered and being run out of town on a rail:

> Well, it made me sick to see it; and I was sorry for them poor
> pitiful rascals, it seemed like I couldn't ever feel any hardness
> against them any more in the world. It was a dreadful thing
> to see. Human beings *can* be awful cruel to one another.
> (1884/1985, pp. 301–2)

Huck's ready sympathy, which doesn't minimise the trouble and
distress the King and Duke have caused but puts it into perspective
in the light of their fate, adds a particular way of looking at people
to our repertoire. It adds to our emotional possibilities, our possibilities of making a response to highly ambiguous situations that is
clear-sighted and unsentimental, but humanly sympathetic. We
have another model, another inflection of discourse and so a new
way of being through which we can respond when appropriate:
"Human beings *can* be awful cruel to one another." Huck's reaction here is instinctive: it is not a matter of weighing up the crimes
of the King and Duke against their fate and rationally judging it to
be inappropriate. His words are so superb a summing up because
they apply as much to the King and Duke—we might think of the
appalling confidence trick they attempt on the Wilks girls—as to
their tormentors. If the move to those final words strikes us as
emotionally right, it has created (or strengthened) through essentially aesthetic means an emotional connection that is a small but
perhaps significant development for us as human beings.

Aesthetic works are continually developing us in this way,
and it would be ridiculous (if not impossible) not to open ourselves up to such possibilities for fear that we might be ideologically corrupted. We need models of thinking and feeling, models
of living, that extend us, which is not to say that we do not at the
same time bring them into the light of ethical evaluation. We do
not abrogate judgment because we are feeling: judgment itself is
as much a matter of feeling as of intellect. Foucault in his later
works was concerned with "technologies of the self" not as something to be avoided because they are constructing unwanted subjectivities, but as a way of human beings taking responsibility for
appropriate "care of the self." Human agency is essential in this:

> What strikes me is the fact that in our society, art has become
> something that is related only to objects and not to individuals
> or to life. That art is something which is specialized or done by

experts who are artists. But couldn't everyone's life become a work of art? Why should the lamp or the house be an art object but not our life? . . . From the idea that the self is not given to us, I think that there is only one practical consequence: we have to create ourselves as a work of art. (1997, p. 350–51)

Aesthetic texts are a significant way in which we develop our subjective repertoires, and so are a major technology for taking proper care of our selves, indeed for that most significant project of creating ourselves, even as a work of art.

The Aesthetic and Pleasure

The third answer to the question of what might be the use of the aesthetic is that the aesthetic experience is good in itself because it gives us pleasure. This answer is at least as significant as the other two—indeed bound up with the other two—but it is in danger of seeming trivial because pleasure is so often thought of as trivial, opposed to the serious things in life.

This is far from new. Mark Twain back in 1884 seemingly subscribed to the view that one could not be intellectually engaged and still experience pleasure when he wrote his "Notice" to stand at the front of *The Adventures of Huckleberry Finn* (1884/1985, p. 48):

> Persons attempting to find a motive in this narrative will be prosecuted; persons attempting to find a moral in it will be banished; persons attempting to find a plot in it will be shot.
>
> BY ORDER OF THE AUTHOR
> Per G. G., CHIEF OF ORDNANCE

Such a "Notice," of course, is both a pre-emptive strike against critics and a populist move, and is undoubtedly not meant literally, but the implicit premise is nevertheless striking: an author would rather not have his book taken seriously because it would get in the way of pleasure.

This is working with a very limited notion of pleasure; pleasure as diversion, pleasure as avoidance of intensity, pleasure as an escape from thinking. While one would not for a moment want to deny that such escape can at times indeed be pleasurable, and that the aesthetic can honourably provide such diversion, one would equally not want to see this as the only kind of pleasure the aesthetic can provide. Pleasure, as we have discussed it, is engagement. It can be engagement with the familiar and clever play of *Friends,* the verbal dexterity and musical wit of a Cole Porter lyric, or the excitement of the developing plot of *The Da Vinci Code.* It can also be engagement with the dark ambiguities of *Six Feet Under,* the bleak psychological and musical exploration of *Die Winterreise,* or the complex reverberations of the interaction of plotlines in Don de Lillo's *Underworld.*

What engaging with the aesthetic offers us is intensity of experience. It offers us a way of fulfilling some of our desires. As we saw in Chapter 4, desire can be seen as arising from lack, in which case pleasure comes from having this lack satisfied, or desire can be seen as a productive force arising from a human drive to make connections, in which case pleasure comes from the exercise of our productive capacities. The pleasure of reading *Huckleberry Finn* can be seen in either way, or there are aspects of both need-fulfilment and the exercise of productive energies in the pleasure we take in this book, as there perhaps are in our engagement with any aesthetic text.

The book certainly satisfies a need we have to see experience as meaningfully structured. The episodic nature of the book, determined largely by the journey narrative, builds up to a broad and diverse but coherent picture of society along the river, just as the journey also maps the trajectory of Huck's developing relationship with Jim. It satisfies the need we have for variety of experience, as we share the adventures of Huckleberry Finn. More profoundly, it gives us the experience of seeing the world afresh through a particular consciousness marked both by naïveté and by strong common sense, and an even stronger instinctive, pre-socialised sense of what is right.

But the experience is not only receptive; it is also productive. As with any book, we need to work with it, fill in the gaps, realise the implications of what we are being shown. Some books may engage us by leaving a lot of room for us to project our fantasies (popular texts often work this way): other books engage us by making us work hard to recuperate the meaning. Because Huck is an unreliable narrator in the sense that we understand more than he does, we are constantly engaged in reading off the reality from what Huck tells us and evaluating (and generally valuing) the Huck perspective. We don't submerge ourselves in Huck's viewpoint and "become" Huck, but instead we are constantly positioning and repositioning ourselves in relation to him, noting his naïveté sometimes, other times assimilating the extraordinary moral implications of his words and action. When Huck races back to Jim on Jackson's Island and rouses him with "Git up and hump yourself, Jim! There ain't a minute to lose. They're after us!" (p. 117), the implications of that "us" is both thrilling and profound, and it takes us a moment's work to realise them. The book is full of such moments, and it is the shock of discovering the deep implications behind simple words—think of the words about covering Buck's face, or "All right, then, I'll *go* to Hell!"— that is part of the pleasure of our engagement with the novel.

Beyond that, we also produce a reading, or a constantly evolving array of readings, as, to take up the Barthesian metaphor, we follow one or other thread through the fabric of the text. Reading is a creative act, and there is great pleasure in exercising creativity. We bring the different threads of the narrative into a kaleidoscopic array of conjunctions with each other. We speculate, we play with possibilities for generating new meaning. In a sense, we rewrite the text, and in this sense reading, almost as much as writing, can be seen as a productive activity.

Which brings us to the matter of writing.

The Use of Writing Aesthetic Texts

We have been looking so far in this chapter at the "use" of the aesthetic in terms of reading, but the question asking what is the use of the aesthetic in writing can be answered in the same terms. In many ways the answers seem even clearer and more obvious in the writing context. It is important to write aesthetic texts because it can give us access to a version of truth, it can help us develop as people, and it gives us pleasure.

Much writing is heuristic: we engage in it to discover what we think and feel. There is, in fact, arguably a heuristic element in all writing. Even when we set out simply to express something we have thought, the act of writing leads us to discover nuances and implications that were certainly not in our mind when we started. This is partly because we inevitably write within particular discursive formations, and these channel and limit what can be said, but just as they do in reading, they also provide frames that can reveal to us different aspects of what we are writing about, can lead us to see new potential in the material, and so we constantly find ourselves discovering (partial) truths that we were not previously aware of.[6]

Aesthetic writing is important because, as we have seen, the aesthetic allows us to discover aspects of reality and experience that can be discovered no other way. Because of its re-creative representational aspects, drawing together the emotional and the intellectual, the reflective and the experiential, it allows us to apprehend things that purely rational, intellectual writing cannot. We can write ourselves into understanding.

We can also write ourselves into being. We develop ourselves, vary who we are by engaging in writing. Foucault has said in an interview:

> for me my books are experiences, in a sense, that I would like to be as full as possible. An experience is something that one comes out of transformed. If I had to write a book to communicate what I'm already thinking before I begin to write, I would never have the courage to begin. I write a book only because I still don't exactly know what to think about this thing I want so much to think about, so that the book transforms me and what I think. I am an experimenter and not a theorist. I call a theorist someone who constructs a general system, either deductive or analytical, and applies it to different fields in a uniform way. I'm an experimenter in the sense that I write in order to change myself and in order not to think the same thing as before. (2001, pp. 239–40)

Those last words express powerfully the self-transformative possibilities of writing, the answer in terms of development of why one should value the aesthetic.

They also express powerfully the deep engagement with writing, the productive energies in it that are the source of pleasure. Writing can be pleasurable, simply in the sense of exercising skill, seeing what we are capable of, how well we can produce something in a particular form. But just as in reading, there are also the deeper pleasures of creativity. There is the ability to engage in intense experience and explore the fulfilment of our desires through imaginative creation. There is the productive pleasure of discovering the new, playing across the space of writing, trying out different configurations of meaning, releasing imaginative energy, and being surprised at what we have created.

Our engagement with aesthetic texts may be useful in the three ways we have been examining—discovering "truth," developing ourselves, and giving ourselves pleasure—but it is important to note that in all three areas the texts work in specifically aesthetic ways. One aspect of this is that in each area, the gain to us is not just intellectual but is felt in a bodily way. As argued in Chapter 2, one of the significant elements of the aesthetic is that it brings together intellectual and bodily experience. It is this that we will go on to investigate in the next chapter.

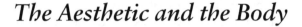

The Aesthetic and the Body

It is paradoxical that for most people these days the aesthetic is thought of as remote and ethereal, whereas historically at least an equal emphasis has been on its materiality, on the aesthetic as a bodily phenomenon. Terry Eagleton begins his book *The Ideology of the Aesthetic* with the assertion, "Aesthetics is born as a discourse of the body" (1990, p. 13). He notes that the term comes from the Greek *aesthesis,* "perception," and, stemming from this:

> The distinction which the term "aesthetic" initially enforces in the mid-eighteenth century is not one between "art" and "life," but between the material and the immaterial: between things and thoughts, sensations and ideas, that which is bound up with our creaturely life as opposed to that which conducts some shadowy existence in the recesses of the mind. It is as though philosophy suddenly wakes up to the fact that there is a dense, swarming territory beyond its own mental enclave which threatens to fall utterly outside its sway. That territory is nothing less than the whole of our sensate life together—the business of affections and aversions, of how the world strikes the body on its sensory surfaces, of that which takes root in the gaze and the guts and all that arises from our most banal, biological insertion in the world. . . . It is thus the first stirrings of a primitive materialism—of the body's long inarticulate rebellion against the tyranny of the theoretical. (1990, p. 13)

This is, of course, in many ways, contrary to the current impression of the aesthetic as that which is nebulous and numinous, ineffable if not downright effeminate. An antonym to *aesthetic* is *anaesthetic,* the suppression or absence of bodily feeling. It is unfortunate that the teaching of many texts in the English classroom has an effect that seems closer to anaesthetic than aesthetic. It could well be argued that if the aesthetic is to be a vital element in English and literacy teaching, we must move beyond suspicion of the corporeal: the aesthetic must be returned to the body.

Theorizing the Body

In the Western tradition at least, there is conceptually a persistent mind/body dichotomy: and, as usual, other binarisms line up behind that one, most significantly for our purposes,

Mind	Body
thought	emotion
reason	imagination
critique	creativity
theory	art

To bring together the "body" terms in those binaries: the *body* is the site of the *emotions,* emotions being powerfully bound up with *imagination,* which drives human *creativity,* and so the body is the instrument through which *art* is created. Even in terms of response to literature, it is no accident that so many of the (often rather clichéd) ways in which we talk about the effect a literary work has on us are couched in bodily terms: heartwarming or heart-stopping, spine-tingling, blood-chilling, creepy, nauseating, breathtaking. Terms like these may seem on the surface to be purely metaphorical and emptied of specific physical meaning, but it is worth insisting that they refer to felt bodily phenomena. At least for those of us with bodily habits learned in an Anglo-European culture, when we reach that magical, epiphanous moment of sudden revelation in a text, for example, there is an intake of breath and an instant of felt stillness in the heart: if we are reading a scary climactic scene in a Stephen King novel, or *Harry Potter* for that matter, the shoulders tense and the spine is involved in a kind of shiver, if not exactly a tingle.

On the other hand, if we take those binaries again and look at the "bodily" terms in the pairs, they can seem abstract and dis-embodied, particularly if put up against terms associated with something like work:

emotion	practicality
imagination	knowledge
creativity	productivity
art	skill

If the aesthetic has the capacity to embrace and hold in tension oppositions, such as mind/body, that in itself means that one or other of the sides of the binary can be privileged both by artists and their public, and the aesthetic can be constituted so as to make one set of terms dominant. Undoubtedly this has happened, especially in schooling. Institutionally, schools, in general, are not centrally concerned with fostering emotion, imagination, creativity, and art. If we consider the mind/body duality, their concern is to develop the mind; in order to do that schools aim to discipline the body, make it manageable, which may be necessary to make classrooms possible. Thus work on literature in schools inevitably stresses the "mind" element, and so the literary experience is often limited to (or translated into) thought, reason, critique, and theory. Emotion, imagination, and so on are displaced to another binary—practical/impractical—and thereby downgraded as useless in comparison with such things as practicality, knowledge, productivity, and skills. This is a pity, since the arts, including literature, can develop students in unique ways that nothing else in schooling can or does. They can also engage students in different ways (and in many cases, more profoundly) than more "practical" subjects.

Perhaps surprisingly, a return of the aesthetic to the body may also be a way of bringing it more closely into alignment with the concerns of critical forms of literacy, although not with critical literacy as generally constituted at the present time. A major movement in critical social/cultural theory in the last decades of the twentieth century hinged on the recognition of the importance of the body. Although the aesthetic is not central to this work, it in fact parallels the philosophical move that

Eagleton was talking about in the initial quotation: there is a recognition that the body is so obviously important in human identity that it must be accounted for in the realm of theory. Inevitably, as a phenomenon of schooling, critical literacy has tended to build up its theoretical framework by favouring the conceptual and abstract in poststructuralist thought and ignoring this strand on the body. It has taken up Foucault's work on discourse, power, and surveillance rather than his more potentially disruptive later work on technologies of the self; it has aligned itself with Bourdieu's concept of cultural capital and largely ignored the bodily element in his work on *habitus;* Judith Butler, with her notion of performativity, is scarcely on the radar. We will look at some of this work in a moment.

Even though critical literacy is largely constructed as a discourse of objectivity and reason, it ignores the body at its peril. A major strand of critical literacy (and in some versions seemingly the whole field) is concerned with identity politics, with speaking out against discrimination based on gender, ethnicity, class, and sexuality (to stop at the big four). All of these have strong bodily elements. It is clearest with gender, since conceptions of gender are so much aligned with biological sex. With ethnicity, too, there are often physical characteristics—skin colour, eye shape—that can be attached to a particular ethnic identity. The connection with the body is less clear with class and sexuality, since there are no genetic indicators that can immediately be read, but on the other hand, it can be argued that both class and sexuality are indeed inscribed on the body. This is not genetic but social (and in fact we will see that there is a strong social element in the bodily inscription of gender and race too, even though there may be biological differences that can be aligned with them as well). As early as the 1930s, Marcel Mauss argued that there were learned bodily dispositions—ways of standing, ways of walking—that marked social background (see Cranny-Francis, 1995, pp. 77–84). This idea was incorporated into the larger notion of *habitus* in the work of Pierre Bourdieu.[1] *Habitus* is a complex concept. To put it briefly, Bourdieu argued that there are internalised ways of thinking and doing things according to our particular position within the social structure. These seem "natural" to us—just the way we are—and so this framework governs all our ways of approaching the world, relating to other people, thinking about the possibilities for our lives. In Bourdieu's words, *habitus* is

> a system of durable, transposable dispositions, structured structures predisposed to function as structuring structures, that is, as principles which generate and organise practices and representations that can be objectively adapted to their outcomes. (1990, p. 53)

These "dispositions" are physical as well as cognitive: we bodily address ourselves differently to the world depending on our social positioning.

This, of course, is not just a matter of class, but of race, gender, and sexuality. In theorizing the embodiment of race, the work of Frantz Fanon (1967) and Homi Bhabha (1994) has been central, but we do not need to turn to their work to see that there is a bodily marking of race more profound than that provided by biologically transmitted features. If we think of the stereotypes of the Italian, the Japanese, and (even) the Australian for a moment, we realise immediately how fundamental certain ways of holding the body, walking, and gesturing are to conceptions of ethnicity; if we think of "attitude," particularly as developed in African American culture, we will see how important the body can be to self-perception in terms of race. *Attitude* is an interesting term, since it can have both a physical and a cognitive meaning: one has particular attitudes (i.e., ways of thinking) about certain topics, but one can also strike an attitude (i.e., take up a particular physical position). In Western youth culture generally today, stemming initially from African American culture, there is a great premium on having "attitude," which is as much (or more) a way of holding the body, moving through the world, doing things, as a particular set of ways of thinking.

When it comes to the embodiment of gender and sexuality, the crucial work is that of Judith Butler.[2] Butler argues against the traditional feminist distinction between sex (which is biological) and gender (which is cultural, being discursively constructed), claiming that the body is always already gendered, caught up in the web of discourse; we cannot conceive of biological sex without bringing with it the whole panoply of our conceptions of gender. This leads to the most influential element of Butler's work: her notion of *performativity*. To put it simply, she sees gender as a performance that brings itself into existence even as it is being performed. From the moment of our birth, we are learning how to perform being male or female; our gender is inscribed on our body by the repeated performance. Related to this is the notion of *citationality*: we are constantly "citing" the ways of being male or female that are current in our society. This is not a conscious choice: it is just something we do, and, of course, society makes us aware by disapproval if we have not cited accurately enough, if our performance is not in line with perceptions of what males and females should be. We can, of course, consciously or unconsciously transgress the social norms and stand out against the limitations of social expectations of gender, but this comes at a cost. For this reason, Butler's work has been influential in queer theory as well as in gender theory. The question of bodily inscription of sexuality is particularly interesting since lesbian and gay people can so easily "pass" as heterosexual. In terms of public perception, this can lead, on the one hand, to the attitude that homosexual people should just shut up and not draw their sexuality to people's attention: the result of this for lesbians or gay people is a sense of alienation and dislocation since they are constantly being read as something they are not, the implicit message being that what they are is shameful. On the other hand, the capacity to "pass" can lead to suspicion and panic that homosexuals are undercover, infiltrating the heterosexual world, and the result of this can be overt or covert discrimination or violence towards anyone who is read as lesbian or gay, whether they actually are homosexual or not. Alternatively, lesbian and gay people may be led to an embodiment of their sexuality in traditional, even stereotyped terms, simply to make an assertion of their right to an open space in the community.[3]

Although Bourdieu has concentrated on social class, Bhabha has written on race, and Judith Butler has written on gender and sexuality, their theorisations can be generalised across the field of embodied identity, since similar processes are at work whichever of the identity areas we are concerned with (and this, of course, includes not only those we have looked at but also abledness, age, etc.). Together, Bourdieu, Butler, Bhabha, and others provide an overwhelming argument for the importance of recognising the body as a key element in the creation of our identity.

The Body, Identity, and the Aesthetic

All this may seem a long way from the aesthetic, and certainly a long way from reading a Shakespeare sonnet or *Huckleberry Finn* or writing a piece on something that happened on my holidays in the average English classroom. But the crucial connecting factor is that so much of our embodied identity does come through representations, through the subject positions texts put us in, through the models that texts give us. The influence of the movie star or the rock star does not stop at our taking on their clothing style, their hair style, their "look," but we can take on their whole way of moving the body, their way of being in space. More subtly, if reading a literary text allows us to rehearse different ways of seeing the world and different emotional reactions, these are felt on the body, and they shape our repertoire of bodily reactions just as they do our mental ones. And to repeat Eagleton's words: "Aesthetics is born as a discourse of the body."

Given the nature of the aesthetic, our involvement with it always contains an element of embodiment. Laughter, tears, groans, turning off the television in disgust, turning it up in excitement, are only the tip of the iceberg when it comes to physical manifestations of the aesthetic response, because it is mostly embodied not in outward behaviour but in an inner awareness of such things as muscular shifts, a change in breathing, a different set to the facial expression, that are outwardly all but imperceptible. This is a kind of bodily rehearsal for (or memory of) physical involvement or emotion, and it is going on continually as we read and write.

The body, being material, exists in space and time; the text also exists in space and time; and the aesthetic experience writes the space and time of the text on the body. There are three (inevitably interrelated) aspects of this: the ways in which texts position their readers; the emotional content being presented, the involvement of readers with that, and their reaction to it; and the textual form and our experience of texts as a structuring of time and space. We will look at each of these in turn. Inevitably much of the argument will be impressionistic. It is impossible to demonstrate through analysis the kind of subtle bodily disposition being taken up towards a text. All that one can do is point to one's own experience and hope desperately that it is not idiosyncratic, aberrant, or crazy, and that others can recognize an equivalent experience in their own reading.

Textual Positioning

Positioning is a spatial metaphor, but it is not just metaphorical: there is an actual physical experience involved. When a text positions us, we rehearse the bodily feeling of being so positioned. Positioning can be in terms of a particular physical placement relative to what is being shown, or it can be in terms of being addressed as a particular kind of person (i.e., subject positioning, as was discussed in Chapter 4).

It is fairly easy to demonstrate our sense of being put into a certain physical placement in relation to the material being shown and our physical adjustments to that. This happens especially in narratives. Cinema is the obvious place to start, since the camera frames the action, and the choice of shot and editing puts us in very obviously different relations with what is being shown on the screen. There is, for example, a sense of movement in panning or tracking shots, of the body, along with the camera, being involved in seeking out the significant things to watch. If we cut from a close-up to a panoramic shot, we adjust ourselves in the seat, leaning back. Such a shift will often be underscored by music on the soundtrack: music is frequently a vital element for heightening the sense of physical involvement in film and multimedia texts.

There is something similar happening with our positioning in prose fiction: indeed it is no accident that much of the writing on narrative theory has moved so easily between film and novels since the two media work positioning their audience in such similar ways. As readers we are placed with a certain perspective on a scene. This is often done through the technique of focalisation—that is, the action within a third-person narrative is seen from the viewpoint of one or other of the characters. This can be a matter of physical positioning—we are positioned with Elizabeth Bennett as she enters the Netherfield ballroom—or it can be a matter of being positioned within the character's understanding of events—as we are, for example, when Elizabeth visits Charlotte after her marriage to Mr Collins.[4] Often, of course, both aspects are in operation. Whose consciousness we have access to and whose is closed to us is frequently a highly significant factor in the ideological patterning of a book, since we are on the whole more likely to align ourselves with the values represented and articulated by a certain character—her or his way of seeing the world—the more we see things from their perspective.

If we are involved in an aesthetic text, we will almost inevitably position ourselves spatially in relation to the situation it is presenting, even if the text leaves open what that positioning might be. We saw this graphically in the two readings of Shakespeare's sonnet 18 in Chapter 5, where one reader (Wendy) positioned herself as the person being spoken to, and the other reader (Ray) aligned himself with the person speaking. The text leaves both possibilities open, and there is no way to argue that one way of reading is more "correct" than the other. What is most interesting, though, is that both of us did imaginatively insert ourselves into the dramatic circumstances of the poem, and position ourselves with one of those involved, which suggests how fundamental an aspect of reading that kind of physical positioning is. There can, of course, be cases where we identify not with one character but with a whole situation: in the scene of Romeo and Juliet's first meeting (and perhaps in "equal" love scenes in general where the text does not position us clearly with one or other of the participants), we may well identify with the whole situation rather than with one of the characters.

When it comes to the second kind of positioning—the way the text puts us into particular subject positions—the physical element is perhaps even more obvious, although in some ways harder to demonstrate. The most influential explanation of the process of being positioned subjectively, interestingly given the argument here, is done in embodied terms. This comes from Althusser, when he is explaining the process he calls *interpellation*, being "hailed" into a subject position:

[Interpellation] can be imagined along the lines of the most commonplace everyday police (or other) hailing: 'Hey, you there!' Assuming that the theoretical scene I have imagined takes place in the street, the hailed individual will turn round. By this mere one-hundred-and-eighty-degree physical conversion, he becomes a *subject*. Why? Because he has recognized that the hail was 'really' addressed to him, and 'that it was *really him* who was hailed' (and not someone else). (1970/1984, p. 48)

The physical movement of turning, the bodily disposition taken up, is a fundamental element of recognising oneself as the person being addressed, and so of becoming subject to the discourse. With aesthetic texts, of course, it is only rarely that they address us, like Althusser's policeman, imperatively in the second person. They sometimes do, or come close to it, when there is a strongly defined narrator:

It hath been a custom long established in the polite world, and that upon very solid and substantial reasons, that a husband shall never enter his wife's apartment without first knocking at the door. The many excellent uses of this custom need scarce be hinted to a reader who hath any knowledge of the world; for by this means the lady hath time to adjust herself, or to remove any disagreeable object out of the way; for there are some situations in which nice and delicate women would not be discovered by their husbands. (Fielding, 1749/1950, pp. 449–50)

Henry Fielding (in *Tom Jones*) positions his reader in a jocular way as a sophisticated person who will have no trouble understanding the irony undercutting the surface discourse of social decorum, as a person very aware of why a lady might want time "to adjust herself," and what kind of "disagreeable object" may need to be got out of the way. There is a kind of clubby proximity created by the light irony. One feels a very different kind of gravity in one's listening when being addressed by George Eliot:

Nor can I suppose that when Mrs Casaubon is discovered in a fit of weeping six weeks after her wedding, the situation will be regarded as tragic. Some discouragement, some faintness of heart at the new real future which replaces the imaginary, is not unusual, and we do not expect people to be deeply moved by what is not unusual. That element of tragedy which lies in the very fact of frequency, has not yet wrought itself into the coarse emotion of mankind; and perhaps our frames could hardly bear much of it. If we had a keen vision and feeling of all ordinary human life, it would be like hearing the grass grow and the squirrel's heart beat, and we should die of that roar which lies on the other side of silence. As it is, the quickest of us walk about well wadded with stupidity. (1871–72/1965, p. 226)

Our positioning here has a very different kind of intimacy. There is an invitation to sober and serious contemplation (although not without its own kind of (self-)irony in the last sentence). We track the trajectory of a deep thinking process, which does in fact ask us to consider our sensory processes in that extraordinary vision of what it would be like to "have a keen vision and feeling of all human life." The body is certainly not divorced from thought here.

In most cases with aesthetic texts, the process of interpellation is more complex than in these examples, since we are being addressed indirectly and so brought into the subject position through a kind of imaginative alignment with the discourse, or, if the discourse is that of an unreliable narrator, with an implied attitude towards the discourse. Still, as with Fielding and Eliot, with each different author we come across there is felt to be a particular kind of attention required in listening to her or his voice and a particular associated bodily feeling:

> Emma was sorry;—to have to pay civilities to a person she did not like three long months!—to be always doing more than she wished, and less than she ought! (Austen, 1815/1981, p. 148)

> And there he sits munching, and gnawing, and looking up at the great Cross on the summit of St Paul's Cathedral, glittering above a red and violet-tinted cloud of smoke. From the boy's face one might suppose that sacred emblem to be, in his eyes, the crowning confusion of the great, confused city;—so golden, so high up, so far out of reach. (Dickens, 1853/1971, p. 326)

He remained only a few minutes longer, then took his leave. When he was gone Ursula felt such a poignant hatred of him that all her brain seemed turned into a sharp crystal of fine hatred. (Lawrence, 1921/1960, p. 221)

The bare facts of Grace Thrale's love, if enumerated, would have appeared familiar, pitiful, and—to some—even comical. Of this, she herself was conscious. It was the sweetness that was unaccountable. (Hazzard, 1981, p. 271)

The security alarm on the west end of the Denon Wing sent the pigeons in the nearby Tuileries gardens scattering as Langdon and Sophie dashed out of the bulkhead into the Paris night. As they ran across the plaza to Sophie's car, Langdon could hear police sirens wailing in the distance. (Brown, 2003, p. 189)

One could go on forever, picking extracts at random that seem to draw out a different sense of one's positioning, a different sense of physical being in the world.

It is difficult to analyse differences in such positioning, but in the end there seem to be two elements. The first involves the social expectations of the attitude one takes up when dealing with particular areas of experience. Our bodies are socialized to experience heavy philosophical thought such as we get with George Eliot with a kind of tensing of the facial muscles—eyes concentrated, the hint of a frown—and a hunching forward of the shoulders in concentration. On the other hand, we are socialized to experience comic ironic thought such as Fielding's in a much more relaxed way related to the bodily reaction of smiling and laughter—face opening up towards a smile, shoulders back.

The second difference, it could be argued, comes from the structure of the language itself, the syntax. Syntactic structure is largely about suspension and closure. It involves holding material in the mind and placing it in relation to the new material that comes, until we have the complete sentence and can reach closure and then begin again. There is a sense of a sentence as blocks of words being put into relative positions, of shifts in direction or changes in level signalled by conjunctions. Fielding's prose is relatively straightforward and flows with urbane ease. The progression is clearly signalled in the conjunctions. George Eliot's prose is more complex. It moves with beautiful serious-ness, but it builds up over longer periods and seems to move in unexpected directions. The difference between them may well, in the end, even in our silent reading, have something to do with breathing, that most fundamental of physical activities. We are aware of the kind of breathing needed to articulate the sentences and, at least in imagination, our body responds.

All of this is important because it is involving us in the world being represented in the text in particular ways, and since we are dealing with aesthetic texts, that involvement will have a strong affective element. If the positioning gives us a sense of the body in space, then the emotional impact of the text gives us a sense of the body's capacity to react to events. It is to this that we now turn.

Feeling Emotions through Texts

When we think about physical reactions to a text, it is the range of phenomena discussed in this section that most immediately comes to mind: laughter at comedy, the tear in the eye at the happy ending, the quickened breathing when the heroine or hero is in a seemingly impossible position, the jumping in our seat when the wizened hand of the undead monster suddenly appears in the frame snatching at the hero, and a thousand other possible reactions, most of them more subtle than these.

One range of reactions arises simply from empathy with what the person we are reading about or seeing in a play or film is going through. It is easy to write this off as low level and simple com-pared with the more complex reactions that we have to texts, but it is a highly significant aspect of our aesthetic experiences. It allows us in a fundamental way to feel intense experience (and remember that intensity is a core aspect of our perception of aes-thetic beauty), and it allows us to engage deeply with emotion (and remember that engagement is a core aspect of aesthetic pleasure). Intensity and engagement can be infinitely more com-plex, ambiguous, and multilayered than simple empathy allows, but that does not mean we should reject what empathy can give. It can allow us to rehearse emotions and extend our emotional repertoire, thus producing (hopefully valuable) development in ourselves. We learn how to perform our selves in a way that Judith Butler would recognize, through the iteration of bodily involvement in the emotional scenarios that books and movies provide. It has often been said, for example, that the most clichéd words in the language are "I love you," but we fill them with meaning by particularisation and physicalisation, through speaking them in particular individual ways in the situations of our own lives. The words inevitably bring a sense of iteration, but we make them meaningful to ourselves (and hopefully the person we are addressing) in ways learned through representations.

Almost as clichéd are expressions of grief. However, take one of Wordsworth's supreme short lyrics:

> A slumber did my spirit seal;
>   I had no human fears:
> She seemed a thing that could not feel
>   The touch of earthly years.
>
> No motion has she now, no force;
>   She neither hears nor sees;
> Rolled round in earth's diurnal course
>   With rocks, and stones, and trees.

("A Slumber Did My Spirit Seal")

This is totally individual, but also universal, a potential education in feeling for anyone who can sympathise with it. We can have enormous empathy here for the speaker, as he expresses the universe-involving experience of his loss. We understand the contrast between the sense of timelessness in his "slumber" of raptness in this person as opposed to her current, truly "timeless" state. It may seem odd to invoke this particular poem when we are talking of the embodiment of aesthetic response, but in some ways that is a tribute to how well the poem works. The experience is of physical unknowing—spirit-sealed "slumber"—succeeded by an overwhelming, understated awareness. The physical experience is one of not being able to comprehend contrasted with comprehending all too clearly. The physical restraint is in fact what makes the poem so utterly physical, the sense of numbness coming through, the sense of the enormity of the earth's movement becoming allied to the enormity of the dead girl's lifelessness.

We might compare this with Kate Chopin's very short story "The Story of an Hour." Mrs Brently Mallard has just learned that her husband has been killed in a train accident:

> She did not hear the story as many women have heard the same, with a paralysed inability to accept its significance. She wept at once, with sudden, wild abandonment, in her sister's arms. (1894/1984, p. 213)

Wordsworth's poem in some ways is about being catapulted beyond the "paralysed inability" to accept the significance of death, while at the same time being unable to intellectualise beyond the emotion. Kate Chopin's protagonist, Louise Mallard, goes to her room, and in the prose, we feel the dawning of the true, totally unexpected significance of the event for her:

> Now her bosom rose and fell tumultuously. She was beginning to recognise the thing that was approaching to possess her, and she was striving to beat it back with her will—as powerless as her two white slender hands would have been.
>
> When she abandoned herself a little whispered word escaped her slightly parted lips. She said it over and over under her breath: "free, free, free!" The vacant stare and the look of terror that had followed it went from her eyes. They stayed keen and bright. Her pulses beat fast, and the coursing blood warmed and relaxed every inch of her body. (1894/1984, p. 214)

The prose beautifully renders the welling up from her subconscious of the unspeakably wonderful implications of her husband's death. The reader's experience, in bodily terms, is of expanding involvement, induced by the suspense of what this thing is "that was approaching to possess her," followed by an elation of discovery of the rightness of what it is, with her whispered, repeated "free." The prose moves from being quite complex and guarded to being simple and direct. (A very different embodiment of a similar experience is Penelope Keith arriving home from her husband's funeral in the first episode of *To the Manor Born*, taking off her mourning veil, checking that there is nobody but her best friend around, and shouting "Yippee!") Such representations are truly subversive, for they allow possibilities, indeed endorse possibilities, that would otherwise be virtually unthinkable, totally undoable.

Beyond empathy, there are all those elements of reaction that are based on our response to the whole text, not just what is happening to one or other of the people involved. In fact, there are probably no responses to literature that are purely empathetic, since there is always an awareness that the text has been constructed purposefully and is meaningful beyond any individual person's experience represented in it. Our response to Wordsworth's poem is not just about this individual experience of grief, but about intimations of the universal inevitability of human subjection to time, of the fragility of human life against the impersonal inexorability and bleakness of the massive machinery of the earth and its movement. The very briefness of the poem can leave a stunned reaction that is related to but distinct from the numbed reaction of the speaker.

The reaction to "The Story of an Hour" is much more obviously quite separate from any empathy we feel with Louise Mallard, although based on that empathy and understanding. Louise has left her room and is coming downstairs:

> Some one was opening the front door with a latchkey. It was Brently Mallard who entered, a little travel-stained, composedly carrying his grip-sack and umbrella. He had been far from the scene of the accident, and did not even know there had been one. He stood amazed at Josephine's piercing cry; at Richards' quick motion to screen him from the view of his wife.
>
> But Richards was too late.
>
> When the doctors came they said she had died of heart disease—of joy that kills. (1894/1984, p. 215)

The savage irony of the last sentence can prompt a kind of humourless laugh, a surprised gasp of grim recognition from the reader. The mind races to take in all the implications of the situation and the irony of the sentimental, socially governed diagnosis.

In a very different way than with the Wordsworth poem, we are left with the bodily sense of reeling under the complexities the text leaves us with.

Of course, this all assumes a compliant reader. It would be easy to imagine, especially back in 1894 when it was first written, that there would be people who refused to see Louise Mallard's reaction to the news of her husband's death as anything but reprehensible—after all, Chopin makes it perfectly clear that he was a "good" husband—and would not accept at all the ironic implications of the ending. One can imagine the growing anger and revulsion as they read the story, and the force of rejection with which it might be thrown down at the end.[5] Some of our strongest physical reactions—groans, under-the-breath mutterings, sighs of exasperation, getting up and walking out—are reserved for those texts we react to negatively, where we can't go along with what they seem to be saying, or when they just seem so "bad." Being "bad" can relate to the banality or unbelievableness of the action we are being shown, but it can also relate to incompetent form and structure. We now turn to such matters.

Registering Form and Structure

We have inevitably already talked about some aspects of form and structure, since positioning and emotional content are both so closely related to how a text is shaped, but it is worth focussing separately on this for a moment.

A text structures time and space. A written text moves sequentially and so is experienced in time. It also structures conceptual space, selecting and placing the elements of content material in some kind of (nonnatural) relationship to each other. As readers, we build a map of the material, noting the connections—the similarities, the differences—between various parts of the text.

Rhythm in poetry is the most obvious example of the formal structuring of time; rhythm is related to physical movement and so is basically a bodily phenomenon. We register physically in reading a text that sense of an underlying repetitive beat that somehow relates to (and can take over) our repetitive bodily rhythms of heartbeat and breathing. Every culture seems to develop forms of music and dance, and so rhythm can be considered a universal pleasure. From an early age, children respond to it, particularly, of course, the rhythm of music but also the rhythm of language. The Dr. Seuss books, for example, are so popular because of their absolutely masterly control of rhythm, that wonderful sense for the weight and movement of words (1957/2003, p. 27):

> "But I like to be here,
> Oh, I like it a lot!"
> Said the Cat in the Hat
> To the fish in the pot.
> "I will NOT go away.
> I do NOT wish to go!
> And so," said the Cat in the Hat,
> "So
> so
> so . . .
> I will show you
> Another good game that I know!"

But, of course, the pleasure one takes in rhythm does not end with childhood: it is a crucial part of the experience offered in much great language use, as in the Wordsworth poem we have been examining. The rhythm in "A Slumber Did My Spirit Seal" is regular, underlining the surface simplicity of the poem, moving us on through it. In the second stanza, however, while the regularity is maintained, the untroubled evenness of the first stanza gives way to an extraordinary rhythmic suggestion of the earth's swinging motion in its "diurnal course." (It probably has something to do with a stronger stress on the second syllable of the lines in the second stanza.) The felt movement of the poem underlines the experience represented. Indeed, the physical experience of reading can often carry a great deal of the experience conveyed in the language, which is why it is important that students develop their sense of the rhythm of language. Take the opening of Shakespeare's Sonnet 18:

Shall I compare thee to a summer's day?
Thou art more lovely and more temperate.
Rough winds do shake the darling buds of May,
And summer's lease hath all too short a date . . .

(SONNET 18, LL. 1–4)

and put it up against the first quatrain of sonnet 129, one of the Dark Lady sonnets:

Th'expense of spirit in a waste of shame
Is lust in action; and, till action, lust
Is perjured, murd'rous, bloody, full of blame,
Savage, extreme, rude, cruel, not to trust . . .

(SONNET 129, LL. 1–4)

The sheer sound, the movement, the physical effort in actually speaking the second as opposed to the flow of the first, conveys a great deal about the two relationships and the kind of contrast there is between them.

Rhythm is important in prose too, of course. The discussion of the different way the syntax works in Fielding and George Eliot was skirting the edges of the matter of rhythm. If we take a small section from "The Story of the Hour," we can see how significant the rhythm is there. Louise is in the bedroom, imagining intensely the implications of her new freedom:

Josephine was kneeling before the closed door with her lips to the keyhole, imploring for admission. "Louise, open the door! I beg; open the door—you will make yourself ill. What are you doing, Louise? For Heaven's sake open the door."

"Go away. I am not making myself ill." No, she was drinking in a very elixir of life through that open window. (1894/1984, p. 215)

The pattering desperation of Josephine's language is set against the calm firmness of Louise's response, which gives way to the exultation of how she was feeling with that arching statement about the "very elixir of life." The three-way rhythmic contrast carries much of the experience.

There is also a larger-scale structuring of the material in a text. This is often experienced as the creation and fulfilment of expectations, as discussed in Chapter 4: a desire for certain things to happen is set in motion, even though we may dread those things (as with horror stories). "A slumber did my spirit seal" works on a simple contrast between the two stanzas. "The Story of the Hour" has a very straightforward three-part structure through which we are led, starting off in the societally constrained, conventional space downstairs with the breaking of the news of Brently Mallard's death, then the core of the story with Louise's expanding realization of her liberation in the private female space of her room, followed by the return to the social space with its destructive outcome. Novels can, of course, have very complex structures with many plot strands interacting or being set in contrast with each other. We actively move between them, building up the connections, processing the material. Good reading, as has often been said, is a very active process: we move around conceptually in the textual space, and even in the physical space of the book, looking back to see if we have remembered something accurately, even at times (it must be confessed) glancing forward to pick up hints as to what will happen.

We cannot move backwards and forwards in a play (although we now can in a movie with videos and DVDs, if not in the cinema). Plays and movies often work by contrasts, lulling us with the everyday or a lyrical patch before hitting us with big emotions, setting up contrasting kinds of experience or ways of life, structuring our emotions as we move through the developing narrative. Shakespeare is, of course, preeminent in this, as in most things. The contrast between court, tavern, and the rebels in *Henry IV, Part One* creates an enormously complex multiple dialectic: the comic scenes in the tragedies are there for contrast, thematic variation, mutual heightening. Cleopatra's scene with the Clown who brings her the asps lulls us for a moment, so that the death scene can be all the more lyrically overpowering by contrast; it thematically underlines the sex/death connection; and it is in a sense a test for Shakespeare's conception of Cleopatra: if she is indeed a creature of "infinite variety," she should be able to take part in a comic scene before one of the grandest deaths in literature. She can.

Again, of course, one can have negative reactions to form and structure. Wordsworth may have been able to exhibit the supreme control of the lyric at which we have been looking, but he was also capable of a stanza such as the following:

> No mate, no comrade Lucy knew;
> She dwelt on a wide moor,
> —The sweetest thing that ever grew
> Beside a human door!

> ("LUCY GRAY," LL. 5–8)

Not even the exclamation mark can help! There are also the overly obvious plot parallels, the overdone contrasts, the overly "significant" symbols: we reject all these things. As Keats said, "We hate poetry [for which, read "any kind of text"] that has a palpable design upon us" (1818/1954, p. 72).

Involving the Body in Reading

The word *palpable* in Keats's statement is interesting because its basic meaning refers to something that can be touched or felt (it comes from the Latin *palpare*—to touch). Keats knew the deep involvement of bodily sensation in all emotion:

> My heart aches, and a drowsy numbness
> Pains my sense. . . .

> ("ODE TO A NIGHTINGALE," LL. 1–2)

Familiarity has perhaps blunted the impact, but the words "drowsy numbness" there are extraordinary, surrounded as they are by the verbs "aches" and "pains"—a "drowsy numbness / *Pains* my sense" (italics added). How can numbness pain? Well, we all know how, although perhaps we did not until Keats showed it to us. Emotional experience is complex, and texts teach us how to experience it more profoundly and how to make sense of it. Keats also knew the deep involvement of bodily feeling in literary experience, as expressed in his sonnet about reading Chapman's translation of Homer:

> Then felt I like some watcher of the skies
>   When a new planet swims into his ken;
> Or like stout Cortez when with eagle eyes
>   He stared at the Pacific—and all his men
> Looked at each other with wild surmise—
>   Silent, upon a peak in Darien.

> ("ON FIRST LOOKING INTO
> CHAPMAN'S HOMER," LL. 9–14)

Aesthetic texts are significant because they acknowledge the importance of the body in human experience and, even more significantly, inscribe the experiences they represent on the body. If English classrooms are going to deal with aesthetic texts, then they need to acknowledge and work with such bodily inscription, whether the purpose be celebration or critique.

This is, of course, easier said than done. The problem for a pedagogy that wants to incorporate such responses as those we have been examining is twofold: that they are inevitably momentary, and that they are inevitably impressionistic. In the end it might seem that all one can do in class is talk about them, and to talk about them at any length would be terminally boring. It would also be excessively self-indulgent and solipsistic, because in the end there is no way to determine what is a justifiable or adequate response. One can imagine (or perhaps cannot imagine) students discussing whether it was a shiver or a tremor and arguing over exactly which part of the anatomy was involved, rather like wine judges discussing whether the nose is raspberry or red currant.

And yet, not to acknowledge the bodily involvement in responding to aesthetic texts, indeed to any texts, is to ignore their contribution to one of the most profound ways in which our identity is constituted if we are to believe the theorists such as Bourdieu and Butler. Texts do write themselves on the body, and we go out into the world shaped by what they have shown us about gender, class, physical reactions, emotional style, and all the other aspects of the self we have been exploring, and we respond to the world in ways they have contributed to.

The dilemma is perhaps not insoluble, because, of course, classrooms are not just about private reactions and reporting on introspection; they are about activity. Underlying pedagogy is the drive to externalise—materialise, corporealise—ideas. English teachers work to bring students to an understanding of textuality, including aesthetic textuality, through a variety of means, and so they can work with the bodily—spatial, temporal—aspects of texts through having students play with rhythm in performance, map structures, undertake parallel writing, and a thousand other possible activities as part of a productive pedagogic practice.

Pleasure is often felt to have a strong bodily element, and part of the productivity of aesthetic texts is producing an intense pleasurable engagement that involves us both cognitively and corporeally. We turn to consider some of the ways in which texts are productive of pleasure in the next chapter.

Productivity and Pleasure

> *No sooner has a word been said, somewhere, about the pleasure of the text, than two policemen are ready to jump on you: the political policeman and the psychoanalytical policeman: futility and/or guilt, pleasure is either idle or vain, a class notion or an illusion.*
>
> ROLAND BARTHES, *Image–Music–Text*

Here and there in previous chapters have been hints about the productivity of the aesthetic: about how multifarious aesthetic forms of language are, how proliferating and irrepressible their play; about how pleasure is released as we engage with aesthetic texts, and how the aesthetic produces readers who take pleasure and make meaning. It is now time to develop this argument for the value of the aesthetic and make a case for the liberation such submission paradoxically brings.

Let us begin with part of a jokey text about excess:

Sprawl is the quality
of the man who cut down his Rolls-Royce
into a farm utility truck, and sprawl
is what the company lacked when it made repeated efforts
to buy the vehicle back and repair its image.

. . . Sprawl is never brutal
though it's often intransigent. Sprawl is never Simon
    de Montfort
at a town-storming: Kill them all! God will know his own.
Knowing the man's name this was said to might be sprawl.

Sprawl occurs in art. The fifteenth to twenty-first
lines in a sonnet, for example. And in certain paintings;
I have sprawl enough to have forgotten which paintings.

(MURRAY, "THE QUALITY OF SPRAWL," 1988, LL. 1–5, 20–26)

Sprawl is not a word artists or writers or readers would generally use to describe pleasure-producing aesthetic texts. The term, derived from an old Frisian word for "kicking about," suggests a body in ungainly, careless relaxation—the very opposite of graceful civility or disciplined artistry. In Murray's poem the term is used as a trope for an attitude of mind, an orientation towards the world marked by a refusal to be bounded by convention and decorum. It's an amusing use of the word, which will crop up here and there in this chapter as we engage, not too sombrely, with something of the excessive, unruly quality in texts and the intensity of engagement, amounting at times even to exhilaration or ecstasy, that readers may experience in response.

The Productivity of Texts (and Their Pleasures)

In an ironic age like ours, it is no longer fashionable to use terms like *ecstasy* and *rapture* in relation to aesthetic pleasure, to suggest a sublime or transcendent experience. Nor would most teachers of English literature these days think of the theories from which they work as an erotics of reading, having forgotten Barthes's use of the word *jouissance* (1990), to suggest the orgasmic "bliss" of certain kinds of pleasure we take in particular kinds of texts.[1]

It is worth dwelling on the words *ecstasy* and *rapture* for a moment, however, to make a point about language. *Ecstasy* is derived from a Greek word meaning to be put out of one's place or stand outside oneself; and *rapture* is not too far in its derivation from "rape," both terms suggesting being seized or carried off. These terms carry with them the strong suggestion of bodies not under the control of one's own will and rationality. (Bodily aspects of the aesthetic were, of course, examined in the previous chapter.)

Today most of us know *ecstasy* and its adjectival form *ecstatic* in their positive, somewhat weakened sense of happy states of mind and feeling. "I'm ecstatic," we say, "I didn't get a parking ticket." Or we think of the chemically induced euphoria of nightclubbers. Novice readers of Shakespeare's *Hamlet* may need to be told of another, older meaning lurking under this sense, when they hear Polonius use it of Hamlet's behaviour. (The Prince had just come to Ophelia, looking, in her words, "as if he had been loosed out of hell / To speak of horrors.") When the old man assesses Hamlet's behaviour in this way—

> This is the very ecstasy of love,
> Whose violent property foredoes itself
> And leads the will to desperate undertakings
> As oft as any passions under heaven
> That does afflict our natures
>
> (II.i.102–106)

—the word *ecstasy* is referring to Hamlet's loss of reason: the Prince has been driven mad by desire.

This is a simple illustration of the point that meanings may slip as words and their users move from one social, cultural, historical, or textual context to another. Like chameleons, they change their colour. Readers are not always the same, nor are contexts for reading. And even within the one cultural context, a word's meaning may slide among several alternatives because of the interplay between the culturally dominant signification, other available meanings, and our more personal, idiosyncratic associations. For instance, *ecstasy* will have a differently coloured aura depending on whether you think that it is the furthest reach of a mystical state or a psychological self-deception fostered by those who stand to gain from such mystification. Such ambiguities may, of course, be used by a writer or a reader to generate a suggestive richness, a light that plays over even a "simple" word. And what is true of single words grows exponentially more complex with extended strings of words in texts. Here is the productivity of language and a source of our pleasure as we know it even from newspaper headlines, advertisements, product labels, and poems that exploit puns and other forms of wordplay on double meanings.

But language is more radically indeterminate than a range of variations on a common meaning, according to deconstructionist writers like Derrida. As Spivak puts it, in her translator's introduction to Derrida's *Of Grammatology*:

> Such is the strange "being" of the sign: half of it always "not there" and the other half always "not that". The structure of the sign is determined by the trace or track of that other which is forever absent. (1976, p. xvii)

What are "not there" in the word (the "signifier") are the object and the meaning (the "signified") that are being referred to. And what is "not that" is the word itself, which points onward to something that is not identical with that word. A verbal sign is not like a coin with two sides, letters on one and referent on the other; there is only a momentary coincidence of two sliding layers that are always in play.

Again, take that word *play.* It may signify a staged drama, the finger painting of preschoolers, the give in a braided rope or the slack in the parts of a machine, the performance of a flute, or a cricket team's batting and bowling in the course of a day. But even when in a particular context we settle on one of these meanings in order to make a common sense of a text, the faint glow of the others may continue to play over or under the word. The potential multiplicity of meanings does not stop simply because we have imposed a temporary halt on their play. One meaning defers to another as meaning is constantly deferred (put off, never finally retrieved) through the play of words in the language. (This is Derrida's famous *différance,* his coinage for this characteristic of language that plays on two similar French words for *deferral* and *difference.*)

This multiplicity is also productive. At one point in *The Pleasure of the Text,* Barthes (1990) observes that where words break down, where the edge of meaning is reached—there is also the realm of possibility. Herein lies the playful freedom from singularity we may enjoy in aesthetic texts. American deconstructionists like Paul de Man, in their readings and theorising of texts, have pushed this insight to that edge, in order to liberate an apparently free play of meanings, and have been notoriously censured for it by more conservative members of the American academy. Nonetheless, it seems indisputable that there is play in language and texts, even if such play is not free of cultural preoccupations.

There are implications in this view for the reading, writing, and teaching of aesthetic texts. As readers and teachers, we will not be searching for the one "real" meaning (intended by the author) on which to focus, even though we may yearn for such stability. Instead we will be more disposed to keep meanings in play. Knowing that a text's meaning potential remains inexhaustible, we may press it till it yields some of those multiplicities. We may take pleasure in sensing frictions in the (inter)play of such possibilities. This orientation corrects the more traditional aesthetic valuing of order, coherence, balance, closure, and the like, and supplements the politically critical search for the covert ideological meaning of a text. It opens up a wider range of aesthetic pleasures.

To further explore these matters of generativity and pleasure, we will consider what Kenneth Burke (1969) called the "master tropes" of rhetoric: metaphor, metonymy, synecdoche, and irony. (These have been identified as the basic tropes since Renaissance times.) These tropes offer a range of ways of indicating that one thing is like another by substituting a new, nonliteral signified for the more literal one. Resemblance is never identity, of course: between the signified and the signifier falls the shadow. And in that shadow lie possibilities of other, perhaps unruly associations. In dealing with tropes like metaphor, readers, viewers, and listeners must differentiate what is said or shown from what is pointed to or meant in order to produce a sense out of the multiple potentials of the language we are given. And as our mind plays over those possibilities, this work can be pleasurably productive: *we* are making the ironic realisations, *we* are creatively completing the metaphorical meaning.

However, as Chandler reminds us (n.d., Introduction), "figurative language is part of the reality maintenance system of a culture or subculture": the tropes that are commonly available within that culture also help shape its discourses and thereby also contribute to its dominant ideologies and practices. A writer directs us to see particular, culturally acceptable similarities, and we are thereby encouraged to ignore as irrelevant those aspects that do not fit. Both the text and the culture within which it is read work together to stop the leakage of other unruly meanings into our consciousness. For example, there are the norms of genres and constraints on what can be acknowledged within a particular discourse. And readers also tend to foreground some aspects and slide over others in order to interpret a trope in such a way that it coheres with the meaning offered by various means in the text, without any untidy bits left over. Now as we habitually accede to those tropes, especially where these have become naturalised, we are also being drawn into those habits of assumption shared within society. To ask whose reality is being privileged by such tropes and to bring back what has been suppressed is part of the "resistant reading" work of critical literacy. But we must remember that language cannot be pinned down to even an oppositional meaning: superfluities remain still.

Excess in Metaphor

The *sprawl* of meaning can readily be seen in metaphor, because it is the nature of metaphor to assert a likeness, even an identity, between things that are similar but cannot be identical. By way of example, consider the sonnet constructed by the dialogue of Romeo and Juliet on their first meeting (*Romeo and Juliet*, I.v.95–108). (It is also a nice example of *sprawl* in that after the sonnet concludes with their kiss, the poetry of their flirtation continues into a second sonnet, which is then interrupted.)

> ROMEO: If I profane with my unworthiest hand
> This holy shrine, the gentle sin is this:
> My lips, two blushing pilgrims, ready stand
> To smooth that rough touch with a tender kiss.
>
> JULIET: Good pilgrim, you do wrong your hand too much,
> Which mannerly devotion shows in this;
> For saints have hands that pilgrims' hands do touch,
> And palm to palm is holy palmers' kiss.
>
> ROMEO: Have not saints lips, and holy palmers too?

JULIET: Ay, pilgrim, lips that they must use in prayer.

ROMEO: O, then, dear saint, let lips do what hands do!
            They pray; grant thou, lest faith turn to despair.

JULIET: Saints do not move, though grant for prayers' sake.

ROMEO: Then move not while my prayers' effect I take.

The sonnet is organised according to a number of contrasts: between what is "gentle" or "mannerly" on the one hand and what is "unworthy" or "rough" on the other; between what is holy and what is profane; between faith and despair. Juliet is located in the realm of the sanctified, approached by Romeo as the supplicant who hopes to be absolved of any profanity. The images are conventional, deriving from a long tradition of courtly love poetry, though sustained in an effective way—effective, that is, in enabling Romeo to claim his kiss. In their neatness and successive turns of play these contrasts are very enjoyable to an audience. Moreover, the refinement of this verbal play suggests an erotic finesse.

Yet we may also find in this sustained metaphor superfluous elements—all the unwanted assumptions and connotations that must be suppressed if we are to rest with the meaning the poem is directing us to accept. Juliet, a living young woman, is cast in the mould (so to speak) of a marble or plaster statue of a dead saint, though one who may be enjoying an eternal life in a metaphysical realm, still capable of hearkening to prayers. Not only is flesh somehow transmuted when transferred to the realm of the holy, even while hands and lips touch, but all the desire and initiative rest with the pilgrim. Paradoxically, while the saint may grant prayers, indeed has power to save the supplicant from the ultimate sin of despair (line 106), in the last line he may command her to remain unmoved so that he may take what he desires.

Now this idealised model of heterosexual interactions may have been not only conventional but even taken to be "natural"; indeed it might be the more unquestioned when it is metaphorically identified with the doctrines of the church. But an audience today, in a different cultural context, can make the repressed associations return. As we saw in the textbook exemplar of

"Valediction" discussed in Chapter 5, it is possible to use the techniques of deconstructive reading to make a text's ideological leanings apparent. But even as we acknowledge the tendencies of this text, we can still enjoy the richness of its play of contradictory meanings, and our mental play with them, without wanting to nail down a single covert meaning as what the text is "really" about.

In general, any metaphors that are not dead ask us to make an imaginative leap from one domain to another—to see for ourselves the resemblance that is being suggested between this and that. This effort is both productive (we complete the link, we see the subject of the metaphor in a new way, we make a conclusion about its significance) and rewarding (we have made the interpretation, and it is richly associative). This may be particularly so when metaphor involves both words and visual images, since meanings across modes are strictly incommensurable (Lemke, 1998) and the play between them can be particularly loose. But in any cases of metaphor, what is suggestive may always spill over in excesses of meaning-potential.

Association through Metonymy

Another way of looking at the play of meanings in texts is to trace the uses of metonymy.[2] This trope involves using one thing (a signified) to stand for another that is closely associated with it, or is part of that whole. While metaphor involves yoking things together through similarity, metonymy works by contiguity, or association. An example of metonymy is the use of the word *suit* to refer to business people who wear such formal dress in their working lives, as in "The café was full of suits."

Metonymic substitutions often draw on codes (that is, social systems of categories and their components). Thus the palm leaf carried or worn by a pilgrim returning from the Holy Land comes to stand, metonymically, for all that is connected with it. Those who are in the know can decode that frond as one signifying element in a larger sign system of the medieval Christian practice of pilgrimage. Hence the word *palmer* in Romeo's words. Codes therefore signify through the contiguity of elements, any one of which can stand, metonymically, for the whole ensemble. Advertisers know very well how to use such codes to suggest more than they can show or say, and we obligingly make the associations for ourselves and get the message—for instance, that wearing a Hugo Boss suit shows that one has the cool sophistication of a certain class of young professionals.

Codes are components of particular discourses and enable them to do their cultural and political work economically. Thus codes, and their metonymic expression, enable us to know what it means to be an insider in a discourse practice. Without such knowledge we would find it almost impossible to behave like a "sane" member of society, one who knows, for instance, the difference between a top hat and a baseball cap and what it means to wear the latter with the visor to the back, with all the accompanying attitudes, beliefs, values, and subject positions that are entailed.

So too codes, and their infringement, can be used to assemble a contrary way of being:

Sprawl lengthens the legs; it trains greyhounds on liver and beer.
Sprawl almost never says Why not? With palms comically raised
nor can it be dressed for, not even in running shoes worn
with mink and a nose ring. That is Society. That's Style.
Sprawl is more like the thirteenth banana in a dozen
or anyway the fourteenth.

(MURRAY, "THE QUALITY OF SPRAWL," 1988, LL. 12–16)

(Of course, even when we thumb our nose at the decorums of any code of behaviour—such as by cutting down a Rolls Royce, with all its metonymic associations of wealth and class snootiness, into a farm utility truck—we are still recognising their force.)

It may seem that there is no excess of meaning potential in codes with their rule-governed systems for affixing meaning. Certainly structuralists and semioticians have often tried to tidy a culture's bits and pieces into codified boxes. But poststructuralists have more recently come to recognise that this project is doomed to failure. The bits will not stay put in the one box; they can be used to form different patterns. This variability derives from the indeterminacy of words and images within different social discourses, the associative richness of the cluster of coded items that they bring in their train, and the particular value they may be given by any one reader operating within a particular discourse. Moreover, in any text a number of codes will be at work across the instances of metonymy. Sometimes their work will apparently converge, but there may be tensions and contradictions among the codes that again can yield up a range of divergent meanings from the potential of the text.

To take a simple instance: in the sonnet above the ostensible religious code, with its elements of saints, palmers, devotional rituals, and the like, is substituted for and counterpointed with a less amplified code of physical erotic desire, signalled by kisses, hand holding. Love, then, is endowed with the qualities of religious aspiration. In Baz Luhrmann's film version, *William Shakespeare's Romeo + Juliet* (Luhrmann, 1996), in the scene where the lovers speak the sonnet, these codes (Juliet now manifest as an angel rather than a saint) are supplemented with another, the code of chivalry and courtly love (in Romeo's chain mail armour). And the courtly dance of religious metaphor is counterpointed with the movements of the young lovers around the fish tank: does this signify mundanity or otherworldliness? Elsewhere in the film a range of contemporary Hispanic American cultural codes speak to the Shakespearian text, confirming or unsettling the original (itself, of course, a tale recontextualised in an Elizabethan context). The interplay of these codes, with their metonymic richness, creates a shimmer of overlaid and underlying meanings.

Reading, then, is more than a simple matter of decoding what has been encoded in order to establish a text's meaning. Rather, codes are dynamic and unstable, both in the way they appear and disappear as hints, like light glancing on shifting water, and in the way they interact, as cross-currents create waves. We know too how our attention may shift among them and imaginatively play to create momentary patterns. That is, even when such codes apparently work in concert, they do not do so in a deterministic way. And each works in relation to our acts of assigning significance and value through association. After all, *we* are the ones who fill in the gaps around the selected bits of the signifiers we're given. Such associations, interpretations, responses, and judgements may differ from writer to reader and from one reader to another, whatever the invitations to read the metonym in a particular, culturally sanctioned way. "What goes without saying" can still be set to speak; but it cannot be made to say only one fixed, alternative thing. The oscillation between this and that still remains.

Disjunctions through Irony

Unlike the other major tropes, which point to similarity, irony involves dissimilarity. Something appears to mean one thing but actually signifies something very different. The reality may be overstated or understated or may be the direct opposite of what is being asserted. As Chandler notes (n.d.), "whereas the other tropes involve shifts in what is being referred to, irony involves a shift in *modality*" ("Rhetorical Tropes"; italics in original). By modality is meant the stance the author takes towards the subject matter about how true, desirable, important, usual, necessary, understandable, or serious it is. Readers and viewers who are in the know can infer that something is not exactly as it first appears, or appears to outsiders. We look again, and we re-evaluate. A simple form of irony leads us to substitute one reality for the other: we are expected to reject the naïve or inadequate view for the more sophisticated one. A more complex use of the trope encourages us to see how each reality ironises the other, so that the two are kept in play. It is rather like a palimpsest: the ostensible is a presence that gleams through the overlay of the actual. In any case, irony involves readers actively in inferring—producing—meaning out of this play of possible meanings.

Complex irony is characteristic of the postmodern. In this case texts often involve *quotation*—intertextual borrowings or allusions from diverse, even incongruous contexts. These quotations take on a very different significance and weight in their new context; each in turn gives a new meaning to what it is now juxtaposed with. Things that are usually taken solemnly, such as elements of high culture, whether institutional architecture or Shakespeare, have that solemnity undercut when combined with elements of popular culture or kitsch. The popular in turn is shown to be worthy of affectionate regard. Meanings are realigned and significance reassessed. Indeed, postmodern texts can offer a transgressive, subversive pleasure in revelling in bad taste. This is marvellously exemplified in Baz Luhrmann's *William Shakespeare's Romeo + Juliet* (1996), with its references to film and television genres and the practices of Hispanic American or youth popular culture.

What Mary Douglas (1975) had to say about jokes in general may be taken to apply to irony in particular:

> It brings into relation disparate elements in such a way that one accepted pattern is challenged by the appearance of another which in some way was hidden in the first. (p. 96)

> The joke merely affords opportunity for realising that an accepted pattern has no necessity. Its excitement lies in the suggestion that any particular ordering of experience may be arbitrary and subjective. It is frivolous in that it produces no real alternative, only an exhilarating sense of freedom from form in general. (p. 96)

Irony therefore releases us into the realisation that one particular way of seeing things (the serious, the given, the ostensible, and sensible) is not absolute: there are other ways of seeing that undermine its sufficiency. Even where irony attempts to stabilise the alternative meaning, it allows our minds to play productively over other possibilities in those incoherences or contradictions.

The Pleasures of Readers and Writers (and Their Productivity)

So far we have been considering some of the ways in which texts' meanings always promise or threaten to seep through any bulwarks of containment. We now turn to the almost infinite variety of pleasures that aesthetic texts afford and how this produces readers who take and make pleasure. This section therefore relates to points made in Chapter 4 about desire, conceived by Deleuze and Guattari as a force of energy that produces connections between objects. Our readerly desires are for the pleasures that texts offer. And as we have seen, this desirous, productive energy cannot necessarily be determined and controlled by logical, rational attempts to pin everything down to a tidy order or pattern. Superfluities remain.

As argued in Chapter 2, the word *pleasure* is used here to encompass the range of our intense feelings during and after reading. Texts can evoke laughter, confirmation when hope is realised, a satisfying sense of balance and harmony, and so on; but there can also be a kind of pleasure in feeling sharp despair, sorrow, fear, revulsion, and horror in our reading or viewing. And we desire to go on desiring and knowing the intensity of feelings that follow. After all, one such sad or horrifying experience does not turn us off from seeking it again. A Stephen King novel, for example, can be almost suffocating in the rush of fear-induced adrenalin it induces. Many of us love the violence of being so "rapt"—seized by almost irresistible feeling. Others seek out the pleasure of feeling our hearts full to overflowing with pity and sadness at a "three hanky" romantic film. Still others may feel shaken with helpless rage at the malicious injustice heaped on a victim like the Fixer in Malamud's novel of that name. Moreover, in the course of reading or viewing a single text we may be swept by a succession of different feelings and know a range of pleasures.

It would therefore be very foolish to try to delimit the multiplicity of textual pleasures by defining and cataloguing them exhaustively. Instead, the following pages offer merely a suggestive range. We consider first the range of pleasures offered by degrees of deliberate ordering and shaping and the meaningfulness this provides. Then we turn to texts whose pleasure lies in their complexity and difficulty, or their simplicity. Finally, we consider those texts that offer pleasure by their very meaninglessness or the heterogeneity of their elements.

In the reading of some texts our pleasure may have to do with our sense of its meaningfulness, to which, of course, we actively and selectively contribute. This may take the form of the "Aha!" moment when we are illuminated, in retrospect, by the revelations of a Hercule Poirot: at that moment the jigsaw shapes lock together into a now complete picture of motives and actions, causes and consequences. With other texts the meaningfulness may take the form of a sense of inherent, even cosmic, system in the ordering of events. For example, watching *Oedipus the King,* we may, if only for a time, come to a terrible sense of a retributive balance in things when unforeseeing Oedipus takes responsibility for his innocent, culpable actions and gouges out his eyes. Or our pleasure in meaningfulness may be stimulated by one of Dickens's contrived but neat coincidences, if we can consent to see the world in these terms, at least for a while. In such cases our satisfaction lies partly in sensing that we are now at last seeing an order that was there all along, and partly in seeing things just now falling into an ordered pattern. We become part of the ordering process, but more than this, we feel we are participating in the making of a pattern that is not merely idiosyncratic. Our alignment with such a meaningful-seeming order can be most satisfying, even where that order is revealed as uncomfortably bleak or starkly retributive: at the very least it makes us meaningful as meaning makers. But, of course, such order can come at the cost of our foregoing the potential for disordering or provisional re-ordering we can make of such stories.

A sense of order, with its pleasures, need not be so all-encompassing but may derive from formal elements in the text. The structural balance we perceive in a poem, the syntactical resolution of a sentence or the clinching rhyme of a couplet can give satisfaction. Or there may be a pleasure in perceiving an order that ironises another form of order:

> Some decry it as criminal presumption, silken-robed
>   Pope Alexander
> dividing the new world between Spain and Portugal.
> If he smiled *in petto* afterwards, perhaps the thing did
>   have sprawl.

(MURRAY, "THE QUALITY OF SPRAWL," 1988, LL. 31–33)

Or our pleasure may be roused by an instance of verbal or visual irony that gives us a particularly neat surprise and an appreciation of its surprising aptness. As we have seen, there is a reduplicated pleasure in the mind's oscillation between the two orders depicted—the ostensible and the ironically different actuality.

By contrast with texts that exhibit an ordering in the world and in their form, other texts are deliberately informal, even to the point of seeming shapeless. Here (the poems of John Ashbery come to mind) a reader's pleasure lies in such texts seeming unforced in form or content. There is little formal beauty of a customary "poetic" kind; but to a reader attuned to this kind of low-key writing, the very naturalism of its apparently meandering discourse can be a source of a different pleasure. The satisfactions here lie in the reader's involvement in apprehending (that is, producing) an unspoken significance, a subtle emotional tone, and a barely discernible patterning of elements.

We now turn to the pleasures of complexity and even difficulty. These terms, even more than some others, cannot merely · describe characteristics of particular texts, since they depend so much on a reader's experiences as well as predilections. What is "hard" about, say, *Lord of the Flies* to a thirteen-year-old who is trying to understand the importance of the conch is "easy" to his or her teacher, who enjoys the sense of authority and expertise such interpretive acts bring.

Of course, *complexity, subtlety,* and other similar terms were part of the now old New Critics' evaluative vocabulary. The literary texts they admired had a view of the world that might be ironically poised but was certainly not seeking a simple answer: discords might linger even in the final chord that brings their closure. We now understand that the subtlety, complexity, and the like are not just "there" in the text, nor simply "here" in the expert reader. Rather, they are produced by certain reading practices that privilege those qualities and prefer the texts that most lend themselves to such interpretations. To read with desire for such a "vision" of complexity is to produce in us a predisposition for those complex and subtle satisfactions.

So difficulty can be a source of pleasure. We may derive enjoyment from our perplexities when we are in the midst of a novel with a complex plot that has raised more questions than it has offered answers. Here the pleasure is in part likely to be anticipatory: puzzles do have solutions, and the greater the patience required in the absence of clear patterning, the greater the pleasure in its eventual revelation. Or we may find a satisfaction in contemplating the entanglements of infinitely subtle emotions and motivations in play. This is notorious in some of Henry James's stories, of course, and here the pleasure lies not so much in expecting a solution but in recognising the indissoluble complexities of thought and feeling in people who have the grace and wit to live (*beautifully,* to use a favourite word of James's) with such eventual self-knowledge.

We can know the pleasures of complexity when we are reading an experimental hyperfiction such as Stuart Moulthrop's *Victory Garden* (1991). We may delight in the multiple threads of narrative, the scraps of conversation, and patches of character whose colours flash momentarily before us as each new node of text appears on the screen when we have activated a link. The sheer difficulty of holding in our minds such a complex array of incomplete information can intrigue. And both the difficulty and the intrigue are enhanced by our knowing that in a hypertextual environment there is no permanent order for all these pieces. Instead, the patterning depends on our mental ability to make associations among such bits and pieces, as if the mind were a kaleidoscope turning shards of coloured glass over until a satisfying pattern is momentarily created by their falling together. This may not, of course, be a source of pleasure to all readers, particularly those brought up with a predilection for an authored ordering.

All these cases of difficulty can produce a self capable of knowing such pleasure, and perhaps also knowing that the difficulties can never fully be comprehended: there will always be something that eludes our presently imperfect grasp and even evades the future state of enlightenment to which we aspire and which the text promises.

At the other end of this spectrum of complexity are texts that offer the subtle pleasure of perceiving the complex in the apparently simple: in a haiku, perhaps, or a laconic Hemingway story. In these instances no authorial commentary explicitly points out the meaning of the observed "data." But readers will perceive a meaning in the details themselves, however sparsely rendered, and in the ways in which the elements are selected and juxtaposed. That is, we are doing the meaning making by identifying an apparent absence of interpretation, giving that absence importance and supplying a meaning. This is not simply to read our own cleverness everywhere, even where we are not invited to do so, though this can also happen. Nonetheless, some texts are palpably simple: they do not seem to gesture towards an ironic or "clever" reading—always begging the question of who finds simplicity there. To contemplate singleness of line or purity of colour and their verbal equivalents may be sufficient: such texts apparently need no commentary to round out the satisfactions they offer.

The pleasures of difficulty and of simplicity are always predicated on meaning and order. We now turn to a rather different source of textual pleasure, in the chaotic. This appears in texts or textual elements that have no easily discernible order of form or meaning, though, as we have just seen, we always tend to seek one. At our most desperately determined we may even find a lack of meaning as the meaning the work is offering. Other texts have an organisation that offends our sense of "normal" harmony, balance, and reason. Yet other texts may rejoice in the heterogeneity of their elements, as in the dream-like sequences of some music videos. The avant-garde texts of any generation are likely to be declared chaotic when they rupture the contemporary boundaries of taste, their offence judged worse than sprawl. One example is L=A=N=G=U=A=G=E P=O=E=T=R=Y, a movement of poets from the 1970s whose experiments have deliberately fractured the structures of language, fragmented or reassembled even words, and thwarted attempts to make referential meanings from their poems. Where is the pleasure to be found here? Perhaps in the vertigo of losing touch with the firm ground of order and reason. This is the pleasure of being exempt for a time from the necessity of meaning: the exhilaration of giving oneself up to the sensory rush of experiences that cannot be comprehended and need not be. Immersion may bring enjoyments of sight and sound, and a provisional, if always uncertain, sense of meaning that is contingent on fleeting associations. This can bring a joyful sense of the plenitude such texts offer, of possibilities beyond what we can presently encompass.

Less chaotic, but still "sprawling," are those postmodern texts that rejoice in the multiplicity, even heterogeneity, of their elements. They may knowingly and wittily "quote" other texts—often suggesting an ironic relation to the forms and norms and good taste of a past culture. Such texts dismantle the barriers between the "elite" arts and kitsch; they blur the distinctions between "original, artistic creation" and mass-produced commodity. They celebrate what is random and fragmentary by making a kind of collage out of the bits and pieces that lie at hand.

Texts of this kind are often called *carnivalesque*. The word, made current by Bakhtin (1984), derives from *carnivale*—Italian popular festivals of medieval and early modern times during which people had licence to satirise the authorities, disrupt civic order, parody their social betters, and the like. When used of language, the term *carnivalesque* suggests those popular forms that overturn the normal hierarchies of taste and refuse to be regulated or unified. Official discourses and respectable genres try to shut out the multiplicity of sometimes competing voices and the potentially riotous play of meanings, but the babble will break out at some point. This is not to suggest a permanent revolt against order: carnival is license to play with and within the institutional forms and norms of society and language. In any social situation certain truths and values will be sanctioned, fixed on; but these are always provisional, always capable of being unfixed. This returns us to those earlier points about the generativity of language.

We now need to bring together again the two threads of this chapter, concerning productivity and pleasure.

The Production of Selves That Take Pleasure and Make Meaning

Aesthetic pleasures can involve us in a submission that is liberating. Giving ourselves over to such involvement is both pleasurable and productive. When we engage with an aesthetic text, desiring the pleasures it can give us, we are active: we improvise on the hints we are given in the text; we play imaginatively over it; we collaborate in creating our experience and making its pleasures ours. An energy is released by such creative activity; indeed, it *is* a form of energy.

In such acts of willing submission and liberation we are becoming our selves—selves as multifarious as texts and the enjoyments they offer. This is rather different from the liberal humanist claim that our human sympathies are enlarged, and we ourselves made more civilised, by our immersion in literature, because that belief is predicated on a coherent, if developing, identity. As Chapter 4 argued, in engaging with texts we can take up a number of subject positions, even contradictory ones, almost simultaneously, and the subjectivities that derive from them. When we experience the various pleasures of feeling and knowing, aesthetically and cognitively, we also thereby know ourselves to be capable of variety of response. That is, as we respond to their invitations, texts help to create us as multifarious beings with such capacities. Moreover, in such engagements we also exercise agency: we collaborate in producing ourselves as aesthetic subjects who take and make pleasure. Neither drugged dupes nor passive dopes, we carry out pleasurably intelligent "work" through participating in the play of associations, the constructing of significant form, and the like. It is for such reasons that taking pleasure in texts is desirable, and productive.

This self-productive work is not accomplished simply in the space between individual text and single reader. As previous chapters have argued, texts and readers are created by means of the social. Therefore our responses, including our pleasures, are likely to be appropriate within our culture or perhaps reactive against its assumptions and norms, but in either case they can be comprehended (articulated, made meaningful) only within its discourses. The point to stress here is that the act of giving ourselves over to a text and giving ourselves up to its pleasures is not to be understood in crass terms as a capitulation to an ideology that can enslave us. It is not a matter of being either in thrall to or free from seductions, ideologies, desires, and pleasures. Certainly we are always subject to cultural, social, and material forces, many of them conveyed through texts. But in these acts of yielding, we do not merely heed the text's beckoning. Our capacity to evaluate is not necessarily impaired thereby. As we saw in Chapter 5, the dynamics of alignment and resistance are often subtle and oscillating, and in fact there is no other route to evaluation except through testing on our pulses the pleasures a text offers.

Pleasure and Productive Play

. . . *In Writing*

No discussion of the productivity and pleasure of the aesthetic would be complete that does not mention creative writing. (And it is only a mention here; the topic deserves a book devoted to it.) This chapter has argued that reading is generative: it involves our thinking, imagining minds in creating a version of the text for ourselves and, in so doing, producing pleasure. The production of texts in various modes (writing, speaking, performing, producing visual or multimodal texts) clearly involves the imagination. Even when we come to write in the factual and functional genres, we still project ourselves into the situation; we envisage addressing someone; we project ourselves into the rhetorical and structural requirements of our chosen genre. So too writing involves us in critique: we need to evaluate how appropriate and effective our developing text is, rhetorically but also aesthetically. This work of creating and crafting can be pleasurable too.

But text making is more than a matter of planning, expressing what we have already thought, and crafting it. Something happens in the act of production that is not always under our conscious control. Ideas and feelings emerge; connections occur to us, ways of putting things we have never been capable of before. At such times something is created which goes beyond what we understood and could do before the process of writing. Here too there is a play of potential—images, associations, tropes, phrases, fragments of dialogue—only some of which may be inscribed in the text. As noted previously, no play is free of the social and cultural contexts within which and out of which it is generated. Nonetheless, where the conditions for this are created in classrooms, such play can permit the return of the repressed, or at least some of the potentials that might otherwise remain suppressed.

And here too, in such textual production, selves are created. The old saying "How do I know what I think until I see what I say?" has a lot of truth in it. When things emerge in the writing, not only what we think and feel and understand will change; so too who we are will change. When we have written, we have become people who think and feel and write these new things. We have an expanded repertoire: we become more variable, more capacious selves through our writing. We become people who know our aesthetic, productive pleasures in writing no less than in reading.

. . . And in Learning

In many English classrooms there is a deep ambivalence about play. The aim of English education is often seen as the promotion of critical rationality, control over texts and the mastery that comes from being a literate self. In such cases play will need to be rationalised as a form of problem solving, if it is not to be dismissed as frivolous indolence and self-indulgence. Or it is brought under the umbrella of creativity and located alongside the discipline of literature. (The dark or nonsensical aspects of the imagination are not so easily accommodated in most forms of English.)

Some teaching principles can be adduced from this chapter, however, that make aesthetically and critically productive use of play and that allow for a range of pleasures. Such principles are mentioned here and elucidated, with examples, in the next chapter. Indeed, much of the productive work on texts dealt with in that chapter depends on the excesses of meaning and the varieties of pleasure texts offer.

It is often less a matter of particular techniques than of creating classroom conditions that permit and produce pleasurable play. Teachers can promote the play of meanings in and around texts by various explorations and activities, rather than settling simply for either the invited or the oppositional meaning. They can model their pleasurable engagement with a range of texts, not just those that are already deemed great. They can work *with* pleasure, and not just critically against it, exploring how texts invite us to take pleasure and knowing something of what those pleasures consist of. They may be able to expand the ways in which they encourage students to engage with texts—playfully, imaginatively. Even when teachers are nudging their students towards critique, it can be possible to do this productively and not too solemnly, perhaps by asking them to explore the possibilities of irony or satire, or to substitute less conventional tropes in a text in order to denaturalise its assumptions. Teachers may invite students to shift the discourse or the perspective of the text, or to "indulge" in the importantly generative work of wordplay, learning thereby how to use such materials as a springboard into the pool of the "undermind" and its creativity. The possibilities for such work are limited only by a teacher's imagination.

Teaching for the Aesthetic and the Critical

The theories discussed in the preceding chapters have been about practices of reading and writing, often outside the more formal contexts of instruction in those practices. Here and there in those pages have been pointers towards a theorised practice of teaching for the aesthetic and the critical. It is this we now turn to as a culmination of the book's discussions. This is "where the rubber hits the road," where the arguments presented to this point are translated into classroom activities.

The more traditional forms of teaching for the aesthetic in literature classrooms may not appear to be easily compatible with critical literacy practices, since both are based on different ways of understanding the nature of texts and the work of readers and writers. To oversimplify somewhat, one encourages submission to the text and close engagement with it, for the experiences it offers; the other promotes suspicion of the text's wiles and distantiation from it. One of the major tasks of this chapter, therefore, is to suggest ways in which aspects of these teaching practices may be synthesised, extended, and transformed into a new form of English teaching practice.

The overall aim of such a practice is to make students better able to create in themselves various aesthetic pleasures in relation to texts; to understand the social, discursive, and ideological means through which those pleasures have been created textually; and to know the consequences of what those texts offer by way of pleasures, meanings, and subjectivities. In such a teaching practice both analytical and aesthetic forms of knowing are valued and are seen as complementary ends in view.

This chapter argues that in their designing of classroom activities and assessment tasks, teachers can help students elicit and enact both the aesthetic and the critical. All these activities and tasks direct students' learning and frame their products. This is nothing to be embarrassed about. All such interventions can be productive. However, to ensure that they are positively productive, two things are involved. First, we need to ensure that the framing has a clear purpose. Second, while being directive about some aspects of the activity or task (directing students' focus to certain aspects of the text being studied or specifying particular aspects of the form their work is to take), we need to ensure that we do not tie down every particular of the activity or task so tightly that all students can do is rehearse an outcome that has already been dictated. What we need is to set up a dilemma or an opportunity to explore or a problem for students to solve, and the purpose for so doing, but not tell them directly and precisely how to do it or what to think and feel.

This chapter, then, will explore various practical strategies to help students understand and appreciate how the aesthetic works in texts and readers, in ideological ways, but also in ways that produce valuably pleasurable experience. Before we come to these strategies, however, several points need to be made about the nature of this chapter.

First, scope: it does not aim (impossibly) to be an all-purpose how-to-teach manual, nor can it directly address the range of English teaching regimes, with their specifics of curricular frameworks, texts lists, the experiences and expectations of students, the school or college contexts, assessment practices, and so on. Teachers who read the suggestions that follow here will need to select and adapt them to suit the particularities of their own contexts and the maturity of their students. In many cases students, whether in junior high or college, could undertake rather similar activities around texts, and what younger students may begin to apprehend through those activities can be built on and articulated in more sophisticated ways by more sophisticated, older students.

Second, no bright new teaching "technologies" will be offered here with the promise that they will always work aesthetic or critical magic on the most resistant students. Some may be new to some teachers, and some will look all too familiar to everybody. In many cases those more customary activities can be adapted and made to serve the new ends mapped here.

Third, as mentioned already, the kind of teaching advocated in this chapter is not "facilitative": it unashamedly intervenes in students' reading and writing, it interferes with texts, and it aims at times to interrupt the "natural" (that is, naturalised) processes of engagement and response. After all, reading and writing are *practices* that have been learned and may therefore be taught, directly or indirectly (that is, demonstrated, modelled, planned for, fostered through particular activities). Thus the teaching practices discussed here meet head-on the preference of those British English teachers whom Peel surveyed about how to "teach and yet not to teach" (Peel, Patterson, & Gerlach, 2000). (Many English teachers elsewhere would hold to the same ideal.) Among these teachers Peel found clear evidence of

> anxiety expressed about direct intervention, about an overtly didactic approach, about being seen to direct and control . . . together with a sense of satisfaction and ease in a discreet facilitative role, in which students seem to be self-motivating, self-correcting and self-directing, with the teacher as presence, supervising indirectly. (pp. 161–62)

In even the most seemingly nondirective classrooms, students' minds and bodies are inevitably if incompletely disciplined. Such disciplining is productive of the particular pleasures students come to know and value, and of the capacities they exercise for engaging with given texts and producing texts of their own. What counts as legitimate response to text, what capacities come to be valued, will vary according to the norms at work in this classroom or that. So it is too with the kinds of classroom envisaged in this chapter. But this does not mean that the kinds of intervention offered here are always "overtly didactic" or that teachers in such classrooms are thought police. As we shall see, negotiation about the multiplicity of textual meanings and readers' responses is key to this practice.

Finally, this chapter must deal with questions of assessment. Some remarks are made towards the end of the chapter about how assessment tasks can promote and evaluate both the aesthetic and the critical in students' responses to texts. However, matters of assessment are implicit and at times explicit throughout the chapter. The choice of tasks is (or should be) an integral part of the design of a unit of study: students' demonstrations of their learning are a proper culmination of their participation in that program. Of course, assessment does not only occur when students submit work for formal evaluation: teachers and students continually assess their performances informally in ongoing classroom interactions. Thus many of the activities discussed in this chapter may be used as formative assessment tasks—that is, as opportunities for students to try out their skills and knowledge, evaluate their developing performance, and get informal feedback from teacher and peers before they embark on summative (culminating) tasks for formal assessment. Indeed, a number of these activities may also be appropriate for such formal assignments.

Mapping Textual Understandings

Before embarking on a discussion of classroom activities, it will be useful to list the key propositions about the aesthetic and the critical that have permeated the book to this point and that will be discussed in more detail later in the chapter.

> Proposition 1. Aesthetic texts offer pleasure in beauty—that is, engagement with intensity of textual experience.
>
> Proposition 2. Aesthetic texts are situated within contexts to which they contribute.
>
> Proposition 3. Aesthetic texts offer partial but potentially illuminating interpretations of experience.
>
> Proposition 4. Aesthetic texts offer meanings that are negotiated with readers.
>
> Proposition 5. Aesthetic texts are multiple, as are readers and the meanings they produce.

As part of their planning and teaching, teachers identify particular concepts or capacities for aesthetic and critical engagement with texts that they want their students to develop, including perhaps those listed here. The activities outlined in the pages below are categorised according to these understandings and suggest some possible means to those ends. One reminder, though: there can be no single ideal activity or task that will enable students to develop and represent every aspect of their response. Any teacher will select a particular aspect of the text and of response for students to attend to and will select activities that accord with his or her purpose and sense of what will be most useful to the students, depending on their learning needs and other elements in a program of study. Such selective direction is not only inevitable but positively productive of teaching and learning.

As a first stage in investigating these understandings and associated activities, we need to look at the kinds of classroom interaction and activities that promote immersion in the text and aim to enhance readers' experiences in reading it. We will then consider those activities that intervene in the text and experiment with (re)readings and (re)writings. This sequence is not meant to suggest that immersion comes first in a set of lessons and is concerned with developing aesthetic response to text, and is then followed by experimentation, which brings students to a more distanced and critical evaluation. In planning a program of study, teachers will undoubtedly make a principled selection from each category and sequence activities according to their judgment about what will most help students enjoy and understand various aspects of the text before, during, and after reading. For some students and some texts, the way towards closer engagement may be through various forms of playful intervention. For others, analytical examination of the text may bring them to a more aesthetically appreciative response.

It is important to understand that both immersive exploration and textual experimentation are complementary: both promote the aesthetic and the critical. Some teachers stick exclusively to immersive experience and therefore forego the learning that can emerge from experimentation; others may move too quickly to the latter, perhaps because they are uncomfortable with discussing literature or impatient to implement a critical literacy agenda as they see it.

Experience: Direct Encounters with Texts

In addition to individual or shared reading, in classroom interactions there are several often complementary ways by which teachers encourage their students to project themselves imaginatively into the world of the aesthetic text under study, to engage emotionally as well as cognitively with its concerns, and to articulate their responses to it. Teachers can enact their own responses and explicate these through teacher-directed discussion or even, in a postsecondary context, through lecturing; students can develop their responses informally in small group work or more formally in presentations to peers and teacher; and particular activities may be employed to focus on the specifics of the text under study. We consider each of these responses in turn, the first two in this section and the third in the section that follows.

When teachers project their own pleasure in the text under study, they point to features they find admirable. They may perform the text with verve. They may model the kind of reading processes and practices they aim to develop in their students. Sometimes they articulate their own felt responses; sometimes they demonstrate where they direct their attention—tracing a repeated motif, for instance, or drawing inferences out of a metaphor, or eliciting implications from a character's dialogue and actions. They may explicate the ways in which various textual elements (symbols, plot events, subplots, themes, and the like) cohere into a meaningful whole. And so they enact their aesthetic engagement, account for their experience, and show how it has been produced. By these means they hope their students will develop their own aesthetic satisfactions. Indeed, engagement can be enhanced by means of such discussion. Teachers also intend that their students should learn how to produce such accounts for themselves.

These forms of performance are all perfectly legitimate. Teachers can and do employ them purposefully and selectively, to generate and enhance students' enjoyment and understanding. They may alternate between these and other activities in which students take the lead. At times they may know that students are having difficulty with a particular aspect of a text, or have become "stuck" at a particular point in their reading, or are going off in a direction that will limit their interpretations. They may want to take their students' responses to a new level of discrimination and sophistication. They may want to offer an alternative focus—on structuring, say, or focalisation.

This teacher-centered practice does, however, raise several issues. First, the mode shifts quickly from initial response to analysis. This is one of the besetting problems of English classrooms in general: there are so few overt techniques for sustaining aesthetic response over the length of a lesson; it is much easier to resort to explication and analysis, for which there is a great array of activities. Teachers, of course, hope that when students practise such analysis on the text in hand, they will be able to apply it in future encounters with other aesthetic texts, thereby enhancing their aesthetic response to those texts. This may well happen; but the mode has certainly shifted from response to critical-cognitive analysis.

Next, this teacher-centric kind of pedagogy may be singular in the line it takes on the text, no matter how much the teacher appears merely to "facilitate" discussion. It aims to induct students into the teacher's responses to and understandings of the text and to instruct them in reproducing those responses for the same or a similar text. There is nothing necessarily wrong with a teacher demonstrating and thereby advocating a reading: many of us have profited enormously by "eavesdropping" now and then on a more experienced reader articulating a reading that is far more subtle and sophisticated than we ourselves could yet manage. However, a risk remains: the text that has been explicated in this way may have been so effectively colonised by the teacher's reading that it may no longer be available for us as a text on which we can develop our readings for our own purposes.

Nevertheless, by this means we have learned what a particular kind of skilled reading performance looks like, what benefits might follow from this kind of discriminating attention, and what we in turn might aspire to produce in time. By this means we are also learning what counts as competence within that culture of reading and what "procedural displays" (Bloome, 1985) will demonstrate this within the particular educational regime. For example, as Pope notes, in literature classrooms in higher education, much academic work "requires or assumes the operation of *linear or binary logic, positivist textual reference,* and, perhaps above all, the ability of the *individual learner* to recognise and reproduce the *dominant critical orthodoxy* in a particular course" (Pope, 1995, p. 196, emphasis in original).

Finally, such teacher-centric explication carries the risk of substituting too quickly the teacher's perception of form, meaning, and response, with all the wisdom of hindsight developed through prior study, for the students' gradual groping towards understanding. This is not to suggest that students' responses can be "authentic" only if they are purely "personal" and somehow unmediated: all readings are produced within readers' past and present contexts, including those of the classroom. When teachers become impatient with students' inchoate, interim, uncertain meaning making en route through a text, they may hurry students along to a conclusive interpretation with all the elements beautifully in perspective. But the sometimes ambivalent oscillations mid-journey, as well as the winning through to moments of perception, when patterns emerge, when elements fall into place—these are some of the pleasures of aesthetic reading, and it is a pity if students do not experience this for themselves.

To be sure, teachers' demonstrations need not lead to a premature packaging or to the imposition of a single reading. Teachers can model and promote a range of plausible readings en route and can keep them in play provisionally.[1] They can demonstrate and so legitimate the dynamics of alignment and resistance. If they value this play of meanings, they are likely to draw on the kinds of intervention activities outlined below.

We now turn to that second way of promoting close encounters with texts. When students are asked to demonstrate their engagement with an aesthetic text, they may share moments of laughter, revulsion, fear, admiration, and the like. They may be able to articulate their responses further and address form and structuring, and not just the text's content or their own feelings. But as their teachers know, it is difficult to dwell in and prolong engagement directly in classroom discussion. Both teachers and learners may feel on more familiar ground when students are asked to convey their responses in a different, analytical and not aesthetic mode, through book reviews, character analyses, expositions of the formal and structural elements of a poem, and so on. After all, students in traditional literature classrooms know that merely reporting on their affective responses is insufficient; they are expected to justify those responses by reference to details of the text. In such cases, for students no less than teachers, the pressure to give a coherent account is likely to lead them to substitute a tidy gestalt of the text for the more uncertain processes of shifting, partial responses.

It is possible that when students undertake such exposition they may come to understand more comprehensively the sources of their engagement and the aesthetic characteristics of the text that have evoked it; but anxiety about their performance, particularly if it is assessed, may set even the memory of any aesthetic responses flying. It can also be difficult when students do not yet have a developed aesthetic-critical vocabulary or the tools for analysing how the specifics of the text have evoked their responses.

Sometimes one cannot see certain aspects until one has the terms for identifying them and describing their workings. Students need such a vocabulary and a discourse in order to gain control of texts, and it is part of a teacher's responsibility to provide them with these tools for analysis. These may be developed informally, as part of the ongoing conversations of the classroom, and they may be deliberately taught. Skilled teachers will know when and how much terminology to present. They will not shovel words and theories in before their students have any experiences to attach these to or any need to draw on them.

Any shortcomings in these ways of encouraging students' responses should not be taken to mean that there is no place in the classroom for students to share their reactions to a text. On the contrary, it is important to allow for ongoing informal conversations during class and to open up opportunities for students to express their affective and cognitive responses. However, because not all students are equally willing or able to take up such opportunities, it is important not to rely on this as the sole means of evoking or communicating those responses.

This brings us to the third means of helping students project themselves imaginatively into the world of the text, to engage with it emotionally as well as cognitively, and to articulate those responses. Because of the dissatisfactions mentioned above with the limited ways in which teachers and students have more traditionally produced and demonstrated aesthetic response, teachers have devised a range of text-focused activities as a different means to the same end. These have been more prevalent in secondary than postsecondary classrooms, but there are strong arguments for the appropriateness of such activities at all levels, to foster textual understanding.

Experiment: Agency through Intervention

We first consider the purposes, principles, strengths, and weaknesses of various practices of textual intervention and then evaluate the use of such practices in critical literacy curricula.

According to Pope, the various forms of intervention in the text involve

> *critique through transformation* as well as interpretation and analysis; *re-coding* as well as decoding; gratification through *re-production* as well as consumption; and *re-creation* in a genuinely active sense rather than 'recreation' in the sense of more or less passive leisure. (Pope, 1995, p. 186, emphasis in original)

Much of the impetus behind the development of these forms of response since the 1970s and 1980s lay in dissatisfaction with traditional literature teaching, including the essay of literary criticism. Various forms of "dependent authorship" promised to allow students to respond to the aesthetic aspects of a text by a parallel act of creativity.

It is sometimes argued that re-creative responses are more open than traditional forms of explication and analysis: they invite students to enter into the imagined world of the studied text and learn to produce in their writing some of the aesthetic qualities they responded to in their reading. Of course, such tasks as assigning students to take a narrative in another direction from a particular plot pivot, change the narrative viewpoint, rewrite (a section of) the text in a different genre, and so on always frame and direct students' imaginations, as do the classroom conversations that precede their writing. As noted already, such framing is inevitable and not necessarily sinister.

Various forms of re-creative responses have been put to various ends, and these tell us a great deal about the particular assumptions regarding the aesthetic on which they are founded.

At times such activities have been framed by a more traditional view of narrative fictions as conveying an imagined world which readers could enter into, explore more fully, and even develop by their dependent authorship (Adams, 1995). In such cases, the teacher has wanted to bring students to value more highly the qualities of the given text that evoked an aesthetic response.

In other cases, teachers working from a poststructuralist stance have set re-creative writing activities as an antidote to students' naïve views of narrative realism (Morgan, 1992), deliberately using base texts of an experimental kind. Yet other teachers have used re-creative responses to help students understand reader-response concepts such as reading positions, textual gaps, and the like. And some others have deliberately framed such activities in order to have students demonstrate a historically or culturally "resistant" reading by writing "against the grain" of the text's discourses and ideologies (Corcoran, 1994). By so doing, students are expected to reveal the discourses and ideologies that constituted it. Teachers have often underplayed the potential of such interventions to give aesthetic satisfactions, but students undoubtedly often do derive pleasure from their reading and writing, within this framing.

The fundamental purpose of such activities, however, is now generally taken to be educative, not purely imaginative (as the expression of a creative self) or therapeutic (as the path to better understanding of oneself and one's life) or even exploratory in an open-ended kind of way. For example, a task offered as an exemplar by the Queensland Board of Senior Secondary School Studies directs students to write a eulogy for Ophelia, developing metaphors other than the images of flowers and fragility that Hamlet, Gertrude, Claudius, and Laertes use to describe her (Queensland Board of Senior Secondary School Studies, n.d.). The task specifies that students are to make another, more positive reading of Ophelia's character possible through these alternative images.

While it can be quite productive to ask students to substitute new metaphors in a text in order to make different meanings, there are several difficulties with this task as framed. It directs students very narrowly: in specifying the substitution of more positive imagery it assumes conformity with feminist critiques of traditional representations of women. The task, then, depends on students' having developed an understanding of such critiques of the discourse of flower-maiden and passive victim and having some acquaintance with alternative feminist stories and metaphors. And then the students must be able to use this knowledge to create a rhetorically effective piece in a specific, perhaps unfamiliar genre—and possibly in Shakespearean diction. (This might come under the category of what Buckingham, Fraser, and Sefton-Green [2000] call the "impossible text": one that encodes oppositional content within a dominant form, such as a radically alternative soap or a nonsexist teenage magazine.)

There is some danger that teachers may move too quickly to assign rewriting activities as the primary means of engaging students with a text. In such cases the task is required to do all the work of developing students' understanding of the text, its discourses and ideologies, on the assumption (not always warranted) that one learns all one needs to know about a text's constructedness by playing around with it.

Sometimes teachers require students to provide an oral or written reflection on their re-creative writing. They want the learners to clarify their purposes in undertaking such transformations (where students have chosen these for themselves) and to explain what they have come to understand about the text through their writing. Teachers are especially likely to insist on such explanations where the creative work takes a visual, dramatic, or multimedia form, since teachers are often less confident of their interpretations and evaluations here than they are with writing. When students undertake these justifications, they shift back into an analytical and objectifying mode of knowing, one that again puts the aesthetic, in both the studied text and in their created text, at a remove.

The use of such interventions in critical literacy classrooms has often been very fruitful. It has enabled politically committed teachers to pursue their social justice agenda in often interesting ways, particularly since critical literacy teachers refuse to take the text at its word, in its own terms. They have reinserted the text (no longer seen as an autonomous unit that contains all its own meaning) back into history. They have seen it within the context of an inequitable society and hegemonic discourses, social structures, and practices that work to the advantage of the few. Hence they have refused to accede to the reading that the text offers but instead read it for other meanings, other implications. The text yields a very different meaning when examined through lenses shaped to detect ideologies of race, gender, ethnicity, sexuality, and the like. This leads them to focus on what is not there in the text—what it omits or conceals—as well as what it offers. For such "reading and writing otherwise," intervention activities have been very useful.

However, this critical approach has been criticised for a number of reasons, three of which are relevant to this chapter. First, it can encourage the teacher to impose an authoritative (re)interpretation of a text that can be just as monologic as that offered in a traditional literature classroom, however different it may be in substance. This raises a question: how is it possible to teach in such a way as to keep the text's meanings in play while also tracing some of the discursive and ideological implications of this reading and that?

Second, when a critical literacy teacher defines and even prescribes a political position, such as feminism, for students to take up for their reading, they may not always align themselves with the ideological positions that undergird a particular "reading against the grain." It can be legitimate to ask students to step into a different position—provided they are given plenty of material to work with imaginatively as they step into another's shoes. However, it can be a problem when students are given no room to develop their own hypotheses about the aesthetic, discursive, and ideological function of this or that aspect of the text and must then choose a particular form of transformative play according to their hunch about the consequences of this intervention. The kind of writing that follows when students are directed to take a particular political stance can become a perfunctory exercise. They may be required in advance to take a writing position "with," "across," or "against" the text (Moon, 2001; Pope, 1995).[2] No less than the analytical essay, this triad is very reductive: our reading responses (developing, changing, sometimes ambivalent, even oscillating) are more multiple than these. Nor does this kind of activity allow for the complexity of relations with the studied text that may develop in the course of the re-creative writing. The question is, how can teachers intervene in students' reading in productive ways without taking on the role of ideological police? How can they ensure that students do not remain in crudely caricatured positions, taking a single line?

Third, such politically critical teaching can encourage teachers to move too quickly to substitute generalisations about the politics of the text (for example, that *The Tempest,* like *Lord of the Rings,* endorses a racist and sexist agenda) without looking at how any such societal interests are interrogated by the text and played out in its details. It is a weakness of much critical literacy that it has sometimes focused almost exclusively on the content of the text, which is seen simply as exemplifying political relations outside the text, and has neglected aspects of form. It thereby misses much of the sociopolitical persuasiveness of the aesthetic, for, as argued in earlier chapters, the aesthetic is deeply imbued with the social and the ideological, not least through its use of discourses and genres. The question here is how to be alert to the ideological while still engaging with (and being engaged by) the aesthetic.

These questions can in part be answered by the kind of disciplined, productive, imaginative work that textual intervention can do, as part of the ongoing classroom discussions and investigations that are grounded in a firm grasp of the understandings about and valuations of the aesthetic outlined in previous chapters.

What follows is a representative range of activities selected for their capacity to promote and enhance students' aesthetic responses and develop understanding of these as socially conditioned. The activities are organised according to the textual understandings, or propositions, listed above. It should be noted that any of the activities can be used to foster more than one such understanding. And none of them will of themselves "do the trick" of enabling students to understand and evaluate this aspect or that of the text studied. Such understanding will depend largely on the preceding classroom activities, the way the teacher introduces and frames the activity, feedback on drafts, the sharing of students' work, and the classroom discussion generated by all this.

The suggested approaches have the advantage of maintaining students' attention in the same creative, aesthetic mode, which also involves critical design decisions and comparisons with the given text. There is thus a continuity between students' engagement with the given text and their own further explorations of other texts; it is a way of sustaining aesthetic enjoyments while almost simultaneously drawing students' attention to various understandings about the constructive, productive nature of textual practice.

A Sampler of Text-Based Activities

Proposition 1

Aesthetic texts offer pleasure in beauty—that is, engagement with intensity of textual experience.

This proposition sums up the book's argument that the aesthetic as a valuable way of knowing depends on readers' apprehending aspects of textual form and content, responding to them in culturally and personally selective ways, and thereby creating in themselves pleasure, a sense of significance, and intensity of feeling. Such aesthetic engagement works to position readers ideologically: to invite them to take up the particular way of seeing the world offered in the text and to become the kind of reader who responds according to that invitation.

Where teachers want to help students engage with the intensity of textual experience, the following activities may be helpful.

PARALLEL TEXTS

It can be useful to begin with a selected text (film, television program, popular literature) that students engage with voluntarily out of school. Recently, for instance, many secondary teachers have made much of the parallels between the film *Clueless* and Austen's *Emma*. The point is not so much to compare the more popular text unfavourably with the text under study, but to make a bridge from one to the other. In this way teachers can model their openness to a range of texts and the peculiar aesthetic satisfactions each offers. Both texts may use a similar patterning of events, repetitions of motifs, image, or symbol; they may draw on similar discourses; or the genres to which they adhere may offer similar satisfactions, such as resolution of a storyline. As well as such aesthetic continuities, there will be differences, in form or content, and in the affective satisfactions they offer. Comparing these can throw into greater relief the specifics of the text under study while still promoting engagement.

PARALLEL COMPOSITION

A similar way of fostering engagement could be set at the outset of a unit, as a lead-in to investigating the concerns of a text. This involves getting students involved in a particular issue, exploring it and creating a text that in some way echoes some aspect(s) of the study text. For instance, a pair of students could each be asked to compose a song lyric from a different viewpoint about a currently contentious issue that in some way parallels an issue in the text. When students later come to consider the given text, the teacher can help the students to compare it with their own work in such a way that the form, emphases, and stance of the text become more salient. A poem may be ostensibly monologic, for instance; a short story may offer details without commentary; an essay or speech may frame others' opinions within the presentation of its own argument; and so on. While this kind of activity can prompt examination of the studied text's content and form, such investigation may be the more engaged because of the bridge created with the students' involvement in their own composition.

ENACTMENT AND IMPROVISATION

English teachers have much to learn here from the repertoire of strategies their drama-teaching colleagues have at hand. What is offered here is a mere sample of a much broader range.

When the text under study is a play, teachers will often involve students in staging a performance, in whole or in part, formally or informally. This entails blocking of moves, which requires students to think about how relationships and interactions are managed by gesture, action, and position relative to others, and how this can involve an audience affectively. Even in learning to speak others' words and make their moves, students are inhabiting more or less vividly another, imagined person. No doubt they have often enough identified with characters on screen. But when students get absorbed for a time in the character they are impersonating, enactment means embodiment with breath and muscles. Their bodies are shaped according to the text and become the means by which the text is projected. The body is crucial here to the kinds of experience the text is creating and representing, and it can open us to deeply felt engagements with these experiences. Such enactment can help bring home to students how they are positioned through language, but also how they might inhabit a number of embodied selves or subject positions and make them their own, if only for the time. (Whether or not that embodied knowledge is articulated through analysis and reflection will depend on the teacher's framing of the activity. But it will remain in the student as a latent resource, all the more vivid if the enactment has been emotionally intense.)

Several forms of dramatic improvisation can be used to maintain engagement and enhance its intensity. Students may be asked to explore a character's thoughts and motivations in an interior monologue or informal soliloquy. They may be invited to present aspects of the given character in a dramatic monologue (thereby concealing or giving a different interpretation to particular aspects of the character to those offered in the text). They may be put in the "hot seat" as a character and subjected to interrogation.

These activities are both imaginative and creative; they need not thereby lead students to conceive of fictional characters as having an extended existence outside the text, in our world. Such characters do, however, exist imaginatively for us, and through such activities students may lend them their imaginations in creative ways that enhance their engagement.

Other forms of enactment may be wordless and more abstract, involving mime or freeze-frame "living sculptures." (Words may, of course, accompany such presentations, as voice-overs or narration.) Such techniques direct students' attention to the expressive range of bodily position and gesture and the ways these can be stylised—stripped back and rendered more starkly. Even more strongly perhaps than the other forms of enactment mentioned above, these require students to "translate" words into posture, transform thoughts, feelings, and desires into gesture, and perhaps grasp how embodiment and articulation are complementary but also distinct.

ABSTRACTION

An equivalent but different form of representation may be selected to encourage students to determine what is significant for them in the text and render visible their affective and aesthetic engagements with it. Here students are asked to abstract the form, or the aesthetic/affective structuring, or the content of the given text by creating diagrams (of plot pivots, for example, or high and low points in the characters' fortunes), symbols (of relationships, or motifs for themes), songs (encapsulating the emotional heart of the text), movie trailers, or back cover blurbs. These are vastly different from plot or character summaries, in giving students more scope to register and value their affective and aesthetic responses.

Proposition 2

Aesthetic texts are situated within contexts to which they contribute.

According to this proposition, every text is a node in a network. The form a text takes and the ideas it represents depend on and contribute to the society within which and for which the text was produced. These contexts are historical, cultural, political, and aesthetic; the genres, discourses, and ideologies that are available to be drawn on are intimately involved in producing the text. Any text also contributes to the proliferation of these "conversations" of texts and discourses.

In exploring this understanding about the situatedness of texts, teachers may be drawing on any of the following elements.

JUXTAPOSING TEXTS

Many teachers give students notes about the historical context of the text, and while this can be useful, such "factual" knowledge may not inform the students' engagement with the text in the same way as juxtaposed texts can. In this version of the parallel

texts activity outlined above, similar texts from different historical or cultural contexts are set alongside the text for study. It may
be helpful to select texts whose discourses and ideologies are
more salient, if in some way equivalent. The texts may, for example, be from other times or cultural contexts. They may be
selected because they are provocative in the clarity of the issues
they present. For example, when some of Rudyard Kipling's stories are set alongside Ruth Prawer Jhabvala's *Heat and Dust,* the
very alien gendered and racial assumptions of the former may
prompt examination of some of the relationships depicted in the
latter—to see how they are or are not similar, to see how these
problematics are worked out in the study text's content and
form. The point of this activity is not to accuse each text of "fundamentally" offering the same aesthetic and formal satisfactions
and solutions. Rather, such comparisons make it possible to trace
the specifics of the "conversations" each text has with the culture
within which it was produced and the influence that has on the
specific satisfactions the text offers.

The juxtaposed texts can, of course, be the students' own, as
in the parallel composition outlined above. During or after reading a novel or play, students could write a version of a key scene,
resituating it in their own context, in order to see how culturally
determined the forms, concerns, and discourses of the original
are and what resolutions now seem peculiar—ideologically but
also aesthetically.

PARALLEL COMPOSITION

Another form of parallel composition may be used to resituate
some aspect of the studied text in another context, perhaps the
students' own. In a novel, those aspects may include the view of
causation, fate, or justice (or whatever) as played out in the text;
the frameworks of discourse and ideology proffered by the text
or by particular characters; the patterns of societal preoccupation
and the resolution, if any, played out in the plot structures; or the
con/textually bound nature of characterisation. For instance, at
the beginning of a unit on *Macbeth,* students could be asked to
devise the storyboard for a short film in which a character reads
his or her day's horoscope in the newspaper and in the course of

that day comes to fulfil it in a most unexpected way, one that gives an unexpected new meaning to the wording of that horoscope. This activity can enable teachers to focus students' investigation on the underlying assumptions about prophecy, coincidence, fate, or chance in the Shakespearian play and in the storyboards, the ways in which that worldview informs the unfolding of the narrative, in each case, and its consequences for the characters' agency, sense of responsibility, and so on.

Such a parallel composition activity provides a fairly flexible frame: it does not specify the writer's stance or dictate the line that is to be followed. It sets up a comparison with only some aspect(s) of the given text. And there is also scope for perhaps ironic play and for perhaps unexpected discoveries to be made about the form and "argument" of both the given text and the student's, as well as acknowledgment of the aesthetic satisfactions of a plot pattern being worked through in each case.

Indeed, teachers may offer students more openly productive prompts. After a class has studied a text and traced the ideologies it espouses, a teacher might say, "Imagine the consequences if this view, promoted by the text, were carried through. Tell me a story about what happens." Here students are given scope to develop their own hypotheses and then choose the narrative pattern that will enact it. (Their stories might or might not involve the setting and characters of the text they have studied.) When they speculate in this way, they may come to understand that writing can be a form of cultural dialogue, one that is not only prompted by social critique but also by a social imagination. They may recognise too that acts of reading and writing are constructed and negotiated in very complex ways—not simply as either endorsements or rejections of a prior text.

PARODY AND IRONY

Another form of activity exploring the situatedness of texts within cultural "conversations" involves using certain forms of humour. In one instance students have been studying a text they have largely disliked. (They might, for example, have objected to the glamorising of a particular form of sexism in D. H. Lawrence's *Women in Love*.) The teacher has invited them to find a parodic way to analyse their dissatisfactions. One group has decided to draw on a popular television talk show that features a relationship counsellor. They identify how the form and language of this show works to present particular ideologies about certain forms of love as normal and valuable, and how they establish identities and persuasive relationships between the presenter, the participants, and the audience. Next the students script and perform an episode of the show, featuring some of the novel's characters and offering solutions for their relationship problems. This is quite complex work, involving analysing the form and language of existing shows, selecting aspects of the satirical target and identifying the peculiarities of its discourses and ideologies, and then devising an episode show that combines both parody and satire. The conversations that go on during its development, the satirical inventiveness of the script, and the parodic enactment of the characters all make this a memorable and illuminating representation of the students' responses to the novel.

In another example students are drawing on a form of collage to do ironic work. A class has been studying a Shakespearian play: *Henry V,* say, or *Romeo and Juliet,* or *The Merchant of Venice.* In order to explore some of the ideals and ideologies endorsed by the play, a teacher has asked students, working in groups, to choose a key speech or scene—say Henry's St. Crispian's Day speech before the Battle of Agincourt, the Balcony scene, Portia's courtroom triumph over Shylock. They will project a film version of this onto a screen, or perhaps perform the scene themselves. At the same time, alongside this they will screen a PowerPoint presentation, to juxtapose a range of images and texts (some of them from the same play), thereby engaging that scene in a "conversation" with the other texts. The aim is to destabilise the certainties offered by those Shakespearian characters, to undercut ironically their discourses about war, romantic love, or justice, and to demonstrate how the arguments that thread through and surround a text may be re-presented in a multimedia performance.

In these examples, again, the work of the aesthetic and the critical is integrated in playful and productive responses to text. There is critique of language use and genres, enjoyment of texts that stand at an oblique angle to mainstream conventions, and appreciation of texts whose rhetoric or commonsense neutrality carries authority and conviction. In the students' own work there is both critique of the norms and enjoyment of the aesthetic. In such cases there can be an affectionate realisation that one may admire or enjoy a text while still being able to critique it play-fully. Tasks like this may enable students to avoid oversimplifying the multiplicity of their responses to a text and represent something of its ambiguities and their ambivalences.

Proposition 3

Aesthetic texts offer partial but potentially illuminating interpretations of experience.

This proposition asserts that any text offers a particular version of a story or a situation and therefore a partial interpretation of the world. A text invites readers to consent to this version and know the aesthetic satisfactions and sense of significance offered by the content, form, and emotional structuring. Readers often find this distinctive version of reality and knowledge valuable, since it offers a way of seeing and understanding that extends their own.

Where teachers are interested in developing this understanding in their students, they may be working with, and adapting, any of the following activities.

TRANSLATION

Students can be asked to translate all or part of an older or more formal text, such as a poem, into the conversational idiom of their own primary discourse. The point of this exercise is to compare the effects of each in order to make the specifics of the given text (its word choices, formal features, discourse) stand out in greater relief.

WHAT IF . . .

While studying a narrative text in class, a teacher may speculate with the students about how their aesthetic and emotional satisfactions would be changed if the storyline were changed at a particular point (the hero does not die; the relationship peters out; a disaster or a stroke of good fortune occurs); or if the tone of a central episode were altered to make it more comic, or bathetic, or laden with tragic significance; or if the narration were focalised through a different character. There are always other stories that can be told out of the given one, and they offer to satisfy very different desires.

GENRE-BENDING

"Genre-bending" can involve changing some of the key characteristics of a genre (such as its constituent discourses or aspects of form), or putting it to a new (unlikely) purpose, or situating it in an unexpected context, or incorporating heterogeneous elements. In one example the genre of autobiography is "bent" by making it discontinuous and nonlinear and using the hypertext medium to permit a range of reading pathways.[3] Having read a number of autobiographical texts and identified some of the discourses that have shaped the subjects' lives and their writing, students are set to trace some of the discourses that have been at work in their own lives. The activity is designed to help students understand how a life, lived and known through language, is a cultural and social project; how a life is a text (or series of texts) crisscrossed by discourses that constitute its reality and give it meaning. Given this diversity, the students are asked to experiment with diverse ways of narrating some of the episodes they have selected from their own lives. And they are to present it in hypertext form, making use of linking to connect or contrast elements that might be widely separated in time or context.

Here form and content are appropriately matched, to explore and represent a self as a multiple, discursively constituted subjectivity, in ways that even secondary students can understand. Through such narrative experimentation, which many students find very engaging and aesthetically satisfying, they are also learning about the work that sequential, conventional autobiographical narratives do: how they create a smoothly consistent, unilinear whole that does not let other potential texts and storylines surface. (Such narratives, of course, also offer aesthetic satisfactions of their own, which teacher and students may explore in discussion after reading.) When students undertake such composition, they can come to understand something about the ideological and aesthetic work that the form of an autobiography can do. Through such incitements to play (in a medium that many adolescents find engaging but also "natural," from their experience of the Web), new forms and new meanings can be created.

Proposition 4

Aesthetic texts offer meanings that are negotiated with readers.

Summed up here is the understanding that texts offer particular meanings, even if these are unstable. Readers in different historical and cultural contexts read selectively and realise particular meanings from a text, and derive different pleasures from it, because of the knowledge, experiences, desires, expectations and subjectivities they bring to the text, and which in turn are produced from their reading of that text. In their cognitive and affective negotiations with any text, readers exercise agency and are not just subject to the ideologies of the text through the arousal and satisfaction of their desires: their responses show complex patterns of alignments and resistances.

This point is central to the immersive experiences of readers. The suggested activities that follow are only some of the many ways by which teachers can validate the knowledge, experiences, desires, and expectations that students bring to the text, by allowing for the diversity and dynamics of alignment and resistance (without presenting these as purely personal) and by investigating their sources, to the extent that these are accessible.

RECONTEXTUALISING

Recontextualising involves taking a text with an aesthetic treatment of a particular topic—such as a poem about a natural phenomenon (birds, perhaps, or weather)—and setting alongside it or inserting into it a text that offers a non-aesthetic treatment of the same topic. It is then possible to see how one's reading strategies for the non-aesthetic text change when it is incorporated into an aesthetic text, how it becomes available for an aesthetic reading, and how it yields different meaning possibilities.

COLLAGE

In one instance, students are asked to compose an oral "collage" of dialogue drawn from two films (such as *Sense and Sensibility* and *Muriel's Wedding*). They are to juxtapose scenes from the films to set up a "conversation" about how discourses of gender, and gendered discourse, work to shape friendly, family, and intimate relationships. Working individually or in pairs, students are to link the segments of dialogue (projected on screen or performed) with their own prose, visuals, music, or movement.[4]

The resituating of those exchanges of dialogue makes them available for different readings at the same time as they evoke their filmic context and viewers' original responses. The multimodal nature of this collage is an important part of the pleasures it offers and the means of critique it affords. When texts in different modes are set alongside one another, the meanings that can be generated from each are expanded because of their enlarged semiotic and discursive range (Lemke, 1998). This is important in enacting and eliciting something of the aesthetic capaciousness of any text, and also in foregrounding the reader's acts of producing meaning. The suggestive richness of such a multimodal collage contributes to the pleasure and sense of significance that both the makers and the audience derive as they draw inferences from what is displayed before them.

In another instance of collage, the activity involves "exploding" a short story. Using a simple hypertext program, the students first scan in the text, perhaps as a linked sequence of segments. Then, working in small groups, they find some texts and create others, in a variety of genres and from a range of viewpoints, which they arrange and link in such a way as to invite other discourses into the space that contains the story at its centre. In this way they open up that central text to other readings. Links may take readers out into the Web for other perspectives.

When readers encounter texts juxtaposed in a hypertext they are more likely to become aware of differences in register, point of view, discourse, genre, and the like. This offers the teacher opportunities to reread these collated texts with the students: to be amused or surprised at telling links between texts, to enjoy the navigational dislocations and relocations, to savour the disjunctions between stances offered in this text or that, and so to investigate some of the textual features of those component texts. Here, then, the aesthetic potential of hypertext linking is indissoluble from the critical work it is set to do.

Note that these satisfactions and opportunities for focused examination are extended when the students' hypertexts are shared with others in the classroom. This raises an important point: too often assignments are submitted at the very end point of a course of study, with no opportunity for public presentation. This denies students the opportunity to challenge, deepen, or develop their understandings and engagements.

Incidentally, such collage work can serve as a corrective to the problem raised earlier in the chapter, that a unified, retrospective impression of a text is both "the" text and "the" reading. Instead, it recognises the potential variousness of the text, the multiplicity of possible responses in reading, and the ways that these are evoked by readers' experience of other texts and discourses.

Proposition 5

Aesthetic texts are multiple, as are readers and the meanings they produce.

When readers activate some of the potential meanings and kinds of affective experience that texts offer, they are enabled to multiply the possible subject positions and pleasures that texts make available. The aesthetic and the ideological are therefore productive: they construct forms and meanings, and they generate desires, satisfactions, and subjectivities.

The following suggestions may be useful where teachers are pursuing this understanding with their students.

PLAY WITH METAPHOR

This could involve students taking a metaphor, symbol, or motif from their text (a poem, a film scene) and putting it to different ends in a similar text. They might substitute a different metaphor-cluster for the given one and see what different emphases and implications are activated. Or they might play with a metaphor, pressing it until it yields other associations—

uninvited, perhaps even unwanted ones. Students may use these to generate a text of their own that speaks back to (but also exceeds) the given text. The point of this exercise is not to dismiss out of hand the work that the metaphors, symbols, or motifs do in the given text, but by comparison with others produced by students to allow each set to be valued for the particular readings and aesthetic satisfactions it offers.

This activity is rather different from the assignment discussed earlier that set students to find alternative images for Ophelia. The present task offers only a loose structure through wordplay rather than specifying the writer's stance or the direction of the narrative. Nonetheless, it encourages students to think about the implications of dead metaphors, to dig out meanings buried by common use, to consider the discourses metaphors may be used to carry, and to consider the politics of the neutral voice of disembodied authority in dictionary and encyclopedia definitions. Then, as they begin to grasp how "language speaks us" and how we live by and through metaphors, students can draw attention to these through their narratives and so begin to produce new forms and meanings.

MULTIPLYING READINGS

A number of the activities described above have as one of their intended effects the creation of a range of reading positions. The following activity does so more overtly by demonstrating something of the multiplicity of readings a text can generate. The teacher has students take part in a panel discussion. They are to debate whether a particular text (it could be anything from a Shakespearean play to a narrative role-playing game) should be an obligatory text for study at their grade level. Different panel members will speak on behalf of particular interest groups or from particular ideological positions, which may or may not coincide with their own. (They will need to be informed about the key concerns of these positions and be rehearsed in speaking the discourse with some degree of fluency and accuracy.) If, for instance, students are debating the value of *The Tempest*, speakers might take up postcolonial, feminist, Marxist, New Historical, or cultural heritage positions. In this way, the students demonstrate how each speaking position, each ideology, has peculiar concerns, and how each conceives of aesthetic value in different terms.

This is a more directly analytical and critical task than some we have considered here, and it carries the risk, mentioned earlier, of crude caricatures of both text and critique. However, the panel format generates a range of motivated readings and keeps the text's meanings in play. And as a role-playing activity, it allows for the pleasures of performance at the same time as those of critique and debate.

PLAY WITH LANGUAGE

In the best English classrooms, play with language is ongoing and incidental. Teachers and students will enjoy puns, invent forms, ring variations on an expression, parody a slogan, and undertake more deliberately crafted experiments. Such playfulness should not be dismissed as frivolous: this play is serious work that can engage students and lead them to understandings about language and texts they might not have arrived at by other means.

Here is one example of productive play, which explores the discursive richness that surrounds any term. Students have been reading an unconventional short story that offers a series of definitions of the word *blanket* and discussions of common expressions using the word (such as "wet blanket")(Jackson, 1987). Through these definitions a story begins to emerge. Students are invited to choose another common term (*seed*, maybe, or *sight*), to explore its primary and secondary meanings, its literal and symbolic uses, its uptake in a range of expressions, and to generate a story out of these hints. This story will be carried and developed through that series of expressions (the word *sight*, for instance, is in both "out of sight, out of mind" and "in his sights"). And it may work against the apparent "innocence" of those commonplace terms. (The story and an example of a student's version are discussed in Morgan [1992].)

ENACTMENT

As we have seen already, there is a range of ways in which students can come to know the currents of argument, emotion, and attitude in texts by embodying them. Enactment may also be used to foster understanding of multiplicity. For instance, pairs of students may be undertaking a role-playing activity in order to explore the discourses at work in the situation in which their characters are involved. (This could entail worker and boss arguing about rights and responsibilities, or people from different walks of life exploring what the good life means to them—or whatever topic is relevant to the text being explored.) The stance of the characters and the outcome of their exchanges may be more or less closely defined in advance by the teacher. Perhaps different pairs would be assigned a particular discourse or relationship or outcome within the same context and the performances compared. Given some of the critiques raised earlier in the chapter, it may be preferable for teachers not to take away from students the scope to follow the discourse where it leads.

In yet other cases, the enactment may be imagined and projected onto paper in the diagrams of a storyboard. Students might be asked to devise the performance of a poem's lyrics in a music video to enable their viewers to see and hear a neglected meaning they have elicited from the poem, or to position them differently vis-à-vis the poem's discourses. The storyboard, with its accompanying notes about lighting, camera movements, sound effects, and the like can enable students to integrate the aesthetic and the critical.

In such forms of actual or projected enactment, students are rehearsing words, emotions and arguments, postures and actions which are not exactly their own, yet become their own in those acts. Through these experiences, students can both inhabit and understand something of a range of subjectivities and can comprehend them when they step back out of role into the different mode of reflection and analysis. In such moves between modes, both an embodied aesthetic and the critical are engaged.

The unexpected cannot be ruled out when students are undertaking such performance activities. They may be surprised at the emotions and desires liberated in their enactments. Of course, these affects may not be so easily regulated, however disciplined they may be in performance. But the engagements they bring can certainly be a resource and a source of energy that can be harnessed (partly at least) to creative, critical, and aesthetic ends.

The harnessing of such productive engagements brings us to the matter of assessment of students' products and performances.

Assessment for the Critical and the Aesthetic

It is something of a commonplace among critical sociologists of education (Bourdieu, 1996) that the "technologies" of formal assessment inevitably involve some forms of regulation and surveillance; that assessment practices entail a struggle for control over knowledge, meaning, and taste; and that they act as a gatekeeping mechanism to maintain the privileges of those who belong to the "right" class, ethnic group, or gender group. Through such assessment practices, it is argued that disadvantaged students may have restricted social mobility and access to social goods, and, worse, that they may be convinced that they "deserve" their lowly place, since the system is ostensibly based on merit. This may happen as much in the assessment practices of critical literacy as in those of more conservative literature-based curricula.

Such matters are not the main focus of our discussion here, although they are implicit. Rather, the major concern is this: Must aesthetic responses to a text always be left behind, or dealt with at one remove, when students undertake assessment tasks? To answer this question we will consider two characteristic forms of task: first the essay, then textual intervention tasks.

The Essay

Our immediate response to this question is likely to be an affirmative when responses to text are presented via the objectifying move of the analytical essay. In fact, it may be rather more complex. Certainly, when students practise critique that they have learned under the teacher's guiding eye and produce an analytical exposition, they can only report selectively on their aesthetic engagements with the text under scrutiny. And, of course, in any regime of teaching only certain kinds of response to the text are likely to be accessible or acceptable. Such selectivity tends to close down the potentialities of the text and the reading.

However, even when the essay is the designated assessment task, it is desirable to look for ways of keeping the text and the readings more open: of allowing for the fact that the shifting responses that occur during one's reading of a text make it difficult to fix on a single meaning, even on the one occasion of reading, let alone across several. This dynamism can be intolerable for some teachers and students, particularly when the essay topic assumes that a synthesised memory, a final, retrospectively unified impression, *is* the reading—is indeed the text. (Teachers and their topics can forget that any report of a reading is inevitably a sampling, taken at a particular moment and should therefore be recognised as always provisional, always subject to change.)

Instead, when it comes to framing literary essays as assignment topics, teachers have characteristically distinguished between readers (as perceiving subjects), readings (as kaleidoscopic, even chaotic), and texts (as aesthetic objects) and in the wording of their topics tend to redirect attention from the former to the latter (Faust, 2001). Thus when teachers ask students to analyse a text by answering a traditional essay question, they (perhaps of necessity) neglect the fact that when one is writing about a text one can only write about one's reading of that text, a reading that is recalled and reconstructed in the writing, so as to become a further text that can be evaluated in turn. And while topics that invite students to explore their personal responses may do much to keep readings open, the teacher may already have exemplified and endorsed in classroom talk, handouts, sample plans, and the like the kinds of interpretation and response that students are to emulate. How far the students feel permitted to diverge from such norms will depend on the teacher's stance towards multiplicity.

More radical critical literacy topics set up new means and ends for the critical analysis of literary texts, ones that are very different from those enshrined in the traditional essay of interpretative literary criticism, with its focus on the reader's individual aesthetic response. These new kinds of topics still tend to focus on the text's strategies. And they may encourage generalizations about "the" invited or intended reader—or "the" resistant, oppositional, reader. They may ask students to demonstrate that they understand how partial texts are, how they marginalize certain groups, how they "silence" particular "voices," and so on. Indeed, as we have seen, what may well actually be "silenced," disallowed from the outset by the directives in the task, are any admissions by students that they had actually enjoyed the text or that their encounters with it had an aesthetic character.

Whether essay topics are situated within the practices of a more traditionally literary criticism or a more radical critical literacy, some teachers, and their students, hope to eliminate surprise from such tasks. The aim is for students to rehearse critical and theoretical positions that have already been learned through the teaching and are identified in the task.

Nonetheless, the possibility for openness in essay topics remains, especially in those classrooms where teachers have set up particular kinds of exploratory activities to engage with multiplicity, based on the understandings outlined above. Good topics can be phrased in such a way that they encourage exploratory writing. They can enable students not so much to report on the learning that has already occurred as to go on learning—to discover more about the workings of the text and its meanings and their responses to it. It is for such ends that these teachers will assign essay topics and will also teach ways of using language to convey the dynamics of response, tentativeness of interpretation, and openness to other plausible meanings.

Re-creative Tasks

As noted earlier in the chapter, these different kinds of tasks were developed partly out of dissatisfaction with the essay and the kind of teaching towards which it was directed. That earlier question now needs to be asked of these alternative kinds of task: Can these allow aesthetic responses to a text to be presented directly, or must they be re-created at one remove? Can such tasks admit also those aspects of the aesthetic that are potentially liberatory, excessive, or subversive? Or are these dimensions of the aesthetic likely to be rendered innocuous, censored, or ignored when students are developing their assignments and teachers are assessing them?

Particularly as they advance through the secondary years, students are likely to attempt to produce work within the bounds set by what they know or think the teacher will find acceptable.

Thus the potentially transgressive or subversive is likely to be self-censored and filtered out. This is as true of re-creative tasks as of the essay.

Assessment tasks are inevitably partial in their focus (but may still be productive), and they may therefore reduce or ignore much of the aesthetic capaciousness in texts and in students' responses. Nevertheless, classroom activities can offer students aesthetic and critical incitements that evade or exceed what is specified and assessed in assignments. This does not mean that when students engage with such activities their work is always necessarily beyond what assessment can value and evaluate. Indeed, some activities and tasks are very productive in directing, and disciplining, students' aesthetic, imaginative, and critical responses. Often these will go beyond, or in a different direction from, what the students could have produced on their own or even imagined themselves capable of. No less than students, teachers may celebrate such surprising achievements and reward work that exceeds their hopes and expectations (knowing how difficult it is to teach students how to produce such surprises).

The point is that teachers cannot entirely predict or control what will happen—cognitively, emotionally, aesthetically, critically—when they offer their students such invitations to engage with texts creatively. Teachers and systems are fooling themselves if they think they can specify in advance or even anticipate all the possible or even likely aspects of such response by means of generic "outcomes" statements or specific criteria. This does not mean subscribing to a romantic view of the aesthetic as being ineffably beyond teaching and learning in assessment practices; it means just recognising that by nature the aesthetic tends to evade rational control. It means acknowledging, with a wry realism as well as a realistic optimism, that there are not only limitations and uncertainties but especially opportunities and serendipities in much teaching and assessment, not least when these deliberately elicit and enact aesthetic as well as critical engagement. As mentioned earlier, the point is to ensure that there is clear purpose in the task and some directives (such as specifying aspects of the given text's form or content to be focused on or determining some elements of the form of response), while also allowing sufficient room in which students can move around.

Teachers Responding to Tasks

Teachers' acts of assessment are framed in multiple ways. Their past experiences, their membership of a professional community with its norms, lore, and know-how, their knowledge of syllabi and curricula—all these and more shape what they do when they turn to a pile of assignments. More immediately, based on their familiarity with drafts or prior work, they will bring expectations of what their students are likely to produce. Our main concern here is not with this framing. Rather, it is with what teachers do (or might do) when they assess products or performances that engage with and enact both the aesthetic and the critical, based on the kinds of tasks sketched in the previous section. Here are some of the key issues.

As indicated earlier, teachers need to create the space, inter-fere in productive ways, but not become the ideological traffic police. This applies to assessing assignments no less than assigning them. As noted above, we must allow for surprise at what students produce and our responses to those products: surprise at an apt argument, at a position taken that we had not anticipated (and might not agree with), at being carried along in the flow of a narrative, and at being caught up in an unexpected image. We need to be open to the capaciousness of a text, knowing that the meanings it offers may exceed what we derive from it. And we need to reward this.

So often, when teachers' pencils hover above a student's work, their critical faculties are hard at work. Correction is a burden, and they are in judgment mode. The task seems straight-forward when teachers are "correcting" an analytical essay and relatively easy when they are responding to a short story. They may be rather more perplexed about the basis of their judgments when they are assessing students' re-creative writing, performa-tive collages, multigeneric hypertexts, and the like.

In assessing re-creative writing, for instance, teachers do not usually expect to find the same pleasures, attend to the same fea-tures, and apply the same evaluative standards as they do in read-ing the original literary text. They may assess the writing for its effectiveness as a student text in its own right. But they are much more likely to read to find the traces of the student's understand-ing—of textual constructedness or political positioning or what-ever—that the task was designed to develop. Teachers can, of course, operate in both aesthetic and analytical modes simultane-ously. It is just that the usual circumstances of their acts of assess-ment work against it.

A piece of re-creative writing may be an illustration of a stu-dent's understanding and application of aesthetic responses and judgments, but an indirect one. Teachers therefore have to work to infer the evidence that is the basis of their judgments. They will need acuity in reading across texts in response to the stu-dent's writing (and reading) across texts. This becomes particu-larly problematic when students experiment with irony, except where this has been explicitly directed in the task. Teachers will also need to recognise that they are collaborating with the text and the student when they make their inferences.

Other forms of text bring particular headaches for the teacher-assessor. Like collages, multimedia products have a "chameleon character" (Sinker, 2000). They are even more com-plex to assess than a single, printed text, since teachers need to make meanings and draw inferences across texts in different gen-res and modes, each with their own semiotic character. (Here we need to remind ourselves of reader-response theories and acknowledge that meaning potentials always exceed what the author may have been conscious of.) Hypertexts bring another issue. Teachers will need to judge the appropriateness and effec-tiveness of the links in creating pathways. In a narrative hyper-text, for instance, they will look for patterns and directions (Bernstein, 1998); in a collage they will want to see how its com-ponent texts are juxtaposed.

Beyond these issues of forms and modes, there is still the question of how teachers hold in balance aesthetic and critical responses to those dimensions of students' texts. The short answer is that they do it in their reading and viewing of texts in their personal (as distinct from professional) lives anyway. If they have developed some consciousness of how their aesthetic satisfactions work on them and in the text—the kind of socially critical aesthetic awareness outlined earlier in this book—and value this kind of reading competence in themselves, then they are more likely to be able to do something similar when they come to students' texts, even though the circumstances and their role are different.

Since teachers attend to and assess what they value, it will be important that any criteria they identify for themselves and their students, any performance outcomes they specify, give due weight to the aesthetic no less than the critical. But then, they will also need to acknowledge, to themselves and their students, that these features are not simply there *in* the text, but depend on the teacher's reading practices and preferences. Teachers are competent in many ways as assessors, but they are not necessarily the only, or best, audience. In cases where they are less than expert (they might not be connoisseurs of music videos, for instance), they might need to seek the advice of those who are, who can at least help them identify some of the key principles and criteria for success in that particular mode or genre. They can learn much from their students as well as from fellow professionals. At times teachers might want to ensure that other audiences supplement the feedback they provide on such products and performances.

Developing the Subject

Classrooms are complex sites of interaction and engagement with texts, ideas, desires, and feelings. What are produced thereby are not only assessable products but also students' subjectivities. Whether activities and tasks are traditional or innovative, narrowly determined or open, they contribute to producing humans who are being educated more or less successfully in valued competencies, and who are developing specific aesthetic and critical abilities. Such people, both subjects and agents, are the ultimate end in view of the kind of critical aesthetic practice advocated here. What both the critical and the aesthetic have in common is imagination. Imagination entails seeing new possibilities, different realities; it entails asking how things (in texts, in society) appear, and how they might be otherwise. Social critique is founded on imagination no less than hope. Such imagination is informed and disciplined, as are all our mental operations, and also productive. As a form of play over possibilities, it releases energy. Through it students may come to see themselves as the kinds of people who can be at once playful and analytical with language and assume different positions in discourse. And so they may come to know themselves as people with these capacities. They may know themselves as people who can take and make a range of pleasures, including those of analysis and critique, of crafting a text rhetorically and aesthetically, of engaging productively with social concerns and textual representations. They may know themselves as people who are making a contribution, according to their abilities, to the broader conversations and creations of their culture, who create or transform their understandings and therefore their selves.

Reconfiguring Critical
Literacy and the Aesthetic

The problem this book has been investigating, as explained in the introduction, is a simple one. Critical literacy is clearly a very valuable movement with the potential to transform English teaching, making it more socially responsible through giving students a powerful understanding of the social nature of textuality, but it seems largely either unable or reluctant to deal with aesthetic texts in a way that does them justice, and indeed it seems reluctant to engage with the literary part of the English curriculum at all. In some ways this is surprising, since one of the paths by which some people came to critical literacy was through their acquaintance with literary theory in the 1980s, so the ways of thinking about texts that underpin much critical literacy were in fact available and, at some level at least, compatible with studying literature. However, a division arose: on the one hand, critical literacy with its social awareness and promise of a serious new agenda for English studies, and on the other, one of two possibilities: either a traditional approach to teaching literature, or a version of critical literacy applied to literature that was obviously not doing justice to the aesthetic elements of the texts. The aim here, therefore, has been to investigate the possibilities for bringing together critical literacy and the aesthetic.

It is important to stress that critical literacy and the aesthetic are in no way set up as alternatives. In fact, they could not be, because that would be a category confusion: the two things work on quite different levels. Critical literacy is a kind of pedagogy with specific aims about making visible to students the inherently social nature of language and how texts are positioning them ideologically. The aesthetic, on the other hand, is a quality inherent in texts, or perhaps, rather, a mode of text that readers recognise and that activates a particular kind of reading. Everything that might be said in critical literacy about language as a social phenomenon that inevitably carries ideology is as true of aesthetic texts as of any other. Plays, poems, movies, and so forth may be different kinds of texts than feature articles or letters to the editor, but they partake of the general conditions of textuality.

In fact, it could well be argued that the aesthetic is an aspect of virtually all texts (see Chapter 2). Whenever one feels that conscious shaping for emotional effect has taken place, then there is an aesthetic element. (This is why some texts can easily make the transition from being read for their original purposes to being read as literature: Donne's Sermons, Francis Bacon's Essays, Johnson's *Lives of the Poets,* Pascal's *Pensées,* Lincoln's or Churchill's speeches.) If critical analysis is not conscious of this aesthetic dimension in a text, then any kind of critique is going to be severely limited.

However, it would not be useful for the argument here to play the game of dissolving the category of the aesthetic and claim that all texts are in fact aesthetic. It is more important to assert the uniqueness of those texts that work predominantly or exclusively in the aesthetic mode. Although there may be elements of the aesthetic, even quite strong ones, in many expository, argumentative, and other kinds of texts, these are deployed rhetorically for different ends.

Aesthetic texts are unique in the ends they pursue, the way they go about it, and the kind of effect they have. They aim to lead us to apprehend certain aspects of the world by creating a structure of textual experience (usually representational in literary texts) that leads us to think and feel in particular ways. This, like any single sentence trying to sum up the aesthetic, is rough and easily contestable. However, there is enough truth in it to show up the differences from, say, expository or argumentative texts: aesthetic texts aim to make us apprehend rather than comprehend, the shaping of the text is vital, and feeling is as important as thinking in the response elicited. The apprehension/comprehension distinction hopefully suggests the dualities on which, as we saw in Chapter 2, the aesthetic works (particular/universal, emotional/ intellectual, material/numinous, etc). Those dualities mean we cannot resolve the texts to rational understanding, or not so quickly. Perhaps, in the end, talking in terms of apprehension simply points to the fact that there is a stronger interpretative element in reading these texts, more room for the reader to expand her or his understanding, whereas expository and argumentative texts aim for tight closure, comprehensive comprehension. It is this interpretative openness that enables us to read a poem or see a movie over and over, whereas once we have understood an expository or argumentative text there is no point in a second reading, unless to remind ourselves of the content or check on detail.

As already noted, it is perfectly possible to do a standard critical literacy reading on aesthetic texts. There are many sets of questions in the critical literacy handbooks that direct us what to ask:

- Whose views are being represented?
- What interests are being served?
- What reading position is one being invited to take up?
- What cultural assumptions is the text taking for granted?
- What is absent from the text that one might expect to be there?

With any aesthetic text, one can ask these questions and one will get answers, many of which will be interesting. It is not that the answers are wrong, or misguided, or even irrelevant: it is that they often seem simply inadequate to the experience that the text is offering if that is as far as you go. We saw this with the example of the work on Donne's "A Valediction: Forbidding Mourning" in Chapter 5. There is no doubt that the poem expresses a view (at points at least) of the woman as dependent, operating in a limited private emotional world, whereas the man goes roaming about. But one has actually not said very much about the poem in saying that, and it would be a very great pity if a student, after that point was made, felt able to write off the poem as sexist and not worthy of the attention of an enlightened twenty-first century person. That reading has been produced by concentrating on the last three stanzas, and not noticing the remarkable mutuality of the poem in the first six. It is actually impossible to read anything in those six stanzas as differentiating between the status in the relationship of the man and the woman: the metaphoric procedures make the two absolutely equal.[1] The only thing one might point to is the fact that it is the sober, seriously intellectual male speaker who is comforting the female (but even then, he does her the credit that she will be able to understand his complex images). Even in those last three stanzas, there is something of a tribute to the woman in the notion of her anchoring firmness. The point is not that the reading of the compass image as masculinist is wrong or uninteresting—it is a point worth making about the poem—but as a response to the whole poem, it gets nowhere near first base. Certainly its engagement with the poem as an aesthetic text is at best superficial.

Critical Literacy: Its Problem with the Aesthetic

Why does critical literacy have such a problem with the aesthetic? There have been several answers suggested either implicitly or explicitly during our investigation, and it will be useful to bring some of them together and to rehearse them here. They have to do with the aesthetic's characteristic ways of working: in particular, its concern with individual experience, its stress on the experiential, and, leading out of that, the kind of engagement it is asking of the reader. In looking at these things we will remind ourselves of the sheer complexity of aesthetic textuality and its ways of establishing its meanings.

The Individual and Particular

It is a characteristic of the aesthetic that it establishes its meaning through a concentration on particulars, and generally on the actions and emotions of particular individual human beings. This means that there is an inherent interest in the uniqueness of the individual personality and the way it is operating in particular situations. This does not imply any common understanding in aesthetic texts of individual psychology and how a personality is constructed: a text might operate on Freudian or Lacanian or purely social constructivist views, and many authors probably have no single view at all but just consider the "people" inhabiting or speaking their texts as people. (It is interesting how often writers talk about characters seeming to take on an individual life separate from their creators.)

Critical literacy is predicated very much on a view of people as socially constructed: their subjectivity is shaped by the discourses in which they participate. The major identity areas—gender, race, and so forth—are seen as crucial in this construction, and this gives critical literacy its political edge, since it is concerned to speak against social restriction or discrimination in these areas. It is not the place here to debate the adequacy of the social construction of identity model. It certainly is a very powerful explanatory thesis. However, in its simple form, it cannot explain very readily human individuality or human agency. There is something inherently deterministic about the notion that the discourses of society imprint themselves on us and thus create our subjectivity. At the very least, it leads us to think of people in terms of categories rather than as individuals. Eve Kosofsky Sedgwick reminds us that "People are different from each other" and goes on to note:

> It is astonishing how few respectable conceptual tools we have for dealing with this self-evident fact. A tiny number of inconceivably coarse axes of categorization have been painstakingly inscribed in current critical and political thought: gender, race, class, nationality, sexual orientation are pretty much the available distinctions. (1990, p. 22)

She makes the rather astonishing, but almost incontrovertible statement that

> in spite of every promise to the contrary . . . every single theoretically or politically interesting project of postwar thought has finally had the effect of deligitimating our space for asking or thinking in detail about the multiple, unstable ways in which people may be like or different from each other. (1990, p. 23)

Of course, there are many theoretical models within the general social constructivist framework that offer interesting explanations that can begin to account for human individuality and human agency (the theory of multiple subjectivity outlined in Chapter 4 is one of them). However, they can be quite complex, and critical literacy, perhaps out of necessity for its school audience, has tended to work with a fairly simple version of the theory of the social construction of identity. This means that it cannot readily acknowledge the individuality of the character or "voice" in an aesthetic text, since it is all the time looking for the social discourse behind it. This largely reduces human beings inhabiting texts to identity categories. Thus, Donne's poem comes to be about gender and the power relations between men and women rather than about two people who love each other parting for a time.

To repeat, this is not to say that that is a misreading of the poem, just not a very comprehensive reading. In fact, one of the fundamental features of the aesthetic, as we have seen, is its ability to reach the general through the particular, and it could well be argued that picking up on the gendered implications of the compass metaphor is working precisely with this aspect of the aesthetic. The text's aesthetic qualities are what have allowed us to analyse the social construction of gender in it. One would not disagree with the argument. The problem is that if the range of concerns in looking at a text is limited to a fairly simple and inflexible view of identity areas and questions of social power and interest, then there is not going to be much depth and richness in the textual study. Before very long, all texts are going to seem boringly the same, because one is going to be discovering over and over again the same things in and about them. This, in fact, was an inherent problem in the whole move to "theory" in literary studies in the 1980s and 1990s. It has often been said that what you get from texts depends totally on the questions you ask: critical literacy has tended to confirm that if you ask a radically limited set of questions, then you get a radically limited set of answers.

Emotional/Experiential Element

When we come to look at the emotional/experiential element in the aesthetic and consider why critical literacy finds this difficult to deal with, there are two aspects that need to be considered: first, the experience and emotion the text represents, and second, the experience the text gives to and the emotion it elicits from the reader. The two, of course, are not identical, although obviously related, the first providing material that is taken up in certain ways to produce the second (see Chapters 2 and 7).

Since it has a limited view of the individual, critical literacy can say very little about represented emotion. It might be seen as the product of socialisation, and so as indicative of how people positioned socially in a certain way are conditioned to behave or not to behave, as the case may be. It could be an indicator of the kind and intensity of feeling that certain sorts of conditions and relations arouse. Whichever way, in a sense the emotion or the experience being described cannot be considered empathetically but must be treated as an indicator of a social phenomenon or a social attitude that can be evaluated.

Critical literacy can deal better with the emotion that the experience of a text can give to a reader, because that is very clearly a product of textual construction. (So is the emotion that is represented in the text, of course, but that is more naturalised.) Critical literacy knows all about textual construction: one of its major aims is to show the constructedness of texts and how they are shaped for particular ideological purposes, shaped to show the world in certain ways. Thus the experience of the text is analysed for its "partiality," for its way of constructing a partial view of the world and for putting the reader into a particular subject position. Without question, part of the text's strategies for doing this is by generating emotion through either its representational or its formal construction. We are caught up in the human situation of two people in love being forced to spend time apart, and we don't notice the gender power relations being played out; or we are caught up in the beautiful formal lyrical movement and lulled by its aesthetic perfection into not noticing the gender power relations being played out. In other words, the experiential/emotional impact of the text is largely there to distract us. Thus arises the suspicion of pleasure and beauty.

This leads us on to look at that third area: the nature of our engagement with the text.

Engagement with the Text

Our engagement with an aesthetic text is very complex (see Chapter 5), especially since it consists of both affective and intellectual elements. Thus we do not simply take the message from the text intellectually, but the message becomes deeply implicated with our emotions, and in a very real sense we experience what it is like to see the world from this particular angle. And this is not just a mental experiencing; as we saw in Chapter 7, the experience has a strong bodily resonance, so that the text is even inviting us to take on its view of things bodily. Besides which, in reading such texts, there is likely to be a considerable degree of interpretation involved, as noted earlier. This means that there is a particular intensity of engagement, since we as readers have contributed so much to the meaning through the interpretative process, thus investing something significant of ourselves in the text even as it is working to position us.

Critical literacy is a rationalist practice. The argument is that texts use various strategies to naturalise their ideology, and if we are not to become subject to the text, we must denaturalise it, show how it is in fact constructed. The force of reason, once we see the constructedness, will defuse the ideological power.

Undoubtedly this can happen, and often does happen to some degree, but it by no means always happens, and particularly not with aesthetic texts. It is easy to see why. If ideology is not carried just by intellectual means, but by experiential—emotional and corporeal—ones, then a rational critique is likely to interfere with the intellectual channel, but it may well leave the experiential ones virtually unimpaired. The intellectual and the experiential can be radically dissociated. We might like to think that reason is the most powerful governing factor in human life, but history, literature, and most personal experience would suggest that emotion can withstand rational onslaughts remarkably well under most conditions.

If you read the Donne "Valediction" and feel a strong emotional engagement, perhaps even feel that this is the kind of relationship you would like to be in, then rationalist critique of the poem in terms of gender power relations is not going to be very effective. Similarly, you can go to a romantic comedy at the movies, know that the ideology it presents is reprehensible on all your best feminist principles, but still be caught up in the tension of how these people are going to get together, and if it has a sentimental streak, you might be quite capable of shedding a tear at appropriate points. One may rationally reject the ideology, but one emotionally lives it out being caught up in the narrative.

The point can perhaps best be made by looking at advertising for a moment. Although not all advertisements could be claimed to be aesthetic texts—their purpose, after all, is fundamentally persuasive—many of them do use aesthetic means very powerfully. Take that classic kind of high-end-of-the-market advertising where you simply have a picture of an exceptionally good-looking, sexy, cool, hot, charismatic person, and the only written text is the product name. The picture may well be black-and-white rather than coloured to add to the arty, aesthetic feeling. The exceptionally good-looking etc. person may be wearing the product, but this is not essential (and obviously in perfume advertisements, for example, we cannot tell). A rational critique will look at the advertising strategy and scoff at the notion that the underwear or the perfume can make you look like that, will perhaps fulminate about the objectification and exploitation of women (and increasingly men) in advertising, and will stress the dangers of glorifying such exceptional body images. All this may be true, but in a sense it is beside the point. No one really believes that a pair of Calvin Klein briefs or a spray of Chanel No 5 is going to transform them, and no one really believes that the models are anything except exceptional physically. We wouldn't enjoy looking at them if they looked just like most of us. The image is not working rationally but aesthetically, drawing on our emotional engagement and desire for this particular fantasy ideal, and so the rational critique scarcely blocks our engagement with it at all. Advertisers know this, of course, and know that they can make outrageous connections and outrageous claims because no one actually believes the claims rationally, but they do feel them emotionally. If you want to intervene critically, then the critique must work at the emotional level somehow, through parody, for example, such as getting the students to imagine what the model is actually thinking.[2]

There is another point worth making on advertisements that suggests the limitations of the view that showing the constructedness of a text somehow defuses its power. Anyone who has done serious critical work on advertisements or taught them in any but the most piously negative way will understand the fascination they exert. One is on the lookout for interesting and clever advertisements, and the analysis of their construction only makes them more interesting, because one is getting more involved with them through working on them. The scary thing is that you can be in the supermarket or department store and find yourself searching for the product, in spite of your full knowledge of the text's constructedness and how it was working to position you, because the awful fascination of the advertisement becomes only stronger because of the analysis. This happened with Barthes's groundbreaking work in *Mythologies:* Jonathan Culler notes the "awkward fact" that

> the mythologist puts himself in complicity with what he attacks, as he articulates what goes without saying, spelling out mythical meaning . . . demystification does not eliminate myth, but, paradoxically, gives it a greater freedom. (1983, p. 39)

Advertisements are a favourite kind of text in critical literacy classrooms, and if the normal way of handling them has serious flaws as suggested here, then critical literacy really does have problems. However, we should not write it off just yet. Let us see what it could learn from considering the aesthetic more closely and reconfiguring itself to accommodate it.

The Aesthetic: Reconfiguring Critical Literacy

The first question to ask is, "Why is critical literacy worth saving?" The answer is that, in spite of the weaknesses we have seen and its uneasiness with aesthetic texts, it has managed to get most things right. It is predicated on the belief that English/literacy teaching should be about developing the students' understanding of textuality—that is, how texts work. It recognises that reading and writing are purposeful activities that are always socially situated, and so the meaning of any text is dependent on its context. It understands the fundamental significance of language and discourse in the construction of human identity and so can provide a justification for English beyond the functional one. It acknowledges how thoroughly implicated language is with ideology, and how language in shaping identity is making us the subject of ideology. To make students aware of this gives

English/literacy a serious ethical and political purpose in the need to give students the tools that will help them understand how they are being positioned and how they are positioning others. One would not give up any of this lightly.

One solution would be to acknowledge that critical literacy does not do very well with aesthetic texts, and simply say that there need to be two different practices of English teaching: one dealing with the aesthetic, and the other dealing with the kinds of texts with which critical literacy does work well. It is a "horses for courses" solution. Operatively something like this has happened in some schools that have taken up critical literacy in the general English program but seem to continue to teach literature in much the same way as ever. This is selling both literature and critical literacy short. If English/literacy teaching is about developing a critical understanding of textuality, then there ought to be a theory of textuality that will cover aesthetic texts as well as all the others. As we have seen, on the one hand, the sort of theoretical framework underpinning critical literacy can work with the aesthetic, and on the other hand, critical literacy is inadequate to deal with some of the texts that are central to it (e.g., advertisements) if it doesn't encompass a theory of the aesthetic. To argue for fundamentally different kinds of practice would be settling for second best for both.

Clearly we need to reconfigure critical literacy so that it can and does take account of the aesthetic, and this has, of course, been the project of this book. While maintaining the fundamental framework of critical literacy, this regenerated version makes three assertions that are absolutely self-evident but have not commonly been emphasised in critical literacy: texts can be valuable and productive; the emotional and experiential elements of texts are significant; and texts are read and written by individuals who are different from each other. These, not surprisingly, can be aligned with the three reasons we were considering before as to why critical literacy has a problem with the aesthetic.

Texts Can Be Valuable and Productive

The basic attitude in much critical literacy practice seems to be that the text is the enemy, constructed to blind the reader ideologically and make her or him subject to its power. The reconfigured critical literacy will acknowledge, as has been stressed throughout this book, that this is true, but that it is also what is valuable about texts: they give us ways of seeing and thinking about the world, different ways of understanding it, by deploying different discourses and modes, such as the aesthetic. The answer to the standard critical literacy question, "Whose interests are being served?" could well often be "Ours." We need to recognise what texts are doing positively, what they are opening up for us, as well as the ways they are framing the world and limiting our view.

This is the productivity of texts. Someone has a purpose, something they want to achieve textually, and they shape language with all its resources as best they can to create something new. They will often discover, as they are creating their text, that the resources of language both constrain what they say and lead them to unexpected insights, so that the final text is never quite what was expected. Someone else then reads or hears or views the text, and they produce the texts for themselves, generally acknowledging the purposes for which it was generated, but making their own construction out of it, their own use of it.

Critical literacy does, of course, acknowledge the value of texts, but it tends to be rather grudging in doing so. A common formulation is that the text is being deconstructed to show the students the ideology, and then they can make up their own minds whether they want to accept the text as valuable or not. This is both disingenuous and out of touch with the processes of reading. Students are very aware that there are major areas where they cannot make up their own minds, but the kind of readings they are able to give are institutionally governed. Apart from the accepted and expected critical practice current in the classroom or assessment regime, there is, at a very simple level, a policy that (rightly) says they are not allowed, for example, to display discrimination on grounds of race or gender. In such cases, we do not want students to make up their own minds, and we let them know if they do so in a way that we do not approve of.

The notion of choice is also limited in that, again, it is on the rationalist model. As we saw in Chapter 5, the processes of our negotiations with texts are very complex and far from purely rational, involving strong affective elements. It is a limitation to assume otherwise. There needs to be a richer sense of the breadth of the kinds of engagement we have with texts and the fluctuations and readjustments that go on as we read.

A great deal of the discussion in the book has been taken up with reading, because critical literacy as currently constituted is very much a pedagogy of reading rather than writing. Writing has tended to be an afterthought or related to critical rereading. But part of the opening out to the productivity of texts will be an opening out to the production of texts, developing in students the capacity to create aesthetic texts (among others), texts that allow them to come to terms with their experience and give their perception on things by shaping it aesthetically. The critical understanding of textuality needs to fuse with a creative understanding of textuality.[3]

The Emotional and Experiential Elements Are Significant

Critical literacy tends to see emotion as a distracter, whereas a fundamental characteristic of how aesthetic texts work is that the meaning is carried as much in the experience the text offers and the emotion it generates as in the more intellectual elements. The experience cannot simply be objectified intellectually and thus defused, but there needs to be an understanding of the kind of desire involving us with the emotion, the subject position being created through it, and why we experience that position as so attractive, before we can begin to weigh up what its advantages and dangers are.

Acknowledging fully that texts work emotionally will not only help critical literacy with texts like advertisements, but will perhaps also allow it to acknowledge something significant about itself. If critical literacy does have a critical agenda to uncover and speak out against discrimination, to expose the ways in which texts make us less free, then it ought to be a passionate practice. Such outcomes are only likely to be achieved if they are felt intensely to matter, and so students must be engaged emotionally as well as intellectually. The objectifying, distancing moves may be necessary, but if that is all there is to critical literacy, and there is not a corresponding emotional understanding of why it matters if black people are depicted as overgrown children or women as passive, then it becomes a set of meaningless exercises.

Texts Are Written and Read by Individuals Who Are Different from Each Other

It may be true that we are all shaped by our society, that we think along the grooves that society gives us, that we are shaped by its discourses as we utilise them, and that we can achieve our purposes linguistically only by working with the conventions that society has agreed to. However, we are all different, and just as social thinking is enshrined in language, that individual difference is created in language too. One person's way of utilising the discourse of school students may be very different from someone else's, just as one person's way of being racist or sexist may be very different from another person's. We ignore these differences and homogenise people (and discourses) at our peril.

We need to acknowledge the differences for two reasons. The first is so that we can understand the range of fronts on which we might need to fight if we do want to counter discrimination or give our students greater social power. The second is so that we can extend ourselves by acknowledging other people's ways of seeing the world. There needs to be a generous acceptance of individual diversity as well as social diversity.

People write aesthetic texts (indeed all texts) out of their own experience. Historically that has been one of the major justifications for valuing aesthetic texts, that they allow us to imaginatively experience things as someone else does, thus extending our sympathies or our capacity for ethical understanding, even if we reject the view of the text. Each of us reads individually as well, out of our own experience, and it is the range of readings that can make an English classroom one of the most exciting places to be, not simply to celebrate diversity, but to understand what generates diversity, and for each person to refine her or his own views through interaction with those of others.

This is perfectly compatible with the critical literacy agenda since understanding the diversity of writings and readings is a fundamental part of understanding textuality, and bringing the texts and readings produced under scrutiny for their ethical and social consequences is a profoundly significant educational and human venture.

Beyond Critical Literacy?

It might be said that this new version of critical literacy is no longer critical literacy at all. So be it. If, indeed, the reconfiguring has produced something that is no longer recognisable as critical literacy, then we will need to find a new name. (It could be said that "critical literacy" has unfortunate negative connotations anyway that may have contributed to the resistance it has met in some places.)

What matters is that critical literacy as conceptualised here will have a richer sense of textuality and be able to deal with all kinds of texts. It will acknowledge that our reading of texts is something that involves us deeply in all sorts of ways, and indeed that it is a major factor in what we are and how we live our lives. The aesthetic may only be one among many ways of knowing that human beings have, but it is a significant one because it acknowledges the breadth, diversity, and even contradictoriness of human experience, as well as the drive to make sense of it. Any version of literacy that fails to acknowledge the aesthetic fully is an impoverished one, both in its sense of language and its sense of human beings. It is one of the greatest pleasures and responsibilities of being an English teacher that we work, critically and creatively, with the aesthetic and its rich sense of human possibility.

NOTES

Introduction

1. Indeed, the keynote address on which this article was based was given in early 1995. The script for the address was even more anxious about and critical of critical literacy, but was toned down somewhat for publication.

Chapter 1

1. For a sympathetic critique, one that acknowledges the ambivalent attitude towards popular culture in both critical pedagogy and cultural studies, see Grossberg (1997). See also the critiques of critical pedagogy by Buckingham (1998); Ellsworth (1989); and Luke and Gore (1992).

Chapter 2

1. Those interested in acquainting themselves with some of the (often fascinating) issues and debates current in philosophical aesthetics can be referred to two anthologies of introductory readings: Gaut and Lopes (2001) and Levinson (2003). The sheer size of these anthologies, 581 and 821 pages, respectively, suggests something of the scope of debates around the term.

2. The question of the aesthetic and the body is taken up specifically in Chapter 7. It is perhaps worth quoting here what is quoted more prominently there, Terry Eagleton's opening to his book *The Ideology of the Aesthetic:* "Aesthetics is born as a discourse of the body" (1990).

3. John Armstrong discusses our emotional involvement with beauty illuminatingly in his excellent book *The Secret Power of Beauty* (2004).

4. This last term, *audience,* is not ideal because it suggests a communal reception of the work rather than an individual one and because it is a term most commonly used for the interpretative arts. However, *reader* or *viewer* suggests limitations on the kind of work, and *consumer* has the wrong connotations, although the term *audience* is perhaps overly passive in its implications. Still, with those qualifications in mind, *audience* seems the most appropriate term.

5. This anti-intentionalist stance has been most famously insisted on by Wimsatt and Beardsley (Wimsatt, 1954), but it is also the position taken by poststructuralists such as Roland Barthes, most notably with his famous concept of the "the death of the author" (1977).

6. As Marvell rather engagingly does imagine, in "The Mower to the Glowworms":

> Ye living lamps, by whose dear light
> The nightingale does sit so late,
> And studying all the summer night,
> Her matchless songs does meditate . . .

("THE MOWER TO THE GLOWWORMS," LL. 1–4)

7. For interesting work on creativity, see Csikszentmihalyi (1996) and Feldman, Csikszentmihalyi, and Gardner (1994).

8. An excellent introduction to ideology, at least for those coming from a literary rather than a sociological background, is Terry Eagleton's *Ideology: An Introduction* (1991). Another useful book is Thompson (1984).

Chapter 4

1. A great deal has been written on subjectivity, and even more on the related concept of identity. Questions of subjectivity and identity are at the very foundation of most poststructuralist theoretical frameworks. A useful, readable introduction to a number of these is Mansfield (2000).

2. Lacan's own writings are notoriously difficult, and one could not refer the unsuspecting beginner to them with much hope of their providing illumination. It is perhaps best for those who want to go further

to begin with some of the early texts that elucidated Lacan in terms of literary studies. Terry Eagleton's account in *Literary Theory: An Introduction* (1983, pp. 163–71) is a remarkably concise and clear introduction to the major concepts. Belsey (1980) and Silverman (1983) give good accounts. More recently, Mansfield (2000) is useful here too.

3. Lacan draws on Saussure's theory of the sign. For Saussure, the sign consists of the "signifier," which is the form of the sign, and the "signified," which is the concept being referred to. With traffic lights, a green light is the signifier, and the signified is that you are permitted to move forward: the black marks on the page—"rose"—are the signifier, the signified is a particular kind of flower.

4. Almost as much as Lacan's writings, those of Deleuze and Guattari are no easy ride for the unsuspecting. The best introduction is probably provided by Claire Colebrook's two books (2002a, 2002b); *Understanding Deleuze* is perhaps the better of the two to begin with.

5. It is worth differentiating between the distinction made here and the one that was popular in the late 1980s and early 1990s: that between analytic and creative responses. This most likely stemmed ultimately from Barthes's distinction between readerly and writerly texts (1975) but found its popular manifestation in such things as Ian Reid's distinction between the literature classroom as "gallery" or "workshop" (1984). The distinction there is between a passive and an active reader, one who consumes against one who produces. There was an implicit valuation. In contrast, the desire for textual engagement in both ways looked at here is active and productive of textual meaning. A Lacanian conceptualisation is certainly not passive, but restlessly searching. It is just that the energy released in the two conceptualisations of reading is very different in each case.

Chapter 5

1. The textbook could also be accused of heterosexist assumptions in the silence here about the possibility that the speaker and addressee are of the same sex.

2. The authors had been invited to present aspects of their work on aesthetic engagement at a Systemic Functional Linguistics conference at the University of Sydney in 1999. As part of the preparation for their address they read the same poem and recorded their responses.

Chapter 6

1. We will not get into the textual problems as to where the closing quotation marks should go, or into the issue of whether Keats was simply equating Truth and Beauty, or if he was making a fine distinction between saying that Beauty is Truth, and the reverse statement.

2. Jonathan Arac (1997), in his fascinating, sceptical study of the novel's growth to iconic status, makes it clear that the "banning" of *Huckleberry Finn* was nowhere near as widespread or as simple as newspaper reports would have one believe. While not entirely a myth, such moves against the book have achieved a kind of mythical status because they provide a never-fail attention-grabbing headline.

3. Cf. Professor Hoxie N. Fairchild: "At all events one thing is certain: whatever his skin pigmentation, any adult who objects to this enlightened work because Huck calls Jim a 'nigger' rather than a 'Negro' simply does not know how to read a great book" (quoted in Arac, 1997, p. 65)

4. It might be noted that, for all their scorn of intentionalism—the belief that the text meant what the author intended—Leavis and the New Critics let intentionalism return through the back door by a kind of anthropomorphisation of the text: the text intended a single meaning that readers had to understand.

5. See, for example, Maxine Greene (1995) and Peter Abbs (1994, 2003). For further discussion on this matter see Misson (2003).

6. For further discussion of this aspect of writing, see Misson (2004).

Chapter 7

1. Two useful introductions to the work of Bourdieu are Swartz (1997) and Thompson (1984). Thompson's long introduction to Bourdieu's *Language and Symbolic Power* (Bourdieu, 1991) is also very helpful.

2. The two crucial books by Judith Butler are *Gender Trouble* (1990) and *Bodies That Matter* (1993). An excellent, lucid introduction to Butler's often difficult thought (and even more difficult prose) is Salih (2002).

3. Much of the work on the body and sexuality stems from Foucault's three-volume (incomplete) *History of Sexuality* (1981, 1990a, 1990b). Lee Edelman's *Homographesis* (1994) is particularly interesting on this topic.

4. Seymour Chatman has usefully suggested the terms *slant* and *filter*, respectively, for these two different aspects of focalisation (see Chatman, 1990, pp. 139–60).

5. A doctoral student tells how he was teaching literature at a university in Vietnam, and the class was looking at an Auden poem. Towards the end of the class, he mentioned that it was addressed to a male. Virtually every member of the group threw down the poem in revulsion, letting out an outraged cry, and did not want to handle it physically again.

Chapter 8

1. Barthes's allusive and celebratory text still has much to offer, although we need not adhere too closely to the polemical distinction he makes between "bliss" (jouissance) and mere pleasure or his argument that bliss may be experienced in reading "writerly" texts, those of the avant-garde, while more conventional, realistic texts generate only pleasure.

2. Some rhetoricians distinguish metonymy from synecdoche; others make the latter a subset of the former. In the discussion here the term *metonymy* in the broad sense is used for both it and *synecdoche* in their narrower senses, since both involve association through contiguity. Even definitions vary, but synecdoche is commonly understood to involve substituting the whole for the part or the part for the whole, the genus for the species and vice versa (Lanham, 1969).

Chapter 9

1. It will be recalled from earlier chapters that by the term *play* we mean the kind of movement that occurs in the strands of a rope—the oscillations of give and take, attraction and repulsion. This frictive play within and across texts is not a matter of indulgent entertainment or trivialising. When we are reading or watching *King Lear*, for instance, it is a matter of the play of serious thought and feeling.

2. While Pope uses this triad, his activities do not insist on students taking a stance in one of the three positions in advance of their intervention.

3. This task, undertaken by Year 11 students at Anglican Church Grammar School, Brisbane, is based on earlier work by Wendy Morgan and Lindsay Williams (Morgan, 1997).

4. Thanks to Bernadine Anning, an undergraduate teacher-education student of Wendy Morgan's at Queensland University of Technology, for this example.

Chapter 10

1. This is actually relatively unusual in Donne: his metaphors do frequently show the woman as dependent or subservient, even gloriously expansive ones like "She is all states, and all Princes, I, / Nothing else is," from "The Sunne Rising." But that doesn't undercut the point being made here about the reading of this poem.

2. For further discussion on advertising, see Misson (1994).

3. For further work on writing within a poststructuralist, critical literacy framework, see Kamler (2001) and Misson (2004).

REFERENCES

Abbs, P. (1989). *A is for aesthetic: Essays on creative and aesthetic education.* New York: Falmer Press.

Abbs, P. (1994). *The educational imperative: A defence of Socratic and aesthetic learning.* London: Falmer Press.

Abbs, P. (2003). *Against the flow: Education, the arts and postmodern culture.* London: RoutledgeFalmer.

Adams, P. (1995). *At the far reach of their capacities: Case studies in dependent authorship.* Norwood, SA: Australian Association for the Teaching of English.

Althusser, L. (1984). Ideology and ideological state apparatuses (Notes towards an investigation). In L. Althusser (Ed.), *Essays on ideology* (pp. 1–60). London: Verso. (Original work published 1970)

Arac, J. (1997). *Huckleberry Finn as idol and target: The functions of criticism in our time.* Madison: University of Wisconsin Press.

Armstrong, J. (2004). *The secret power of beauty.* London: Allen Lane.

Austen, J. (1981). *Emma.* Oxford: Oxford University Press. (Original work published 1815)

Bakhtin, M. M. (1984). *Rabelais and his world* (H. Iswolsky, Trans.). Bloomington: Indiana University Press.

Bakhtin, M. M. (1994). *The Bakhtin reader: Selected writings of Bakhtin, Medvedev and Voloshinov* (Pam Morris, Ed.). London: Edward Arnold.

Ball, S., Kenny, A., & Gardiner, D. (1990). Literacy, politics and the teaching of English. In I. Goodson & P. Medway. (Eds.), *Bringing English to order: The history and politics of a school subject* (pp. 47–86). London: Falmer Press.

Barthes, R. (1968). *Elements of semiology* (C. S. A. Lavers, Trans.). New York: Hill and Wang.

Barthes, R. (1975). *S/Z* (R. Miller, Trans.). London: Jonathan Cape.

Barthes, R. (1977). *Image-music-text* (S. Heath, Trans.). New York: Hill and Wang.

Barthes, R. (1990). *The pleasure of the text* (R. Miller, Trans.). Oxford: Basil Blackwell.

Bazalgette, C., & Buckingham, D. (Eds.). (1995). *In front of the children: Screen education and young audiences.* London: British Film Institute.

Belsey, C. (1980). *Critical practice.* London: Methuen.

Belsey, C. (1982). Re-reading the great tradition. In P. Widdowson (Ed.), *Re-reading English* (pp. 121–35). London: Methuen.

Bernstein, M. (1998). *Patterns of hypertext.* Paper presented at the Hypertext '98, Ninth ACM Conference on Hypertext and Hypermedia: Links, Objects, Time and Space, Pittsburgh. Electronic version of paper retrieved November 25, 2005, from http://www.informatik.uni-trier.de/~ley/db/conf/ht/ht98.html.

Bhabha, H. K. (1994). *The location of culture.* London and New York: Routledge.

Bloom, A. (1987). *The closing of the American mind: How higher education has failed democracy and impoverished the souls of today's students.* New York: Simon and Schuster.

Bloom, H. (1997). *The anxiety of influence: A theory of poetry.* New York: Oxford University Press.

Bloome, D. (1985). Reading as a social process. *Language Arts, 62*(2), 134–42.

Bourdieu, P. (1990). *The logic of practice* (R. Nice, Trans.). Stanford, CA: Stanford University Press.

Bourdieu, P. (1991). *Language and symbolic power* (J. B. Thompson, Ed.; G. Raymond & M. Adamson, Trans.). London: Polity Press.

Bourdieu, P. (1996). *The state nobility: Elite schools in the field of power* (L. C. Clough, Trans.). Cambridge: Polity Press.

Brooks, C. (1949). *The well-wrought urn: Studies in the structure of poetry.* London: Methuen.

Brown, D. (2003). *The Da Vinci code.* London: Corgi.

Buckingham, D. (Ed.). (1998). *Teaching popular culture: Beyond radical pedagogy*. London: UCL Press.

Buckingham, D., Fraser, P., & Sefton-Green, J. (2000). Making the grade: Evaluating student production in media studies. In J. Sefton-Green & R. Sinker (Eds.), *Evaluating creativity: Making and learning by young people* (pp. 129–53). London: Routledge.

Buckingham, D., & Sefton-Green, J. (1994). *Cultural studies goes to school: Reading and teaching popular media*. London: Taylor and Francis.

Burke, K. (1953). *Counter-statement* (2nd ed.). Berkeley: University of California Press.

Burke, K. (1969). *A rhetoric of motives*. Berkeley: University of California Press.

Butler, J. (1990). *Gender trouble: Feminism and the subversion of identity*. New York: Routledge.

Butler, J. (1993). *Bodies that matter: On the discursive limits of 'sex.'* New York and London: Routledge.

Chandler, D. (n.d.). *Semiotics for beginners*. Retrieved 24 January 2005 from http://www.aber.ac.uk/media/Documents/S4B/semiotic.html

Chatman, S. (1978). *Story and discourse: Narrative structure in fiction and film*. Ithaca, NY: Cornell University Press.

Chatman, S. (1990). *Coming to terms: The rhetoric of narrative in fiction and film*. Ithaca, NY: Cornell University Press.

Chopin, K. (1984). The story of an hour. In S. M. Gilbert (Ed.), *The awakening, and selected stories* (pp. 213–15). New York: Penguin. (Original work published 1894)

Colebrook, C. (2002a). *Gilles Deleuze*. London: Routledge.

Colebrook, C. (2002b). *Understanding Deleuze*. Crow's Nest, NSW: Allen & Unwin.

Corcoran, B. (1994). Balancing reader response and cultural theory and practice. In B. Corcoran, M. Hayhoe, & G. Pradl (Eds.), *Knowledge in the making: Challenging the text in the classroom*. Portsmouth, NH: Boynton Cook / Heinemann.

Cox, B. (1991). *Cox on Cox: An English curriculum for the 1990s*. London: Hodder and Stoughton.

Cranny-Francis, A. (1990). *Feminist fiction: Feminist uses of generic fiction*. Cambridge: Polity Press.

Cranny-Francis, A. (1995). *The body in the text*. Melbourne: Melbourne University Press.

Csikszentmihalyi, M. (1996). *Creativity: Flow and the psychology of discovery and invention*. New York: HarperCollins.

Culler, J. (1975). *Structuralist poetics: Structuralism, linguistics and the study of literature*. London: Routledge.

Culler, J. (1983). *Barthes*. Glasgow: Fontana.

Department for Education and Skills (DfES) (United Kingdom). (2004). *English: Key stage 3*. Retrieved 20 January 2005, from http://www.standards.dfes.gov.uk/keystage3/subjects/english/.

Derrida, J. (1976). *Of grammatology* (G. C. Spivak, Trans.). Baltimore: Johns Hopkins University Press.

Dickens, C. (1971). *Bleak House*. Harmondsworth: Penguin. (Original work published 1853)

Dickens, C. (1983). *Hard times*. London: Macmillan. (Original work published 1854)

Douglas, M. (1975). *Implicit meanings: Essays in anthropology*. London: Routledge and Kegan Paul.

Eagleton, T. (1983). *Literary theory: An introduction*. Oxford: Blackwell.

Eagleton, T. (1985/86). The subject of literature. *Cultural Critique, 2*, 95–104.

Eagleton, T. (1990). *The ideology of the aesthetic*. Oxford: Basil Blackwell.

Eagleton, T. (1991). *Ideology: An introduction*. London: Verso.

Easthope, A. (1991). *Literary into cultural studies*. London: Routledge.

Edelman, L. (1994). *Homographesis: Essays in gay literary and cultural theory*. New York: Routledge.

Eliot, G. (1965). *Middlemarch*. Harmondsworth: Penguin. (Original work published 1871/72)

Eliot, T. S. (1991). Introduction to *The adventures of Huckleberry Finn*. In L. Champion (Ed.), *The critical response to Mark Twain's* Huckleberry Finn (pp. 44–49). Westport, CT: Greenwood. (Original work published in 1950)

Ellsworth, E. (1989). Why doesn't this feel empowering? Working through the repressive myths of critical pedagogy. *Harvard Educational Review, 59*(3), 297–324.

English learning area statement. (1998). Perth: Curriculum Council, Western Australia.

Fairclough, N. (1989). *Language and power.* London: Longman.

Fairclough, N. (1992a). *Discourse and social change.* Cambridge: Polity Press.

Fairclough, N. (Ed.). (1992b). *Critical language awareness.* London: Longman.

Fanon, F. (1967). *Black skin, white masks.* New York: Grove Press.

Faust, M. (2001). Literary art as experience: A transactional perspective on the interface between scholarship and pedagogy. *Journal of Aesthetic Education, 35*(3), 37–50.

Feldman, D., Csikszentmihalyi, M., & Gardner, H. (1994). *Changing the world: A framework for the study of creativity.* Westport, CT: Praeger.

Fielding, H. (1950). *The history of Tom Jones.* New York: Modern Library. (Original work published 1749)

Fish, S. (1980). *Is there a text in this class? The authority of interpretive communities.* Cambridge, MA: Harvard University Press.

Foucault, M. (1972). *The archaeology of knowledge* (A. M. Sheridan Smith, Trans.). London: Tavistock.

Foucault, M. (1981). *The history of sexuality: Vol. 1: An introduction* (R. Hurley, Trans.). Harmondsworth, UK: Penguin.

Foucault, M. (1990a). *The history of sexuality: Vol. 2: The use of pleasure* (R. Hurley, Trans.). Harmondsworth, UK: Penguin.

Foucault, M. (1990b). *The history of sexuality: Vol. 3: The care of the self* (R. Hurley, Trans.). Harmondsworth, UK: Penguin.

Foucault, M. (1997). *The essential works: Vol. 1: Ethics: Subjectivity and truth* (P. Rabinow, Ed.; R. Hurley, Trans.). London: Allen Lane, Penguin Press.

Foucault, M. (2001). *The essential works: Vol. 3: Power* (J. D. Faubion, Ed.; R. Hurley, Trans.). London: Allen Lane, Penguin Press.

Fowler, R. (1986). *Linguistic criticism*. Oxford: Oxford University Press.

Freire, P. (1970). *Pedagogy of the oppressed*. New York: Seabury Press.

Freire, P. (1985). *The politics of education: Culture, power, and liberation* (D. Macedo, Trans.). South Hadley, MA: Bergin and Garvey.

Freire, P., & Macedo, D. (1987). *Literacy: Reading the word and the world*. South Hadley, MA: Bergin and Garvey.

Gardner, H. (1999). *The disciplined mind: What all students should understand*. New York: Simon and Schuster.

Gaut, B., & Lopes, D. M. (Eds.). (2001). *The Routledge companion to aesthetics*. London: Routledge.

Gee, J. P. (1990). *Social linguistics and literacies: Ideology in discourses*. London: Falmer Press.

Giroux, H. (1983). *Schooling and the struggle for public life: Critical pedagogy in the modern age*. Minneapolis: University of Minnesota Press.

Giroux, H. (1992a). Decentering the canon: Refiguring disciplinary and pedagogical boundaries. In *Border crossings: Cultural workers and the politics of education* (pp. 89–110). New York: Routledge.

Giroux, H. (1992b). Popular culture as a pedagogy of pleasure and meaning: Decolonising the body. In *Border crossings: Cultural workers and the politics of education* (pp. 180–206). New York: Routledge.

Greene, M. (1995). *Releasing the imagination: Essays on education, the arts, and social change*. San Francisco: Jossey-Bass.

Grossberg, L. (1993). *Cultural studies: What's in a name?* Paper presented at the B. Aubrey Fisher Memorial Lecture, University of Utah, Salt Lake City, Utah.

Grossberg, L. (1997). *Bringing it all back home: Essays on cultural studies*. Durham, NC: Duke University Press.

Hall, S., & Whannel, Paddy. (1964). *The popular arts*. London: Hutchinson.

Hartley, J. (2003). *A short history of cultural studies*. London: Sage.

Hazzard, S. (1981). *The transit of Venus*. Harmondsworth, UK: Penguin.

Hoggart, R. (1957). *The uses of literacy: Aspects of working class life with special reference to publications and entertainments*. Harmondsworth, UK: Penguin.

Iser, W. (1974). *The implied reader: Patterns of communication in prose fiction from Bunyan to Beckett*. Baltimore: Johns Hopkins University Press.

Iser, W. (1978). *The act of reading: A theory of aesthetic response*. Baltimore: Johns Hopkins University Press.

Jackson, G. (1987). The blanket. In W. Morgan (Ed.), *Border territory: An anthology of unorthodox Australian writing* (pp. 66–68). Melbourne: Thomas Nelson.

Janks, H. (1993a). *Language and position*. Johannesburg: Witwatersrand University Press and Hodder and Stoughton Educational.

Janks, H. (1993b). *Language, identity and power*. Johannesburg: Witwatersrand University Press and Hodder and Stoughton Educational.

Joyce, M. (1990). *Afternoon, a story*. Storyspace software for Macintosh and Windows. Cambridge, MA: Eastgate Systems.

Kamler, B. (2001). *Relocating the personal: A critical writing pedagogy*. Albany: State University of New York Press.

Keats, J. (1954). Letter from John Keats to John Hamilton Reynolds, 3 February 1818. In F. Page (Ed.), *Letters of John Keats*. London: Oxford University Press.

Knoblauch, C., & Brannon, L. (1993). *Critical teaching and the idea of literacy*. Portsmouth, NH: Heinemann / Boynton Cook.

Kress, G. (2000). Design and transformation: New theories of meaning. In B. Cope & M. Kalantzis (Eds.), *Multiliteracies: Literacy learning and the design of social futures* (pp. 153–61). Melbourne: Macmillan.

Kress, G., & Hodge, R. (1979). *Language as ideology*. London: Routledge and Kegan Paul.

Lanham, R. A. (1969). *A handlist of rhetorical terms*. Berkeley: University of California Press.

Lankshear, C. (1994). *Critical literacy*. Canberra: Australian Curriculum Studies Association.

Lankshear, C., & McLaren, P. (Eds.). (1993). *Critical literacy: Politics, praxis, and the postmodern*. Albany: State University of New York Press.

Lawrence, D. H. (1960). *Women in love*. Harmondworth, UK: Penguin. (Original work published 1921)

Leavis, F. R. (1962). *The great tradition*. Harmondsworth, UK: Penguin.

Leavis, F. R. (1964). *D. H. Lawrence: Novelist*. Harmondsworth, UK: Penguin.

Lee, H. (1960). *To kill a mockingbird*. London: Heinemann.

Lembeck, M. (Director) (1999). The one where everybody finds out [Television series episode], *Friends*. New York: NBC.

Lemke, J. L. (1998). Metamedia literacy: Transforming meanings and media. In D. Reinking, M. McKenna, & L. Labbo (Eds.), *Handbook of literacy and technology: Transformations in a post-typographic world* (pp. 283–301). Hillsdale, NJ: Lawrence Erlbaum.

Lentricchia, F. (1983). *Criticism and social change*. Princeton, NJ: Princeton University Press.

Levinson, J. (Ed.). (2003). *The Oxford handbook of aesthetics*. Oxford: Oxford University Press.

Livingstone, T. (2004, 7 June). Give classics a dose of reality. *Courier-Mail* (Queensland), p. 11.

Lowell, R. (2003). *Collected Poems*. (Eds. F. Bidart and D. Gewanter). New York: Farrar, Straus and Giroux.

Luhrmann, B. (Director). (1996). *William Shakespeare's Romeo + Juliet* [Motion picture]. (Available from Twentieth Century Fox Film Corporation, Beverley Hills, CA.)

Luke, A. (2000). Critical literacy in Australia: A matter of context and standpoint. In J. Elkins & A. Luke (Eds.), *Re/mediating adolescent literacies* (pp. 47–60). Newark, DE: International Reading Association.

References

Luke, A., O'Brien, J., & Comber, B. (1994). Making community texts the objects of study. *Australian Journal of Language and Literacy, 17*(2), 139–49.

Luke, C. (1997). Media literacy and cultural studies. In S. Muspratt, A. Luke, & P. Freebody (Eds.), *Constructing critical literacies: Teaching and learning textual practice* (pp. 19–49). Sydney: Allen & Unwin.

Luke, C., & Gore, J. (Eds.). (1992). *Feminisms and critical pedagogy.* London: Routledge.

Mansfield, N. (2000). *Subjectivity: Theories of the self from Freud to Haraway.* St. Leonards, NSW: Allen & Unwin.

McLaren, P. (1989). On ideology and education: Critical pedagogy and the politics of resistance. In H. Giroux & P. McLaren (Eds.), *Critical pedagogy, the state, and cultural struggle.* Albany: State University of New York Press.

McLaren, P. (1995). *Critical pedagogy and predatory culture: Oppositional politics in a postmodern era.* London: Routledge.

Mellor, B., and Patterson, A. (1994). "Producing readings: Freedom versus normativity." *English in Australia,* no. 109, 42–56.

Misson, R. (1994). Advertising textuality. *Interpretations, 27*(1), 16–27.

Misson, R. (1996). Character building. *Idiom, 31*(2), 88–97.

Misson, R. (1997). You can't change the world in every lesson (but you can at least try). *Interpretations, 30*(2), 16–35.

Misson, R. (2003). Imagining the self: The individual imagination in the English classroom. *English in Australia,* no. 138, 24–33.

Misson, R. (2004). What are we creating in creative writing? *English in Australia,* no. 141, 32–40.

Moon, B. (1990). *Studying literature: Theory and practice for senior students.* Scarborough, Western Australia: Chalkface Press.

Moon, B. (2001). *Literary terms: A practical glossary* (2nd ed.). Cottesloe, Western Australia: Chalkface Press.

Morgan, W. (1992). Changing the face of the body of literature: Deviant writing in the secondary classroom. In J. Thomson (Ed.), *Reconstructing literature teaching* (pp. 88–107). Norwood, South Australia: Australian Association for the Teaching of English.

Morgan, W. (1997). *Critical literacy in the classroom: The art of the possible*. London: Routledge.

Morris, M. (1997). A question of cultural studies. In A. McRobbie (Ed.), *Back to reality? Social experience and cultural studies* (pp. 36–57). Manchester: Manchester University Press.

Moulthrop, S. (1991). *Victory Garden*. Storyspace software for Macintosh and Windows. Cambridge, MA: Eastgate Systems.

Murray, L. A. (1988). *The vernacular republic: Poems, 1961–1983* (Enlarged and rev. ed.). Sydney: Angus and Robertson.

National Endowment for the Arts (NEA). (2004). *Reading at risk: A survey of literary reading in America* (Research Division Report No. 46). Washington, DC: National Endowment for the Arts.

New London Group. (2000). A pedagogy of multiliteracies: Designing social futures. In B. Cope & M. Kalantzis (Eds.), *Multiliteracies: Literacy learning and the design of social futures*. Melbourne: Macmillan.

O'Malley, S., Rosen, R., & Vogt, L. (Eds.). (1990). *Politics of education: Essays from 'Radical teacher.'* Albany: State University of New York Press.

Peel, P., Patterson, A., & Gerlach, J. (2000). *Questions of English: Ethics, aesthetics, rhetoric and the formation of the subject in England, Australia and the United States*. London: Routledge-Falmer.

Pennycook, A. (2001). *Critical applied linguistics: A critical introduction*. Mahwah, NJ: Lawrence Erlbaum.

Pope, R. (1995). *Textual intervention: Critical and creative strategies for literary studies*. London: Routledge.

Queensland Board of Senior Secondary School Studies. (n.d.). *Framing topics: Then and now*. Brisbane: Queensland Board of Senior Secondary School Studies.

Ransom, J. C. (1941). *The new criticism*. Norfolk, CT: New Directions.

Reid, I. (1984). *The making of literature: Texts, contexts and classroom practices*. Norwood, South Australia: Australian Association for the Teaching of English.

Richards, I. A. (1929). *Practical criticism*. London: Kegan Paul.

Salih, S. (2002). *Judith Butler*. London: Routledge.

Searle, C. (1998). *None but our words: Critical literacy in classroom and community*. Buckingham, UK: Open University Press.

Sedgwick, E. K. (1990). *Epistemology of the closet*. Berkeley: University of California Press.

Seuss, Dr. (2003). *The cat in the hat*. London: HarperCollins. (Original work published 1957)

Shor, I. (1980). *Critical teaching and everyday life*. Chicago: University of Chicago Press.

Silverman, K. (1983). *The subject of semiotics*. New York: Oxford University Press.

Sinker, R. (2000). Making multimedia: Evaluating young people's creative multimedia production. In J. Sefton-Green & R. Sinker (Eds.), *Evaluating creativity: Making and learning by young people* (pp. 187–215). London: Routledge.

Swartz, D. (1997). *Culture and power: The sociology of Pierre Bourdieu*. Chicago: University of Chicago Press.

Thompson, E. P. (Ed.). (1964). *Discrimination and popular culture*. Harmondsworth, UK: Penguin.

Thompson, E. P. (1968). *The making of the English working class*. Harmonsworth, UK: Penguin.

Thompson, J. B. (1984). *Studies in the theory of ideology*. Cambridge: Polity Press.

Tompkins, J. (1985). *Sensational designs: The cultural work of American fiction, 1790–1860*. Oxford: Oxford University Press.

Turnbull, S. (1993). Accounting for taste: The moral and aesthetic dimensions of media practices. In L. Yates (Ed.), *Feminism and education*. Melbourne: La Trobe University Press.

Twain, M. (1985). *The adventures of Huckleberry Finn*. London: Penguin. (Original work published 1884)

Tyner, K. (1998). *Literacy in a digital world: Teaching and learning in the age of information*. Mahwah, NJ: Erlbaum.

Wilde, O. (1974). *The picture of Dorian Gray*. In R. Aldington & S. Weintraub (Eds.), *The portable Oscar Wilde* (pp. 138–391). New York: Penguin. (Original work published 1891)

Williams, R. (1958). *Culture and society, 1780–1950*. Harmondsworth, UK: Penguin.

Williams, R. (1980). Base and superstructure in Marxist cultural theory. In *Problems in materialism and culture*. London: Verso. (Original work published 1973)

Wimsatt, W. K., Jr. (1954). *The verbal icon: Studies in the meaning of poetry*. Lexington: University of Kentucky Press.

Yellowlees Douglas, J. (2000). *The end of books—or books without end? Reading interactive narratives*. Ann Arbor: University of Michigan Press.

INDEX

AUTHORS

Ray Misson is associate professor and director, Learning and Teaching in the Faculty of Education at the University of Melbourne, Australia. His main area of interest centres on the significance of cultural studies for classroom practice, and he has written extensively on popular culture, critical literacy, narrative, sexuality studies, and the place of creativity and imagination in a socially critical curriculum. His publications include *A Brief Introduction to Literary Theory* and *Literacy and Schooling* (coedited with Frances Christie).

Wendy Morgan is senior lecturer in the School of Cultural and Language Studies in Education, Queensland University of Technology, Australia. Her research and writing build on her commitment to making literary and critical theory practicable in English classrooms. This resulted in her book, *Critical Literacy in the Classroom: The Art of the Possible* (1997). She has given keynote addresses at national conferences of English teachers on critical literacy, information and communications technologies, and new forms of textual practice.

This book was typeset in Sabon
by Precision Graphics.
Typefaces used on the cover
include Eric Sans and Trebuchet.
The book was printed on
50-lb. White Williamsburg Offset paper by Versa Press, Inc.